A
Smattering
of Monsters

A
Smattering
of Monsters

A KIND OF
MEMOIR

George Greenfield

CAMDEN HOUSE

First published in the United States in 1995
by Camden House, Inc.

The moral right of the author has been asserted.

Printed on acid-free paper.
Binding materials are chosen for strength and
durability.

Printed in Great Britain.
First Edition

ISBN 1-57113-071-3

A CIP catalog record for this book is
available from the Library of Congress.

Camden House, Inc.
Drawer 2025
Columbia, SC 29202 USA

Turning down an empty glass

for

those Jackies, Jillys, Julies,

Sallys, Shirleys and their like

who all too often put

the litter into literature

CONTENTS

AUTHOR'S NOTE

In the Second World War, I was a member of the battalion
tug o' war team. Our coach was Regimental Sergeant-Major
Martin, a bull of a man, who crouched like a sumo wrestler
and grunted in a rhythmical chant, ''Eave! ''Eave!'

Between bouts, when I was able to talk again, I once asked
him: 'Mr Martin, why don't you join the team? We could use
a strong man like you.'

'No, sir,' came the prompt reply. 'I know my job, sir. '*I*
grunt, *you* 'eave.'

RSM Martin would have made a useful literary agent.

Where the memory is sufficiently vivid, I have recreated the
dialogue of long ago, instead of adopting the more orthodox
technique of paraphrase.

If the purists cavil, with admitted reason, I can only say in
defence that this is my story, told as I remember it, dialogue
and all.

I

A SMATTERING OF MONSTERS

Authorship is an abnormal occupation. The average wage-earner gets up in the morning, goes to work, comes home at night, eats his or her supper and then watches television. That is the norm. To sit at a table or desk, putting black symbols on to white paper and actually being paid to do so is, when one stops and thinks about it, quite crazy. No wonder perhaps the American insurance man's response when Irwin Shaw admitted he was a writer: 'Yes – but what do you do for a living?'

Most authors, it has to be said, earn less per hour than an office cleaner. Of the 6,000 or so novels published every year in Great Britain, probably over 4,000 receive a publishing advance of £5,000 or considerably less. What with spasmodic failure of the imagination, false starts, crossings-out, fresh starts, even most experienced professional novelists would count themselves fortunate to average 100 publishable words an hour. So, for a novel 100,000 words in length, at least 1,000 hours would be required. £3 to £5 per hour cannot be considered a high rate of pay.

Of course, many – perhaps most – novelists hold down a daytime job and write in their spare time. There are other perquisites, apart from the niggardly return on their efforts.

Good reviews and a growing reputation in the literary field may enhance career prospects; even at its lowest, to be recognised at the golf club as 'our local novelist' can be socially rewarding. And, above all, to have succeeded in getting published when at least ninety per cent of full-length fiction typescripts submitted to publishers are rejected brings real private satisfaction.

Years ago, a TV producer set up an interview with an Oxford don in his rooms in college. When the filming was done, the producer said: 'Now I'm afraid we come to the embarrassing part – the matter of a fee.'

'Ah yes,' said the don, reaching in a drawer for his cheque book. 'How much do you want?'

In like manner, I find it fair to say from my many years' experience that almost any author would pay to get his first novel published. And when a publisher, either directly or through the author's agent, accepts the work and actually offers to pay for the privilege, the writer's immediate gratitude is boundless. The sad corollary is familiarity does often breed contempt. The more a publisher pushes a new author's work, the more he is whittling a stout rod for his own back. If his protégé succeeds, the terms required for successive books will become higher and higher. The author will have acquired a public reputation and other publishers will be making seductive noises. By now, those early grateful thanks and promises of eternal loyalty have slipped through the cracks of memory. Very few long-term novelists – perhaps fewer than one in ten – stay with the same publisher throughout their careers.

I am not suggesting that, if a publisher has the wit or the luck to catch a good author young, he should confidently sit back and expect to keep him indefinitely without making an effort. Loyalty is a two-way street. Many writers who change publishers have a genuine reason or a grievance. In the last twenty years or so, the swallowing up of private firms by conglomerates has often led to the sacking or resignation of senior editors. A novelist over the years has learned to trust and rely on his editor, who has probably become a close friend. Then, sometimes with no warning, he finds the editor has disappeared in a welter of cuts and changes. It is little wonder if he grows restless and asks his agent to move him to another house.

But over the last decade or so, many of the better known novelists seem to have become 'guns for hire', mercenaries prepared to do battle on behalf of the highest payer. It ill becomes an agent, whether current or ex-, to turn up his nose at big money. A fool – and there have been plenty of them around in publishing circles since the war – and the shareholders' money are easily parted. If a publishing house is throwing around excessive amounts, the author's agent, it can be argued, almost has a solemn duty on his client's behalf to relieve that house of the surplus cash before someone else does. After all, the more they pay, the harder they have to work to get their money back and so the better the book will sell. At least, that is the theory. *Caveat emptor* all too often is closely followed by *nunc dimittis*.

In line with the spread of television commercials, about a score of authors, almost all of them novelists, have become brand names. Booksellers, particularly those with high-street shops, will confirm that at least half the potential buyers go into their shops and ask not for a title but for 'the new Jeffrey Archer' or 'the new Dick Francis' or 'the new Wilbur Smith'. That pressure in turn forces the novelist to continue in the same *genre*. Most of them would probably have stayed there happily, but the inventive and experimental risk of losing the 'brand image' is great – and with that loss the automatic high income.

Apart from the questionnaires which are sent every few years by the Society of Authors to its members, I do not know of any careful statistical attempts to evaluate the annual incomes of leading British novelists. (The PLR findings are fascinating but, as the ceiling is comparatively low, they cannot focus on the upper earnings of the few.) My guess, based on over thirty years of direct experience, knowledge gleaned from the trade papers and gossip with publishers and one's friendly rivals, is that, lumping in film rights, TV rights, audio-cassette rights, paperback rights, translation rights and – possibly the biggest source of income – US volume rights,

there are perhaps 300 British-born novelists who regularly earn
more than £50,000 a year before tax. One hundred of them will
earn upwards of £100,000 and at least ten of that hundred will
be in the £1 million-or-more bracket each year. In this context,
'British' includes authors born in the Commonwealth.

If a novelist reaches such peaks of fame and fortune –
say, upwards of £500,000 a year before tax – he is certain
to be lapped in adulation. With each new book, there will
be even more journalists queuing up for interviews, yet
more wheedling television producers, bookshop managers
desperate for signing sessions, guest appearances on this or
that celebrity show. And the big man becomes Sir Oracle both
to his agent and to the managing director, the senior editor and
the marketing executives in the publishing house fortunate
enough to be putting out his books for the time being.

Even at the height of their fame, several authors I have
known well – men like Ed Hillary, Leonard Cheshire, Chris
Bonington, Robin Knox-Johnston, George MacDonald Fraser
– have remained their natural modest selves. Significantly,
perhaps, they are all men of action; although Fraser is best
known for his fictional *Flashman* stories, as a very young
man he acquitted himself well in the Burma campaign. It
is the novelist, particularly one on whom the sun suddenly
shines, who is at most risk of acquiring *les idées au-dessus de
sa gare*.

Step forward, Sidney Sheldon, known to the house of
William Morrow, then on Madison Avenue, as 'El Sid'.
A Hollywood graduate, with numerous screenplays and
television scripts, including many of the famous *I Love
Lucy* series, and the successful *Hart to Hart* format behind
him, he decided at the age of sixty or thereabouts to duplicate
his success – improve on it, indeed – as a novelist. His first
full-length fiction, *The Naked Face*, perhaps the best novel he
has ever written, was a tightly sprung and graphic thriller that
made a mark. But it was his next, *The Other Side of Midnight*,
the story of a Greek shipping tycoon who might almost have
been Aristotle Onassis, that really struck gold. From then on,
each new biennial Sidney Sheldon novel went straight to the
top of the American bestseller list, where it stayed for many

weeks; film rights were snapped up for enormous sums almost before the bulky book copies had been stacked in the main windows of B. Dalton and the Doubleday shops. In fact, *Bloodline* was launched in its movie form as *Sidney Sheldon's Bloodline*, which evoked the comment from one British film critic, 'Now we know who to blame.'

Once firmly established, Sidney felt he should enjoy the trappings of a resident British literary agent. He installed himself in a suite at the Dorchester Hotel. Heather Jeeves, then his editor at Pan Books, rang me up one afternoon and generously said that she had recommended me. She added that, as self-protection, she had had to mention a few names of other agents as well. Sidney was on his way back to the Dorchester from lunch and she suggested I should call him there in about ten minutes. I did. An imperious voice ordered me to attend punctually at 4.45 p.m. that day. I was to be granted exactly fifteen minutes – no more, no less – in which to state my case. It appeared that the great man had split his valuable time that afternoon into fifteen-minute segments, inside which the lucky applicants (supplicants?) would make their respective pitches. I was slightly tempted to tell him to stuff his quarter of an hour but curiosity and, to be honest, the hope of some juicy commission won the day.

Sharp on a quarter to five, I rang the doorbell to his suite. Tall, white-haired, with a brick-red complexion, Sidney Sheldon was surprisingly affable – almost deferential in his treatment. Would I like a cup of tea? Or coffee? Or a real drink? – all of which I declined with thanks. Was that chair comfortable enough? Good of me to drop every-thing like this. I sat facing him. He had his back to the fireplace and there was a clock on the mantelpiece behind his head.

I told him something about the Farquharson operation (my agency) and mentioned the names of a few leading clients like John le Carré and Morris West. The only recent British adventurer/explorers Americans seem to have heard of are Sir Francis Chichester and Sir Edmund Hillary and so I trotted out both names. All the time, I was keeping a covert eye on the mantelpiece clock. When the minute hand reached the perpendicular, I stood up in mid-sentence and moved towards the door.

'Hey, what gives?' he said.

'It's five o'clock, Mr Sheldon. My time's up.'

'Forget it,' he said. 'Come back and sit down. Now, what's that you were saying, George?'

At that moment, I knew I had him. No one else was going to turn up for the parade.

When he had finished the draft of a new novel, Sidney Sheldon had the neat trick of summoning his American hardcover editor, his American paperback publisher and his agent, which ended up as myself in those days since he appeared not to have an active agent in the States, wherever he happened to be in the world. They each had a copy of the typescript to read, while the author prowled around in other rooms, ostentatiously avoiding putting pressure on them, which of course added to the pressure. My introduction to this barbaric practice was with *Bloodline*. Sidney and his wife Jorja (yes, really) were then living in a *castello* outside Rome. I flew in on the Saturday. Hillel Black, the William Morrow senior editor, and Howard Kaminsky, the Warner Books chief executive, were due to arrive the following day on their return from the Jerusalem Book Fair.

For the minority who have not read the novel, *Bloodline* is the story of a lovely young girl who inherits a huge pharmacological-*cum*-chemical outfit in Switzerland, a sort of Ciba-Geigy or Hoffman-Roche, and the machinations of a British aristocrat and MP, a director of the firm, who tries to wrest control from her, first by financial skulduggery and then plain murder. The villain just happens to be impotent as well and so is a notorious cuckold.

After a somewhat tense lunch and a cursory tour of the faded grandeur of the *castello*, I was left in a vast vaulted room at a large oak desk on which lay a pile of several hundred virginal sheets of typescript. There were protestations that I should take my time, don't rush it, kid, you've got all the time in the world – except that pre-dinner drinks would be served around six o'clock and (the inference to be drawn was) heaven help me if I had not reached The End by then. So there I was, the tethered sacrifice while the tiger of an author padded restlessly around a neighbouring room. It was summer, the windows were open, there were few tapestries on the marble walls to soak up sounds and my powers of hearing are probably above average. As my eyes flickered across line after line and page after page, my ears could pick up the noises in the next room, Sidney's coughing or shifting the feet of a chair or making a telephone call on the antiquated Italian instrument.

Popular novelists should take as their motto those defiant words from Galileo on the rack, *Eppur si muove*. And yet it moves. Above all, keep the story moving, even if, as Chandler put it, you have to bring in a man with a gun in his hand. I was less than a quarter of the way into the story when I realised – with considerable relief – that *Bloodline* was okay. It moved. And the episode where the young boy has to rush back to the ghetto in Tsarist Russia before the main gate closed for the night was good, strong writing in anyone's terms.

I already knew the rudiments of the plot because over the previous six months or so, Sidney had often called me from the United States to pick my brains over the landed gentleman Member of Parliament who was the villain of the piece. I had given the opinion that, as a true-blue Conservative, Sir Jasper (or whatever his name was) would almost certainly have belonged to the Carlton Club and probably White's or Boodles as well. When the House was sitting, he would have been likely to lunch at Locket's, a short walk from the Commons, rather than more distant and exquisite restaurants like Wilton's or La Napoule. He would hunt during the winter months, and go North for the grouse and pheasant shooting in August and September. Sidney Sheldon never appreciated that whatever such knowledge I had was not from first-hand experience but rested on a 'friends of friends' basis.

I just managed to scan the final pages as the six o'clock deadline approached and walked into the next-door room where Sidney stood like an expectant father with Jorja beside him, like a reserve midwife. Luckily, I was able to deliver genuine praise. It was a strong story, I said; I liked it a lot. It was a real page-turner, as we used to say in the business.

The ice was splintered into a thousand fragments, several of which seemed to find their way into the stream of scotches on the rocks that I drank in quick succession. Sidney was not the only one to feel relieved.

That evening, he told me something that has stuck in my mind ever since and which I pass on for the benefit of would-be popular novelists. It was his practice with every one of his novels that, when he had studied all the editorial points and accepted or rejected them, he would go through the complete typescript one last time *and cut ten per cent of the text*. Two and a half lines out of every page, an average of fifty or sixty pages deleted from the full-length script. This way, he reckoned, the last ounces of 'fat' would be cut away from the book – any repetitious dialogue, over-detailed descriptions of the characters, superfluous phrases. The resulting story would be leaner, harder, faster-paced. It is an interesting technique which certainly worked well for him.

The following morning before my departure and while Sidney was preparing for the arrival of the remaining Kings of Orient, Jorja and I went for a stroll round the grounds of the ancient fort. She was a warm, comfortable woman, an expert interior decorator and designer, who was proud of her husband's success but, unlike so many authors' wives, not at all prone to supervise it. We strolled along in the pleasant sunshine until she stopped and, looking me in the eye, said, 'George, give me a straight answer to a straight question.'

'I usually try to.'

'What do you really feel about the book? Were you just being polite to Sidney last night?'

'Not a bit,' I said. 'I like it. I honestly do.'

'Cross your heart?'

'Cross my heart.'

'Oh, that's nice,' she said, 'I'm so glad you really like it. By the way, did you recognise any of the characters?'

'No – should I have done?'

'Yes – Sir Jasper. Sidney modelled him on you.'

'Well, thanks,' I said.

*   *   *

The next such occasion was a year or two later and 7,000 miles to the west. *Rape of Angels*, as it was then titled, was the novel to be read and reported on; the venue was the newly acquired Sheldon home on Sunset Boulevard. Once again, as things worked out, I was due to arrive the day before Hillel Black and Howard Kaminsky, and was to be the guest of the Sheldons.

Knowing that I would be jetlagged after an eleven-hour flight, I decided to arrive a day early, spend the night at one of the Los Angeles Airport hotels and rent a car the following morning to drive at my leisure up the coast and along the twenty miles or so of Sunset Boulevard as it snakes and climbs up to Beverly Hills. Between the entrance to Bel Air and the Beverly Hills Hotel but on the other side of the road lay the Sheldon mansion. You drove up a steep laneway to be confronted by a tall iron gate with a voice-box protruding by the driver's door. Once oral credentials were established, the gate swung back and the drive continued up to a spacious forecourt. The neo-Georgian house was flanked by a double garage that housed the Rolls Royce and the Cadillac. The floor of the garage was covered in the best Wilton carpeting.

Inside the house, Jorja's decorating taste, unhampered by financial restrictions, had been indulged to the full. (Sidney once confided to me that she liked to buy a house, do it over, live in it briefly and then sell it at a profit, when the process would begin all over again. As a result, he said, in thirty years of marriage, they had had over twenty different homes.) The washroom on the ground floor must alone have cost more than the average suburban house in its plethora of shining marble, onyx basins and gold taps. Beyond it was a room I christened 'the snug', all black stuffed leather with buttons and a mahogany bar with a stag's head on the wall. The main room, which was huge, had a wall-to-wall fitted Chinese carpet which had been specially woven as a one-off to Jorja's design. In the centre was a grand piano and on it an exquisite small painting. ('How do you like my hand-painted Renoir?' Sidney asked me.) Through the french windows one could see several acres of garden with flower beds tended by Japanese gardeners, sloping down to the obligatory swimming pool and the bathhouse, resplendent in black and white marble and brass fittings. Two vicious-looking Alsatians prowled in an alley closed off by wire netting at the side of the house.

I noticed that Jorja, who had flown in from their other home in Palm Springs that morning, seemed a little depressed and by now I knew her well enough to ask if something was bothering her.

'You bet it is,' she said. 'It's that husband of mine. He's just told me that when I was there at the Springs, he turned down an $8 million offer for this place. More than twice what it cost us. Can you beat it?'

Sidney lowered his left eyelid a fraction. I knew exactly how he must be feeling. The mere thought of leaving the home he had just grown accustomed to, packing – even if it were done by hired hands – the removal, setting up again with the smell of new paint and wispy interior designers in a high-pitched and arcane discussion with Jorja . . . I was reminded of the old story of the asylum psychiatrist who asked an inmate why he banged his head against the wall of his room and the man replied, 'Because it's so nice when you stop.'

Rape of Angels was another fast and easy read, full of action, credible if somewhat overblown characters and a clever plot. I had only one constructive comment to make. I urged Sidney to change the first word in the title to *Rage*. Being Jewish, he might not appreciate the full implications for a devout Roman Catholic or a convinced Methodist of associating angels with rape. It was a pity, I argued, to risk losing a wide slice of his likely readership for the sake of one letter. As Hillel Black and Howard Kaminsky also happened to be Jewish, they too might not spot the risk in using the current title. An experienced professional, hardened from years of writing to order for film producers and television directors, Sidney had no false pride in his work. If he found a contrary argument convincing, he accepted it. He changed the title with one curve of the pen.

That night, we dined at Hollywood's latest 'in' restaurant. I felt as though I were a bit-player in a Hollywood movie. When Sidney brought the Rolls Royce to a silent halt outside the awning, a parking attendant, dressed like a Swiss admiral, was at hand. The interior of the restaurant was of that rustic plainness that only the most expensive Californian eating places can achieve. The three of us were ushered by a smirking *maître d'* into a booth consisting of high-backed wooden sides, hard wooden benches and a plain scrubbed wooden table. The Sheldons ordered steaks, so I followed suit.

While we were waiting and sipping our drinks, a tall, sunburnt man wearing dark glasses, a gold necklace with a large gold medal clanking against his exposed bronzed chest, a gold bracelet round one wrist and a weighty gold Rolex watch round the other, walked past our booth. Spotting my host, he did a dramatic doubletake and exclaimed, 'Sidney, baby, where ya bin?'

Sidney stood up, squeezed out between his bench and the table, and shook his friend's outstretched hand. The man put an arm round his shoulders and gathered him to his bosom, declaiming all the while, 'I love ya, baby. Jesus H. Christ, you're my friend – and they don' come better!'

It was an affecting moment as they hugged and virtually kissed each other. With a final embrace, the friend walked off to join his party at a table in the centre of the room, waving farewell as he sat down. Sidney plomped back on to the bench opposite me and said in a sibilant undertone, 'Gee, I hate that sonofabitch! He shafted me up over a movie one time. One day, I'll screw him – but good.'

The steaks arrived, over an inch thick, pinkly tender and overlapping the plates. Jorja cut two or three small triangles out of hers, ate them and then pushed the plate away. Sidney did the same after a few mouthfuls. I was thoroughly enjoying my steak and, having a healthy appetite, would have happily cleared my plate but solitary chewing, watched over by an audience, soon dries up the gastric juices. Ruefully, I lowered my knife and fork.

Sidney summoned a passing waiter and asked him to fetch a doggy bag. When the man had gone off, I said, 'But surely, steaks like these are far too good for those Alsatians of yours?'

'It's not for the dogs,' Jorja explained. 'I have an electric carving knife which cuts very fine. I can slice those steaks into six, maybe ten, slices. Heated up with a toasted bun, they'll do Sidney and me for lunch all next week.'

At present, although many influential members of the two professions have urged a change, barristers and solicitors practising in England are not permitted to charge contingency fees ('no win, no pay') on a percentage basis but only fees based on reputation, time spent and out-of-pocket expenses – in other words, what they can, reasonably or unreasonably, get away with. United States lawyers can and do charge contingency fees, and are able to act for authors as both agent and legal advisor. But, with the notable exception of Paul Gitlin, who became prominent around 1960 through representing such successful novelists of the day as Harold Robbins and Irving Wallace, most New York lawyers did not realise the rich pickings involved at the top end of authorship.

The scene changed abruptly about a decade later when Allan Drury, author of the blockbusting novel, *Advise and Consent*, sued his publishers for breach of contract on his next novel. It became a *cause célèbre* and the hundreds of thousands of dollars in question became headline news in the press and the subject of green-eyed comment on television. New York lawyers raised their eyes from the communal trough to the slippery slopes of Parnassus; none more so than Morton Janklow, who had married the daughter of a Hollywood magnate, occasioning the quip, 'The son-in-law also rises', and who ran a smallish firm, Janklow Traum. He awoke from his 'dream' and set to work.

Orthodox agents have sub-agencies throughout the main publishing centres in Europe and what were the Iron Curtain countries; they will also have a reciprocal transatlantic agency with which they will be in virtually daily contact. The American-lawyer approach is different. Setting up ten or more sub-agencies is a fiddly business and having to keep in touch and supply them with finished copies an expense of money, effort and time. Far better to hold rights auctions at the Frankfurt Book Fair once a year or call up a large

American publishing house and sell it world language rights in the big author's next work, adding on a million or so dollars to the advance. Better still, as even New York lawyers rarely have service contracts with their clients, sell world language rights in the next *three* novels. If the author wants to fire his lawyer-agent after Book I, he will still find himself paying commission to his ex-friend on the next two books.

In spite of his boisterous prose, Sidney Sheldon is a man of some delicacy. He also was, perhaps still is, something of a hypochondriac. He told me he was coming to London and, having been his British agent for over five years, I naturally invited him to have lunch with me. He arrived with eyes and nose streaming, the victim of an allergy. There was to be no lunch for either of us at the Savoy Grill that day. I managed to get hold of the great Dr Goldman of Upper Wimpole Street, who had saved Elizabeth Taylor's life and had been GP to Kay Kendall, her husband Rex Harrison, David Niven and other film stars. (I knew this would mean much to Sidney, who had graduated from Hollywood with an Oscar for screenplay-writing.)

Dr Goldman, who was my own GP as well, agreed to see him right away. He was so much in demand that appointments usually had to be made at least a week in advance, but he cured the ailing author within forty-eight hours. A New York publisher – even if he held world rights on the next three unwritten novels – or a Madison Avenue lawyer could hardly have done as much from a range of 3,000 miles.

Restored to his normal vigour, my friend Sidney informed me at our next meeting that the main reason he had come to London was to break off our relationship, as he had decided to move to Morton Janklow. Mort, as he was known, would never use a sub-agent. I had driven half a mile from his hotel before the quip *juste* came to mind. I should have replied, 'Timor mortis conturbat me' – but I don't suppose Sidney had ever heard of William Dunbar.

'You know, George, life is demnably unfair. Take me and Niv. He screwed every woman in Hollywood who stood still long enough. But he's only had two wives – Primmy, who died so tragically, and then Hjordis. So the world reckons he's Mr Nice Guy. With me, when I fall in love with a woman, I want to do the decent thing and marry her. Because I've had six wives, I believe they call me "Sexy Rexy"!'

We were lunching at Les Ambassadeurs in Park Lane and my host was, of course, Rex Harrison. Encouraged by the great success of David Niven's *The Moon's a Balloon*, I was pursuing an even more likely actor for his memoirs. Harrison was an international star and his personal story was a gossip columnist's delight, as the plaintive little speech just quoted helped to prove. Not for nothing had Alan J. Lerner, himself the survivor of seven wives, once said to him, 'You know, Rex, between us we've supported more women than Playtex!' Early on in his Hollywood career, Rex had been briefly suspected of murder when Carole Landis, a starlet with whom he had had a rather public affair, committed suicide. Many years later, when his third wife, Kay Kendall, was slowly dying of leukaemia, he had to behave as normal to keep the secret from her. There must be a heap of good anecdotes connected with the stage version and the film of *My Fair Lady*. He had played the part of Caesar in *Cleopatra*, when life imitated art to an overblown degree through Richard Burton's and Elizabeth Taylor's notorious affair. Beyond all this, he was one of the most outstanding actors of his generation. With no formal training but the grind of weekly repertory, he had polished his talents to a glittering level.

Rex, I soon learned, had a high regard for his own status and would go to extreme lengths to protect it. He was living in Portofino and drove an elderly drophead Rolls Royce when the casting for the film of *My Fair Lady* was being carried out. The Hollywood production company thought he was too old to play Professor Higgins and at first tried to attract stars like Cary Grant, all of whom wisely refused. When Rex finally got the part on the strength of a colour photograph of himself naked on his boat with a champagne bottle concealing his genitals, he insisted in the film contract that his own Rolls Royce must be the vehicle to transport him the few miles from his private bungalow at the Beverly Hills

Hotel to the studio and back again each day. That meant the film company would have to hire a chauffeur to drive the old car from Portofino to the French coast a thousand miles away, thence to be shipped to Southampton and crossing the Atlantic aboard *Queen Elizabeth II*. From New York, the chauffeur would spend over a week driving it the 3,000-odd miles to Los Angeles. All this for two short journeys a day, totalling perhaps ten miles.

In vain, the studio pleaded with Rex. They calculated it would be cheaper to buy a brand-new Rolls Royce for the assignment and give it to him at the end of shooting. But he was adamant. He liked his old veteran of a car. He was used to its faded charms. If he was going to play Professor Higgins in the film, then only a car old enough for George Bernard Shaw himself to recognise would do. And so it did.

When first approached to have his memoirs published, Rex Harrison demurred. It is always flattering to be asked, even when one has a keen sense of one's own worth. But he was chary of overmuch intrusion into his private life – all the more when one American publisher crassly proposed the book should be entitled *My Fair Ladies*. On the other hand, he must have felt it was high time to set the record straight on the acting side. Here he was at the age of sixty-three, a rich man, a distinguished actor and yet somehow . . . unaccepted? Of his contemporaries, Olivier was a peer, Gielgud and Richardson had both been knighted, as had Guinness, a younger man. Perhaps a good book and the surrounding publicity would help to provide that acceptance. If he did decide to go ahead, to a large degree he wanted it both ways. He wanted the wide sales that the 'Sexy Rexy' image would ensure without providing any real details of how that image had been created.

After a few weeks of meetings and discussions, I had come to realise that when a decision loomed Rex could be cautious to the point of dithering. He had caused Lerner and Loewe months of anguish and innumerable transatlantic flights before he finally committed himself to *My Fair Lady*. And that, apart from the singing problem, was his practised medium. Having left school and gone into repertory at the age of sixteen, with no exams passed, he was fairly close to illiteracy. His handwriting was clumsy and his spelling atrocious. Being almost blind in one eye from a youthful bout of measles, he was also a very slow reader.

Gradually he came round to the idea – with several strong provisos. First, the American rights were to be sold before the British. Second, the New York publisher must be clearly informed that there would be no emphasis at all on scandal or the reasons behind the break-up of any of his previous marriages. Third, the publisher must at his own expense nominate an acceptable editor who would stay in London throughout the time required to tape-record, transcribe and edit the text. Fourth and finally, all these points were to be incorporated in the publishing agreement, which had to be approved by his New York lawyer, Aaron Frosch, before Rex signed it.

Everyone in the publishing scene knew how well Niven's *The Moon's a Balloon* had done and was doing. The thought of a bigger star with a juicier story to tell concentrated many minds around mid-town Manhattan but gradually the would-be bidders stole away when they learned of the onerous conditions. But the house of William Morrow was one that had let Niven slip by and Lawrence Hughes, their president, was determined to catch Harrison if he could. He offered an advance of $150,000 (about $900,000 today). I thought it quite generous. In addition, the firm would have to stand the cost of a senior editor's salary for possibly two or three months while he worked exclusively on Rex's book – plus his living expenses and accommodation. That in all could amount to another $50,000.

I was in New York to peddle my wares and felt it useful to pay a courtesy call on the lawyer. The firm was known as Weissberger, Frosch and Leavy, with oak-panelled offices in the East Fifties. Arnold Weissberger, tall, pink-cheeked, white-haired, epicene – a Judge Hardy figure straight from central casting – with those wonderful Elmyr de Hory forgeries of Matisse hanging on the panelled corridor outside his room, was the *doyen* of theatrical lawyers. Every year, he would take his aged and formidable mother to London for two or three weeks; in a suite at the Savoy Hotel he would hold court for such clients as Laurence Olivier and Noël Coward. He would have been at home in a Marquand novel.

I would have expected Rex, with his eye for elegance, to be another of his clients, as Aaron Frosch was a very different breed. He had clawed his way up from the meanest Brooklyn sidewalks and there was still something about the hard stare and the lack of digraphs – 'dese and dose' for 'these and those' – that betrayed the background. (A few years later, he was to suffer grievously from a rare form of osteo-sclerosis in which his neck and shoulders were locked rigid and his vocal chords were so affected that all he could speak was a a kind of guttural glugging. He gallantly went on working; his visitors had to sit exactly opposite him, since he could not move his upper body an inch either way, and they had to strain to understand, often in vain, what he was desperately trying to say.)

When I first met him, he had been much in the news over the doings, both joint and several, of Richard Burton and Elizabeth Taylor. At one stage, she had lost her small fluffy dog – a pekinese, I seem to recall – and at a vast expense of time and money, Frosch had been nominated to find it; which he eventually did, after first scouring Europe. On another occasion, she had undergone an emergency tracheotomy in Harley Street and again he had to be summoned. For quite what purpose it is hard to assess, unless he had hopes of slapping a negligence suit on someone. With two such flamboyant clients spending millions of dollars on legal expenses and many others in the queue for his expensive attention, Aaron Frosch gave me the clear impression that scrutinising a standard publishing contract with a negligible advance in six figures came pretty low on his list of priorities.

As indeed it proved. That contract sat on his desk for well over three months. This was long before the advent of facsimile correspondence but I tried my best to chivvy him with frequent airmail letters and then, when they achieved no response, telephone calls. Rex was busy rehearsing a play and tended to dismiss the problem with the airy attitude of 'the lawyer knows best'. I knew better: hope deferred is the worst recipe for a publisher's enthusiasm. When at last Mr Frosch got round to approving the contract, Larry

Hughes of William Morrow said the firm was most upset over the delays, which seemed to imply that either the would-be author lacked confidence in the house or, worse still, having secured a firm offer, his representatives were stealthily trying to improve it elsewhere. Impetus had been lost, the whole publishing world now knew that the Harrison memoirs were on the table and the unexplained delays must hurt the project. Worse still, in the expectation that work on the book would begin shortly, Morrow had taken a senior editor, Howard Cady, off all his urgent tasks and he had been kicking his heels these past months. The end result, said Larry, was that they were now reducing their offer to an advance of $75,000, half the previous figure. Take it or leave it.

To my considerable surprise, Rex took it. Nor did he – at least, to my knowledge – make any move to wrest from his dilatory lawyer the $67,500 he had lost. My firm, John Farquharson Limited, had in its turn lost $7,500 in commission. (The eventual American edition of *Rex* did not earn enough in royalties to surpass the reduced advance.) There was no point in trying to threaten the threat-maker or, worse still, hire another expensive legal 'fast gun' from Madison Avenue in an effort to outdraw him. The only answer was to shrug and smile, and recall the old story of how the architect and the lawyer argued over which was the older profession. The architect brought in the Book of Genesis to endorse his claim: God had created the world in six days out of chaos.

'Granted,' said the lawyer. 'But who created the chaos?'

In his latter years, Rex Harrison lived in a big apartment overlooking the East River on Manhattan; a recluse named Greta Garbo was his downstairs neighbour. Whenever he was invited to London by a film or stage company for discussions, he had only two simple stipulations. The host company at its own expense must provide him with a suite at the Ritz overlooking Green Park; and for transport to and from Shaftesbury Avenue, about half a mile each way, a chauffeur-driven Rolls.

In the summer of 1981, he and I had lunch at Scott's in Mount Street. Like so many other upper-middle-class

Englishmen, with strangers he would put on that brittle charm and smooth polish which the recipient, particularly if American, could think emanated from a genuine feeling of warmth. I recall the time when a Californian journalist, who was supposed to be interviewing him about his book *Rex*, asked if he could recommend any West End plays. Rex politely went off to fetch a copy of that day's *Times* and worked through the whole list, making barbed but informed comments. When after an interminable time the man departed, Rex turned to me darkly and said, 'Who was that facking feg? Why waste my time with that kind of shit?' But he dropped the bland courtesy with people he knew well and by the date of our lunch at Scott's, I had known him for about ten years.

It was a bright, sunny day and he was in a comparable mood. A few tables away sat a mature actress whose enduring old charms were enjoying a latish flowering as the bitchy star of a successful TV soap opera. 'Dah-h-h-ling,' Rex purred as we walked past, 'you're looking particularly gorgeous today.'

She beamed.

A little later, he raised a glass of white wine to her in silent tribute and then said to me quietly, 'You know, in Hollywood they call her the British Open!'

The lunch continued in that vein. He was interesting, amusing, modest – if one can ever call an international star modest. Not long before, he had put together a personal selection of love poems under the title of *If Love Be Love*, with introductory notes he had written to explain the appeal in each case. The anthology had enjoyed success in Britain and had also been presented on commercial radio in five consecutive programmes. Our meeting was to discuss American publication, which gave him the opportunity for sarcastic comments on the New York publishing scene. But he was in urbane good humour when he called for his Higginsonian tweed hat and left the restaurant with me in tow.

A large highly polished black Ford stood at the kerb. The chauffeur alongside touched his peaked cap and held open the rear door. Rex's eyebrows drew down and his eyes narrowed. 'Where's my Rolls?' he demanded. 'I'm not getting in that hunk of tin!'

The chauffeur apologised. The Rolls had broken down. It was Ascot Week – I thought instantly of the Cecil Beaton costumes, and Gladys Cooper, and Audrey Hepburn fluting 'And gin was mother's milk to 'er' – and all the other Rolls Royces were booked. The large Ford was the next best car available.

Without actually howling or banging a spoon on the table, Rex gave a highly accurate imitation of a small child denied a favourite toy. He glared at the innocent chauffeur and grated, 'I'm supposed to have a Rolls. Get me a facking Rolls!'

'But I've just explained, sir. I'm very sorry but there aren't any spare Rollses. It's Ascot Week. They're all booked up, sir.'

'Then facking well unbook one. Go on – ring your bloody boss. Get him to send a Rolls.'

The man walked off to find a public phone box. It was a hopeless quest – and he knew it.

I said to Rex, 'It's a lovely afternoon – and all downhill to the Ritz. Why don't we walk it? Ten minutes – by the time the driver gets back, we could be there.'

All we would have to do on foot was walk two sides of Berkeley Square, along Berkeley Street, cross Piccadilly and – bingo! – there was the Ritz. In a car, once at the bottom of Berkeley Street, we would have to drive along Piccadilly, turn south into Duke Street, west along King Street, north up St James's Street, west again on Bennet Street and north again on Arlington Street, to reach the side entrance of the Ritz. Depending on the traffic, which would be heavy in mid-afternoon, the car journey might take anything between a quarter and half an hour.

Rex gave me a contemptuous glance. I was obviously one of those 'peace at any price' merchants. Imaginary cigar aloft, Sir Winston Harrison was determined to fight 'em on the beaches.

The chauffeur returned. He was still polite, almost deferential, but you could sense from the way he squared his shoulders and, this time, looked Rex straight in the eye that he was not going to stand much more of this nonsense. 'I've spoken to the boss, sir,' he said. 'He's very sorry indeed – but there just isn't another Rolls in the garage and the broken-down one won't be repaired in under two hours. This is the only car available. The boss apologises – and says he won't charge for today's rental. But it's either the Ford or nothing.'

The graceful gesture of withdrawing the charge meant nothing to Rex. He was not due to pay in any case. I wondered what he would do next. Hail a passing cab? Unlikely: that would cost him money. Stride off, nose in air? Again unlikely: he had rejected my suggestion outright. There was only one thing for it – but the spoiled child had to have the last word.

'You get in the back, George. There's no room in the back of these Fords for my long legs.'

It must appear that Rex Harrison and I measured out our lives with luncheon forks because on this next occasion we were sharing a table in the restaurant of a newly opened smart hotel. At the time, he was married to his fifth wife, Elizabeth, and living in some style in a large house in Belgravia on four floors, with a lift, a butler, a houseman and several maids. Unlike many public performers who have been poor in their formative years, Rex was always a generous host. I had been his guest on numerous occasions and so I insisted that when we broke for lunch – we were going through his draft memoirs in his study and I was desperately trying to persuade him to leave in the most entertaining stories – I would pick up the tab.

The restaurant, as I recall, had a purple ceiling with silver stars painted on it. The other tables were occupied mainly by elderly ladies lunching in twos. There was a ripple of interest when they spotted Rex entering the room. He was shortly to go to New York to play on Broadway and was getting into training, so we both ate and drank sparingly. He had smoked salmon as a main course with a salad on the side and we shared a half bottle of Chablis. The bill came to a little over £14. When I proffered my American Express Gold Card, the waiter regarded it dubiously – in Rex's *sotto voce* to me, 'like a plate of steaming horse-shit'. Nevertheless, he walked off with it, holding the plate well away from his body.

A few minutes later, the head waiter, a swarthy foreigner, came up to our table and announced brusquely, 'We don't accepta credit cards.'

This was a poser. Expecting to pay with my 'that will do nicely' card, I had only a few pounds in my pocket. I said, 'Then you'd better get me a cheque form.'

It was produced and I filled in the details. The waiter went off again and ten minutes crawled by. My guest was ominously quiet. As it happened, my bank was only a few hundred yards away in Piccadilly. I even began to wonder whether the hotel management had sent a member of staff to cash the cheque in person. At the least, it was clear that a telephone call to the bank was being made, to ensure that my current account would stand the massive charge. Rex was one of the most recognisable men in the world at the time. Did the head waiter really think he would be party to a £14 cheque fiddle? Or that the holder of an American Express Gold Card would not be good for that amount?

Rex could play his voice like an ill-tempered clavier. Without depressing the loud pedal more than an inch or two, he gave it a timbre that carried it to the far corners of the restaurant and even aloft to that ghastly purple ceiling. He said coldly, 'I'm never going to lunch in this facking place again!' At the tables around us, the crêpey, liver-spotted hands, clutching their knives and forks, were arrested midway between plate and mouth.

As if on cue, the head waiter reappeared. Even in the wilds of Calabria or wherever he had spent his formative years, films like *The Ghost and Mrs Muir*, *Anna and the King of Siam*, *My Fair Lady*, *The Agony and the Ecstasy*, *Cleopatra* and *Doctor Doolittle* must have penetrated far enough for him to realise suddenly the identity of his distinguished guest. He was now bowing and scraping, his face split in an ingratiating grin. He hopa-ed the gentlemen had enjoyed their lunch? Rex strode past him in a dangerous silence. I knew the signs all too well. The next few minutes could be like learning to juggle with three pinless Mills grenades.

As we threaded our way through the foyer, a little old lady in a shapeless woollen two-piece garment and a grey hat pulled down on her white curls confronted us. She said in a sweet, piping voice, 'Do excuse me, I know how rude it is to accost a total stranger – but aren't you Mr Rex Harrison?'

'I am, madam.'

Her eyes were mist-filled. She said, 'I saw you in *French Without Tears*, Mr Harrison. That other young man – oh, what was his name now? . . .'

'Trevor Howard.'

'. . . Yes, of course, Trevor Howard. He was good – but you were better, Mr Harrison. You were wonderful.'

'Thank you, madam. I am obliged.'

She said musingly, 'Yes, wonderful. Oh, it was all so long ago. Tell me, Mr Harrison, what have you been doing since *French Without Tears*?'

I thought, Hell, that was back in the mid-1930s. Now those grenades will explode. Poor woman – at least it will be instantaneous. She won't know what's hit her.

I was wrong. Rex bowed and gave her a charming smile. He said, 'This and that, madam. This and that.'

The final worth of a writer is what resides on the printed page. He may be a liar, a thief, a drunk, perverted, promiscuous, but if the words continue to sing a siren song long after his death, his squalid life will be justified. From a different starting place, because his life is filled with people (whereas a writer has long stretches of loneliness), the actor's sole justification is how he performs on the stage or the screen. Alas, stage performances can only be measured in the memory or – to a later generation – through the tributes of a Hazlitt or a Tynan.

It would be vastly unfair to pass on from Rex Harrison without a comment on the one thing he loved perhaps beyond all else – his acting. Even at eighty-two, when his memory was failing and he was within a few months of his death, he appeared in Somerset Maugham's *The Circle* at The Ambassador's Theatre in New York. He may have drunk deep in his youth and womanised far more widely than the prim speech which opened this sub-section would allow. But acting took precedence. Just as the public concept of David Niven as the more 'ideal husband' struck him as grossly unfair, so too did the general feeling among audiences and even theatre critics that performing a tragedy was far more difficult than playing in a drawing-room comedy. Indeed, he reckoned the reverse was true.

He would say, 'With tragedy, you open your lungs and you open your arms and you let it all go. That's fine. It takes courage, you risk falling flat on your face. But it's not as difficult as playing comedy. Comedy needs total control. You have to hold it all in, you're playing on a tight rein the whole time' – and here he would slowly clench his fist and present the back of his knuckles, like a coachman reining back the spirited steeds. 'It needs *timing*.'

As an occasional and amateur theatre-goer, I can testify to that – twice over. In the spring of 1974, I went to see Rex in *Enrico Quattro* by Pirandello at His Majesty's. Some time later, I tape-recorded the experience and here is an extract.

The play starts with the figure of a king, a man with an archaic regal manner – sitting on a high throne in an ermine robe. We are in mediaeval times. The servants who scuttle around are dressed in tabards and hose. There are stained-glass windows.

With an imperious command, the king sends his courtiers and staff away. Then a sly look of malicious humour comes over his face and with one extraordinary, almost simian, movement he delves into his voluminous robe and plucks out a large cigar and a box of matches. He handles the cigar as a precious object, holds it up for inspection, lights it very carefully, then puffs out clouds of blue smoke.

It was an absolute show-stopper. With that one little bit of business he conveyed that something very strange was going on. The audience realised that we were not in mediaeval times, as we had thought, but in the present day and perhaps the regal figure we were contemplating was not as royal as we had supposed. Without a word being spoken, Rex Harrison's genius lay in the fantastic control and timing of that gesture. Had he taken longer it would have spoilt the tension. Had he rushed it, he'd have ruined it. As it was, it put a catch in my throat and – judging from the attentive silence in the house – in everyone else's throat as well.

Just over a year later, I saw Rex in New York in a very different play, Terence Rattigan's *In Praise of Love*. They were friends of long standing. Nearly forty years earlier, each had contributed to the other's success when Rex made his West End début in *French Without Tears* but playwrights and novelists have few qualms when a likely plot suggests itself. Rattigan based his new play on Rex's bewitched but tragically brief love affair/marriage with Kay Kendall. Kay had died of leukaemia at the age of thirty-two. The marriage lasted two years and, even as he entered into it, Rex had been told secretly by the doctors that she was already suffering from the disease, unknown to herself, and had only two years to live. To explain her feelings of lassitude and the gradual sapping of her health, she had been officially told she was suffering from anaemia. Knowing the truth, the medicos reckoned, would only hasten the inevitable end.

Rattigan had altered the dramatic details. In his play, the couple are middle-aged and have been married more than twenty years. The hook that this kind of well carpentered play needs was that, while the husband has to go on being the rude, chauvinistic pig he has always been, even though his heart is breaking, in order to keep the secret, the wife *knows* she has the fatal disease. The audience, of course, soon knows that she knows but nothing in her demeanour on stage or her conversation tips the husband off.

As Rex Harrison himself puts it in his last and posthumously published book, *A Damned Serious Business: My Life in Comedy*, 'All through my career . . . I have been employed for the sole purpose of making people love the villain or the cad. Almost all my major roles have been of the self-centred type, who, in Higgins' words, "desires nothing more than just the ordinary chance to live exactly as he likes and do precisely what he wants", and my task has been to get an audience to find something sympathetic in them, so they can identify, and even grow to *like* them.'

This time, he is playing Sebastian Cruttwell, a literary critic

of international renown and very much a Professor Higgins
figure in his intellectual arrogance, his selfishness and his
abrasive wit. He has always treated his wife as an inferior being
– a woman, indeed – and dim into the bargain. And even now
he has to keep up the pretence. The Cruttwells' apartment in
New York forms the set, a combination of drawing room and
study with an upper balcony and shelves of books stretching
across three sides of the stage.

It was not much of a play, despite Rex's acting and that
of Julie Harris as the wife. I have used the phrase 'well
carpentered'. The sides of the box were at right angles, the
hinges deftly concealed, and the lid fitted flush but, when
you came to open it back, there was not much inside. But
after nearly twenty years, one small moment remains vividly
in my mind. Julie Harris is sitting at a desk on the ground
floor while Rex is ascending the steep flight of stairs to
fetch a book from the balcony shelves. As he climbs up, he
delivers a brutally sarcastic speech, a typical diatribe aimed
at her shortcomings. He reaches the climax of his peroration
and the top of the bookshelves simultaneously. His back is
to the audience throughout and his face still out of view as he
stretches to pick out the book. Then he stops talking and half
glances across his left shoulder. She is not looking at him; her
head is bowed.

For the briefest of moments, his shoulders sagged. The erect
back and stiff neck crumpled. The audience held its breath.
One could suddenly sense all the concentrated effort, the
control, needed to keep on playing a false role convin-
cingly; a touchingly wasted effort because we, the audience,
already knew she was aware of her own fate. Then the back
straightened again, the shoulders squared and the sarcastic
voice picked up its theme. The whole episode lasted two,
perhaps three, seconds but it has remained with me for close
on twenty years.

That skill, that technique, that imaginative leap by a man
rooted in himself – for what he brought, he could be
forgiven much.

*   *   *

There was a hoary old story in the trade that went something like this. A famous author has been banging on about himself for at least half an hour. Then he turns to his friend and says, 'That's enough about me. Let's talk about you for a change. What do *you* really think about my latest novel?'

A vague association of ideas brings me on to the interesting case of Jeffrey Archer. During my active career as an agent, I never had the privilege of representing Mr (as he then was) Archer. Deborah Owen had been in that capacity from the start and had performed with great skill. She had shown particular – and welcome – stubbornness in offering his first novel, *Not a Penny More, Not a Penny Less*, to at least a dozen publishers until at last, on the second time round, Jonathan Cape accepted it. For his next novel, Deborah Owen moved Archer to Hodder & Stoughton where he remained with ever-increasing success for his next six novels and two collections of short stories.

Conscientious agents always try to handle their clients on a 'horses for courses' basis. A delicately clever novel which would wither away on a big popular list needs good reviews to bring it to full blossom. Over the years, that might mean trying houses favoured by the literary editors, such as Secker & Warburg, Jonathan Cape, Chatto & Windus, Hamish Hamilton, Weidenfeld & Nicolson and Sinclair-Stevenson. A big adventure novel with a wide potential sales appeal would probably be aimed at Collins or Heinemann or Hodder & Stoughton. Hodder was – and still is, I believe – pre-eminent for true adventure and exploration books as well. It so happened that many of my clients, such as John le Carré, Morris West, Noel Barber, William McIlvanney, Clive Egleton, Sir Edmund Hillary, Sir Ranulph Fiennes, Sir Francis Chichester, Chris Bonington and Robin Knox-Johnston had gravitated to the Hodder list. Jeffrey Archer may have heard my name mentioned along the Bedford Square corridors.

However it came about, at irregular intervals he would telephone me in crisp, military tones. Having made it clear in his opening remarks that he had no intention of coming to me as a client, which evoked the silent response that no one, as far as I knew, had ever suggested he should, he would go on to tell me that he had recommended X or Y – perhaps a new novelist or a politician – to seek my advice. Sometimes, the result was good for both parties, sometimes not; but at least I was grateful to Jeffrey for mentioning my name. At first, I wondered why he had not steered them towards his own agent, Debbie Owen, but then I realised that she kept a very small and select list. Besides, as sometimes happened in my own case, an author who was really happy with his agent might avoid spreading the word and so have to share that agent's time and attention with the newcomer.

It is always worth recalling that in his twenties Jeffrey Archer held the Inter-Varsity 100-yard sprint record and represented Great Britain at that distance. Apart from physical aptitude, the successful sprinter needs absolute concentration, fast reflexes to leave the starting blocks a split second after the gun goes off and blinkered vision. Glancing at the opponents in the other lanes loses precious milliseconds. And he must have concentrated arrogance and a formidable will to win. At university level or international level or Olympic level, there will not be much to choose between the eight finalists in the way of physical condition or power-to-weight ratio. At that stage, winning is in the mind; nice guys do indeed come second – or worse.

The world knows how, more than twenty years ago from the depths of near-bankruptcy, Jeffrey Archer vowed that he would write novels to repay his debts and earn himself a fortune, which he duly did. From the financial shadow over his early political career and, a few years ago, the notoriety of his ultimately successful High Court libel action, he has now found haven in the House of Lords and another fortune through a clever switch of publishers. Only a quick-footed driving ambition and tunnel vision focused on breaking the tape first could achieve this quality of success.

Towards the end of 1983, I was for once involved in active negotiations on his behalf – with, of course, Debbie Owen's full knowledge and approval. Hugh Begg, a one-time director of the Thomson Group and then running Seymour Press, had sought my assistance over a bright idea of his. It was to publish the complete text of a popular novel in consecutive instalments in a national newspaper. In Victorian times novelists like Dickens had written books in instalments published in magazines before their appearance in book form but under Begg's scheme the newspaper editor would have the benefit of assessing the full novel before making a commitment. Obviously, only an author with wide public appeal would be in the running and there were few of those. Some would be between books, others might feel that newspaper coverage of the whole text would endanger their subsequent hardcover and paperback sales. There was also an interesting legal question: under what sub-division of copyright would the form of publication fall? Several book publishers claimed that it constituted 'volume rights'. Hugh Begg and I, having taken counsel's opinion, maintained that a 'volume' in publishing terms could only be a collection of printed pages firmly attached together by some form of binding including staples. As a national newspaper consists of several sheets folded in half and placed together but not attached in any way, anything incomplete it published could not be a 'volume'.

The *Mail on Sunday*, owned by Associated Newspapers, was due for a relaunching under its new editor, Stewart Steven, who had written several topical and cogent non-fiction books, and who just happened to be a client of mine. The idea behind the relaunch was to set the paper at the upper end of the popular market where the moving of lips was not an automatic accompaniment to reading. But it was first necessary to convince the management of Associated Newspapers, in particular the shrewd John Winnington-Ingram, son of a previous Bishop of London. Hugh Begg was well up to that task and there we were, all set to advance with two potential candidates, Frederick Forsyth and Jeffrey Archer, both of whom had new novels scheduled for the appropriate time-slot.

It has to be said that of the two the newspaper preferred Forsyth. But his paperback publisher, Corgi Books, had just paid the then enormous sum of £800,000 (about £1.35 million today), for softcover rights in his new novel and they were convinced that the *Mail on Sunday*'s coverage would seriously prejudice their sales prospects. They and Hutchinson, his hardcover publishers, who benefited substantially from the paperback sale, combined to press Forsyth – through his agent, Diana Baring of Curtis Brown – to withdraw from negotiations. Reasonably enough, he took their urgent advice and duly withdrew. (In the event, Jeffrey Archer's *First Among Equals*, probably because of rather than in spite of the extensive newspaper coverage, outsold its predecessor in hardcovers by 20 per cent and in paperback sales by about the same percentage.)

But that success was blanked off by the future. On the principle of the excess of cooks and spoilt broth, Deborah Owen had generously agreed that I should represent her and Jeffrey's interests in the negotiations – on the understanding, of course, that no commitment was made without his (and her) prior approval, and that any fees for my firm's services should not be deducted from the purchase price due to him, which came to a nice round £100,000. So far, so good: yet I knew that, just as Hutchinson and Corgi had had qualms on behalf of Forsyth, Hodder & Stoughton, who published Jeffrey both in hard covers and in paperback through their subsidiary, Coronet Books, were feeling uneasy. Had Jeffrey's decisiveness twitched by even a fraction, the deal would have been abandoned.

Jeffrey Archer has always been something of a card. Arnold Bennett's notebook would have been out and open had the lives of the two successful novelists overlapped. Jeffrey has the bounce of the short-distance runner and the firmness of the man of action. But just as Hamlet had to walk the battlements alone, speaking his solitary thoughts aloud, so Henry the Fifth needed soldiers around him before he could strike heroic attitudes and rally the troops. At the emergency meeting held in his tenth-floor apartment overlooking the Thames and that recurring target, the Houses of Parliament, on the opposite bank – Virgil's 'love of the further shore' – Jeffrey stood firm. He has made so many speeches in his time that even when he is having a supposedly relaxed chat with one individual, he often appears to be addressing a public meeting. On this occasion, the ability served him well. As he had also said to me in that published interview, 'I by nature like to be an experimenter, the man who tries something that's never been done before. It doesn't worry me to see something fail. If you throw the ball into the ring ten times and it comes back five times, you're damn lucky!'

The deal was agreed and any residual unease on the part of his publishers was soothed by the balm of a generous share of the newspaper payment, donated by the author. All he now had to do was finish *First Among Equals* in good time for the *Mail on Sunday* to run it in four consecutive issues in the early summer of 1984, with book publication occurring towards the end of the serialisation.

Christmas Day in 1983 fell on a Sunday. As I remember, the directors of John Farquharson had decided that attendance on the previous Friday would be voluntary. In any case, the office would close at twelve noon that day. Those who did attend would have a celebratory drink or two and then perhaps do some last-minute shopping before going home for the holiday. At about ten o'clock that morning, the telephone rang. It was Jeffrey.

He came straight to the point, as usual. 'George, how long will you be there?'

'The office closes at twelve noon, Jeffrey. Back again next Thursday.'

'That's not good enough,' he said.

'How do you mean?'

He explained. As I already knew, he often did ten or more drafts of a novel. Now he had inserted the final corrections into the final draft and the script was even now being photocopied. He needed two copies for the United States, two copies for Hodder & Stoughton, one copy for Deborah Owen, one copy for me, another copy for this one and that one – and even no doubt a file copy for himself. Delivery of all these copies had been promised by mid-afternoon that very Friday. He had even booked a motorcycle courier to deliver my copy to me in Regent Street. It should be with me by about four-thirty.

I had been thinking as the clipped phrases entered my left ear. There was no editorial need for me to read the novel at all. But there were still a few minor negotiations to complete with Associated Newspapers and it was obviously essential

for me to know what was in the package I would eventually
hand over. Besides, my firm was due a substantial fee from the
deal; although it did not come from his pocket, I should at the
least show willing. I had never yet read an Archer novel, as his
writing had fallen neither within my bounds of duty nor taste.
Perhaps I should not delay the experience; I might even find an
hour or two towards the end of the Christmas break to read
the opening chapters and then with luck finish the task over
the long New Year weekend.

'Okay, Jeffrey,' I said. 'I'll be out at lunch between twelve
and two but then I'll come back here and hold the fort until
five p.m. But not a moment later. My wife was expecting me
home soon after lunch. She'll probably kill me!'

He promised the courier would be with me before five, we
exchanged Christmas wishes, and that was that.

1983 had been a good year for John Farquharson. Although
inflation was still running at over 5 per cent, it had come well
down from the 20 per cent-plus of three years before. We
were set to make a solid profit on the fiscal year and the
prospects ahead were fine. So the few of us who had come
in that morning had a pleasantly congratulatory drink or two
and then broke up. After a solitary lunch in a pizza parlour
where young and erratically mobile people shouted at one
another and spilled drinks, I returned to my office to sit out
the afternoon. It was gloomy and I could hear the laughter of
revellers and the shouts of late shoppers below on the Regent
Street pavements. There was no one else in our suite of offices
– and probably no one else in the large building except for
the commissionaire at the front desk. Files had been locked
away for the holidays and typewriters switched off. I had
read nearly all the many books that crowded the shelves in
my room and I was in no mood to begin reading one of the
heap of incoming typescripts that sat on a low table close to
my desk. The minutes dragged by.

With nothing else to do, I checked my watch with the
speaking clock. I was determined not to stay one moment
after five o'clock. The traffic might be thick, the courier
might have a puncture or lose his way or be held up by
a traffic warden; in any such event – too bad. Once the

promised hour arrived, I was away, Archer novel or no Archer novel.

At about twenty to five, the commissionaire on the ground floor rang to say that the courier was on his way up in the lift. I met the man at the lift exit and signed for the bulky parcel he handed over. Within five minutes I had locked the office front door and was walking briskly, although lugging the great weight of paper under one arm, to the Poland Street garage to get my car.

Christmas Eve and Christmas Day passed quietly in a pleasant family reunion. On Boxing Day morning, my wife and I were alone once more. After a late breakfast, I was pottering around in my dressing gown, unshaven, hair uncombed, enjoying that world-without-end atmosphere of a holiday that still had some days to go. The telephone rang. We were not expecting anyone to ring and there was that short stab of fear. Could it be bad news? I grabbed the handset off its base.

There was that crisp 'Montgomery at Alamein' voice. 'Well, George, what do you think of it?'

'Er . . .'

'The book, of course. *First Among Equals*. How did it grab you?'

'Er, you see, Jeffrey, I haven't actually read it yet.'

'You . . . what? You mean, you haven't even started it?'

'No, not yet.'

'Well, all I can say is – I'm damn disappointed. Damn disappointed.' There was a loud crackle in my left ear as he slammed his telephone down.

My wife put her head round the door and asked, 'Who was that? Don't tell me one of your clients rang you. On Boxing Day? What nerve!'

'Not a client,' I said. 'More of a friend. I think.'

That was a dozen years ago. Having come to know him much better since then, I can now admit an error. Jeffrey Archer should never have strayed into this compound of monsters. For instance, he lacks that self-deluding arrogance about his writing gift; he considers himself to be just a storyteller and he speaks with genuine humility about the literary skills of a le Carré. Next, he has almost a phobia about paying his bills by return of post and, although he will drive the hardest of bargains with his publishers, he shows real generosity towards his advisors. It is indeed an irony that his more recent public problems have derived from attempts to help others.

Dorothy Parker wanted as her epitaph: 'Her sins were scarlet but her books were read.' In my view, the Archer sins are of the palest pink but the rest of the sentence applies worldwide.

On 13 February 1991, Jeffrey took me to meet Mrs Thatcher. It was Ash Wednesday. In his poem for that day, T.S. Eliot had asked, 'Why should the agèd eagle stretch its wings?' I could only be classified as an agèd cuckoo, having often slipped my authors into the nests of unsuspecting publishers. But, after retiring more than four years earlier, I too had no urge to stretch my wings by a return to active agenting. Jeffrey's plan was for me to act as private advisor to his friend, who had lost an empire but not yet found a role. She had already declared her intention to write a book. Indeed, there were to be three books: her memoirs in two separate volumes and a round-up book on the greatness of England – this scepter'd isle, this precious stone set in a silver sea and so forth – with, it seemed, heavy hints on the identity of the leading statesperson who had restored that greatness.

She sat in a chintzy armchair and I was placed opposite her, about eight feet away, on a slippery and equally chintzy sofa. Fixing me with a blank, self-absorbed stare, she began a peroration that lasted twenty minutes. (I had been allotted half an hour of her time.) Senior politicians, on being Paxmanised in an aggressive television interview, soon learn the trick of rolling on regardless, every time the interrogator prepares to shoot an awkward question. 'And when I ope my mouth, let no dog bark' becomes their motto. I only wanted to be helpful, to comment positively from my experience of the literary world but, whenever I took a deep breath, she pressed on, non-stop, giving me a lecture on how to write a book and then how to market it, various aspects of editing, the pros and cons of the publishing world and how to improve it. The extent of her ill-conceived ignorance at that time was only matched by the brazen vigour with which she expressed it.

When I did finally manage to interject a suggestion, it was that in my opinion the first volume of her memoirs should cover her prime-ministerial career, events that would be freshest in the reading public's memory, and the second volume should deal with her life before 1979. The advice was pretty obvious and I am sure that at least nine out of ten editors or agents would have said the same. But the spunglass halo of hair almost quivered with contempt and the unctuous 'talking posh' accent sounded a harsher timbre. I was totally wrong, it declared. Chronology was the thing. You started at the beginning and went straight on through to the end. It was that simple, apparently.

Fortunately for her sales, her publishers and other advisors must later have persuaded her into accepting the obvious. Otherwise, in October 1993, the bookshops would have been displaying *The Grantham Shop Years*, perhaps for a long time.

When I thought about that meeting afterwards, I was irresistibly reminded of Oliver Cromwell. Not that Mrs Thatcher had ever to my knowledge entertained plans for regicide, although she had, of course, stolen the Queen's role after the Falklands War when taking the salute on the steps of St Paul's. Cromwell had written a letter to the Elders of the Kirk of Scotland, which said, 'I beseech you, in the bowels of Christ, think it possible you may be mistaken.' Great advice for all of us – but, alas, those temperamentally incapable of accepting it are the self-important and the self-obsessed.

After that inauspicious beginning, I spent the next few months as a private consultant, helping to draft various contracts and advising Mark Thatcher, who was spending much of his time in England on his mother's behalf. By the late summer, she had decided to take on an American agent named Marvin Josephson to place her book and serial rights. As I withdrew from the favoured circle, I did wonder why the woman who claimed to have regenerated Britain's pride and position in the world should have looked to a foreigner, who was primarily a lawyer, to represent her when there were at least half a dozen first-rate British agents who would have performed with equal, if not greater, effect.

Mark was always pleasant, polite and punctual – welcome attributes in a successful businessman. His was a difficult task, to live up to the expectations of a famous parent. Over the years, I had often noted that extra urge to succeed, to impress the parent, that can drive the son of a Sir Malcolm Campbell, a Hillary or a Chichester. If Mark ever seemed brusque or thick-skinned in his dealings, I was sure it derived from that need. He was always the soul of friendly courtesy throughout our acquaintance.

On the morning of 4 June – the Glorious Fourth – he and I were ushered by a butler in full fig into Robert Maxwell's dreadful marble, gilt and lacquer eyrie on top of the Shoe Lane building that adjoined the Mirror Group printing and editorial offices. After being kept waiting for a quarter of an hour, presumably to lower our resistance, we summoned the butler and told him that, if nothing happened meanwhile, we would be leaving in exactly five minutes' time. Four minutes later, a vastly fat man lumbered in, still with the jet-black hair I had first seen more than four decades earlier – though now quite obviously dyed – and the thick, black half-hoops of clown's eyebrows. He greeted us with an apology in that melodious upper-class voice that seemed to owe nothing to the guttural echoes of *Mittel Europa*.

In all my long experience, Ian Robert Maxwell was by the length of a Roman road the biggest monster I ever encountered. Later on, I describe how he took over Simpkin Marshall, the famous book wholesaling firm, and by wild spending sent it sliding into liquidation, although he walked away without a dent in his wallet. Indeed, word around the trade had it that the said wallet was then considerably thicker than it had been when he first encountered Simpkin Marshall. But long before this, he had become a byword for slick dealing. In 1946, the story went, when he was still an army captain, he had been duty officer at the main railway station in Vienna, which was then run by the Tripartite – American, Russian, British – Commission. He spotted a lengthy line of goods wagons being shunted into sidings in the Russian zone. He spoke fluent German and asked the station master what was happening. It turned out that, when the Russian troops were closing in on Berlin, Ullstein, one of the biggest German publishing houses, decided to shift its medical and scientific stocks to its sub-office in Vienna. The stocks had been seized by the USSR as war reparations and were to be transported by rail to Moscow.

Maxwell bribed the station master to have the goods wagons shunted into the British zone yards. Next morning, he rushed round to the Town Major, who was responsible for enemy property, told him a yarn about coming across some dud old books and officially bought the stocks for virtually nothing. Armed with the bill of sale and a licence to remove the goods, he managed to have them shipped to England. For some years after the war, until the Ullstein stocks were exhausted, Lange, Springer & Maxwell, book importers and exporters, operated out of that triangular building that separates Shaftesbury Avenue from Monmouth Street, and is now a theatre-ticket office.

If the story is true – and it has all the ring of an honest Maxwell anecdote (if that is not a contradiction in terms) – he learned two valuable lessons from it. One is that after a long war there is a desperate need among institutions – colleges, universities, research centres, reference libraries and so on – for copies of up-to-date and accurate medical and scientific works. The second is that those very same institutions, unlike private citizens, have money to burn. Captain Maxwell MC – he may have sounded like an English gentleman but he never understood the ambiguities, the apparent modesty and the silent confidence that distinguishes the breed – set to work with gusto. Academics, he quickly learned or sensed, are often more interested in career advancement than the royalty rates offered on their books. And so the setting up of Pergamon Press was a brilliant stroke. In the words of Roy Thomson, describing around that time the advent of commercial television, it was a licence to print money.

Institutions all round the world were desperate to replenish their worn-out shelves; academics and scientists among the victorious countries were equally desperate to burst into print. Maxwell brought them together – and the crowning touch of respectability was when he persuaded Oxford City Council to lease Headington Hill Hall, an empty mansion on its outskirts, for a peppercorn rent. Pergamon Press of Oxford – it had the right ring.

He could have spent the rest of his working life quietly building up a great scientific publishing house with prosperous overseas branches, and died a rich and highly respected man. But there was a streak of the actor *manqué* in him and an arrogance that conceived itself to be above the law. He became a Labour MP for a neighbouring constituency but ruined his political career by bumptiously making his maiden speech on the very day he took his seat. He was cautioned by the police for driving his Rolls Royce one-handed while at the same time shaving with an electric razor. His conduct in running his firm was equally eccentric.

Once or twice a year, Pergamon Press took a full-page advertisement in the *Observer* to announce all its titles for the coming months. On one occasion, a minor Scottish novelist named Milne wrote to Maxwell congratulating him on the spread but saying that he was surprised by the omission of a treatise on an esoteric subject – let us say, for instance, thermodynamics. Maxwell replied by return, offering him an advance of £500 on account of a 7½% royalty to write such a book. The novelist, in alarm, wrote back to say he knew nothing at all about thermodynamics except that it was an important scientific subject. Maxwell's follow-up, again by return, was on the lines of 'Let us cut out all this bluffing. I am increasing my offer to £750 advance against a flat 10% royalty. So there.'

Mr Milne began to realise he had a tiger by the tail. He happened to be a client of my colleague, Innes Rose, and sent copies of the correspondence to Innes, beseeching him to put an end to the charade. Innes wrote a blunt letter to the Captain, stressing yet again that his client knew absolutely nothing about the arcane subject of thermodynamics and had only pointed out its absence from the Pergamon list in an effort to be helpful. I can almost remember verbatim Maxwell's reply. It went something like this: 'I am sick and tired of all this double-crossing and now this latest insult of introducing a literary agent. Here is my final word on the subject. My offer is increased to £1,000 advance but the royalties cannot be improved beyond 10%.'

Innes ignored it.

My personal contacts with Robert Maxwell consisted of annual visits in June to Headington Hill Hall for a buffet luncheon to celebrate his birthday and, when he became more widely involved with book publishing, occasional meetings with other senior agents whom he tried to impress, usually by berating his own executives in public. Several hundred guests attended the birthday parties in an enormous marquee erected alongside the Hall. To provide a suitably martial air for the 'Captain', the band of the Royal Marines would march and counter-march on the slippery lawns. Sometimes – a true *deus ex machina* – the host would make a dramatically late entrance in his clattering helicopter.

By the late 1960s, I had struck up a friendship with Harold Evans, then the editor of the *Sunday Times*. We played squash regularly and over a pint of beer afterwards would gossip about Fleet Street and the book world. Harry's Insight Team had already made its mark with investigative reports and I suggested he should put them on to Maxwell. There was a lot of dirt to be dug up, I said. The name, it seemed, meant nothing to Harry and so I told him a few anecdotes. Later on, he followed the advice and in spite of the usual threats of injunctions and libel suits from the irate quarry, ran a solid two-parter on the rise and rise of the 'bouncing Czech'.

By the early 1970s, several agents and publishers, and no doubt the shrewder City dealers, knew that Maxwell was a crook. The criminal method was simple but no less culpable. Pergamon (UK) was a public company, as was Pergamon (NY). There was a constant two-way flow across the Atlantic of book copies published in one country and shipped for sale in the other. But neither company was permitted to deal direct with the other. Maxwell would interpose one of his private,

wholly owned companies. For example, a book published
in the UK for £10 would normally be shipped for export
at 50% off – that is, £5. But Pergamon (UK) would have
to sell that book to the Maxwell private company for, say,
£4 and the latter would sell it on to New York for, say, £6.
The same technique would apply in reverse. It was purely –
if that is the right adverb – a paper transaction; the stocks
were not physically transported by the intervening private
company. But when one recalls the tens of thousands of
books that Pergamon shipped in each direction every year,
the illegal profits, fleeced from the shareholders, must have
been enormous. They silently disappeared into the central
Maxwell bank account in Liechtenstein. Around that time,
the Captain was conspicuous in the van of the 'I'm Backing
Britain' campaign but I doubt if he relished the irony. A sense
of humour is often dependent on a feeling for moderation and
self-mockery, neither of which attributes figured largely in his
make-up.

One assumes that the uncovering of the frauds was behind
Leasco's sudden withdrawal from the planned takeover of
Pergamon and the subsequent Board of Trade enquiry which
found him unfit to be associated with a public company.
It seems odd that he was not charged and tried for fraud,
because there must have been thousands of incriminating
invoices in the London and New York export and shipping
departments. It seems even more odd that when, a few years
later, he bought back the Pergamon group and built it up
again with great vigour, banks rushed to lend him money
and 'blue-blooded' City firms flung a cloak of respectability
over the conniving villain. Of course, he was ruthless in using
the legal system to protect himself from too close scrutiny.
He tried desperately to suppress Tom Bower's thorough
investigative biography by issuing writs for libel that he never
intended to pursue. But it is still a blatant criticism of the Bank
of England, the Stock Exchange and the whole City ethos that
a repeated offender could be supported through the Pergamon
débâcle, the acquiring of the British Printing Corporation,
followed by the Mirror Group, the fiasco of a second London
evening paper and finally the *Götterdämmerung* of buying

Macmillan Inc. and its subsidiaries and the *New York Post*
for crazy amounts, financed by raiding the Mirror Group's
pension funds.

This overlong detour may explain why I approached what
was to be my last encounter with him warily, although I did
not then know, of course, that he was living on borrowed
time and on borrowed funds. Just as his physical condition
was more flabby and gross than at our previous meeting
two or three years earlier, so his mood was less abrasive,
less would-be dominant. He fussed over Mark, extolling
repeatedly his enormous admiration for Mark's mother and
insisting on autographing a copy of the Joe Haines biography
as a humble gift for the great lady. He turned to me with a hard
stare from under those sinister elliptical eyebrows and asked,
'We have met before, have we not?'

I replied, as I always did on the dozen or more times he had
asked the same question in the past, 'Yes, at the relaunching
of Simpkin Marshall.'

'Ah,' he said. As he always did.

We then got down to business. Two acolytes from the
States were present; a senior editor from Macmillan Inc.,
which would be the leading publisher if all went well, and
an intelligent woman trouble-shooter. Neither of them at
that stage had the slightest notion that their employer was
an honours graduate in villainy.

The discussions slowly crystallised. A new publishing house
with the aim of issuing titles by famous personalities was to be
formed – with the unsurprising name of Maxwell Macmillan.
Mrs Thatcher's three books would naturally lead the field.
Delivery dates were tentatively agreed, as were royalty rates
and bonus payments if one or other of the books remained
on the bestseller lists for so many weeks. And finally we
reached the guaranteed, non-returnable advance. It was to be
$10 million. We were sitting at a round table. I happened to be
on Maxwell's left with, clockwise, the editor next to me, then
Mark and the woman advisor next to her boss. He turned to
me and said, 'I could live with that.'

A messenger then arrived to say that his helicopter was
waiting to whisk him off to other meetings. On his departure,

Mark and I stayed on for the best part of an hour, discussing
further details. We both took Maxwell's remark as an oral
agreement to the $10 million. Indeed, the editor produced a
closely typed five-page memorandum which stated that figure
in its third line. So, when we departed for lunch, it was with
the sense of a mission well completed.

Next morning, Mark received a faxed message to say that
the deal was off. Over the following week, abortive attempts
to put it together again were made but without success. Which
was just as well. Captain Robert Maxwell was then within five
months of his final plunge.

For a long time, I felt it was both ironic and inappropriate
that the doubly corrupt hulk should buried on the slopes of
the Mount of Olives. And then I suddenly saw the exquisite
rightness of it all, remembering Byron's terse remark to John
Murray: 'Barabbas was a publisher.'

2

THE SORCERER

Appropriately enough, it all began outside Hatchards book-shop in Piccadilly on a bright summer's day in 1946. A month earlier, I had been demobilised from the army after six years' service; I was indeed wearing the heavy serge 'demob suit' that a grateful government doled out to returning heroes. Having served continuously for more than four years overseas, I was entitled to six months' leave on full pay and, sensing that never again in my lifetime would I be paid for doing nothing, was determined to enjoy every moment of it.

As I was gazing at the book display in the windows of Hatchards, a familiar figure walked out of the shop. It was Cecil Hatry, a wartime friend who had served in the Rifle Brigade. I was both pleased and indeed surprised to see him, for he was not the most bookish of men.

'What on earth are you doing here?'

He made an ample gesture. 'My father owns the shop. You free for lunch? There's an interesting new place opened up round the corner – The Caprice.'

We had not met for nearly two years and so spent most of the lunch getting up to date. He asked me what I intended to do and I said that, when my leave was up, I reckoned to become a schoolmaster. I had, in fact, attended an interview with the Gabbitas & Thring scholastic agency that morning in nearby Sackville Street. He said his father had recently bought a publishing house and was looking for someone to run it. Why not me? Little realising then in my ignorance – I had, after all, put in some 'long service in hot stations', away from cultural centres – what a magnet the publishing world was (and still is) to ambitious young men and women, I demurred. All right, I had read a good many books as a pre-war pupil of Dr F.R. Leavis at Downing College, Cambridge, and had recently had a war novel published with some success but did not know the first thing about the publishing trade. What was more, it sounded a rather speculative business. It was a very friendly gesture on his part, I added, but really . . .?

Cecil continued to urge me at least to meet his father. Lulled by the good wine and his enthusiasm, I was finally persuaded. He went off to telephone his father and no doubt brief him about me. Half an hour later, we were ushered into Clarence Hatry's impressive room in his headquarters at Tudor Street, next door to the then offices of the *Observer*.

Of all the noteworthy men I have met in a longish lifetime, Clarence Hatry was one of the most remarkable. He was a small, bird-like man, bald-headed apart from curly grey hair above each ear, with an enormous scimitar of a nose, a close-cropped grey moustache and the strangest pale blue eyes. He had a soft, sibilant voice – in all the years I knew him, I never heard it raised in sorrow or anger – and a laugh that was a cross between a chuckle and a giggle. He had the quickest of minds and innate charm. Much later, a colleague of his, who had made a fortune in the tough pre-war steel industry and who was as dour as the metal itself, confessed to me that a meeting with CCH, as he was known to friends and employees, was like drinking champagne on an empty stomach. You went in to see him, he said, full of insuperable problems, and in a quarter of an hour he had plucked out figures, juggled with them and then proved conclusively that the problems did not exist. Of course, when the bubbles subsided, you realised the problems had not gone away but while you were the target of CCH's battery of wit and charm, everything seemed not only possible but likely as well.

At our first meeting, he flattered me excessively but with a twinkle in those blue eyes that said, 'We both know I'm exaggerating but just think why I should go to the trouble of doing so' – the most insidious form of flattery. He explained what great prospects there were in post-war publishing and how the trade needed new talent, young men whose horizons had been expanded through their war service, men with no set preconceptions who could sweep away the dusty old practices. It could have been Montgomery addressing his troops before D-Day and not a City magnate devoting his precious time to one raw individual. I soon succumbed.

After I had agreed to try my hand at running the house of T. Werner Laurie Ltd – after forty-five years, my heart can still quicken over the combined force of folly and vanity – we began to discuss my starting salary. He suggested £750 a year. I replied that, with a pregnant wife, I could not accept a penny under £1,000. (The present-day equivalents would be, respectively, about £14,500 and £19,500.) He might have been impressed by my bargaining powers or, more likely, nonplussed by my innocence but, after a short pause, he agreed.

He next suggested I should start my duties at the beginning of September, a few weeks hence. To which, I explained my determination to enjoy my paid leave to the end. Once again, he accepted the condition, although with the compromise that I should play myself in gently by acting as an outside reader of manuscripts submitted to Werner Laurie during the intervening months. We shook hands on the deal.

Thus it was that on Monday 1 January 1947, I walked through the side door of 187 Piccadilly, took the lift to the third floor and was shown into a large oak-panelled room. The polished surface of the big mahogany desk was bare, apart from a pristine leatherbound blotter, a telephone, a new notepad and an in-tray and an out-tray, both empty. It was the first and last time in forty years that I was to greet an uncluttered desk. I sat there in solitude for about half an hour, when there was a tap on the closed door. There entered a flustered and – to my then twenty-nine-year-old eyes – elderly woman, who announced she was Miss Claus, the company secretary.

'There's a big problem,' she declared.

'What's that?'

'The new Upton Sinclair has to go into production this afternoon at the latest. No one's done a blurb!'

I had never heard the word before. Could it be some esoteric part of the printing process? But, towards the end of the war, I had not spent six months at the Staff College for nothing.

'Tell me – who's normally responsible for this . . . er . . . blurb?'

She mentioned a name.

'Well, please give X my compliments and tell him I expect everything to be ready before lunch!'

Miss Claus thanked me and went out. When the door was safely closed behind her, I scribbled on my virginal notepad – *find out what a blurb is.*

Clarence Hatry was to be so much part of my life until his death in the early 1960s and was such an extraordinary character in himself that he deserves space for a biographical sketch. The son of a silk merchant, he had been educated at St Paul's School; on leaving, he had been briefly an inventor. In those far-off Edwardian days, the master or mistress of a large house summoned the servants from their basement quarters by tugging on a bell pull, which caused the corresponding bell far below, joined by wires, to jangle. Throughout his life, Hatry's quick mind was always attracted to new ideas and inventions, latterly to his great detriment. So with the new-fangled electricity becoming modish in the mid-Edwardian era, he invented a system by which a bell rang softly in the servants' quarters and a shutter, like an eyelid, dropped over one of the spaces in a row on the basement wall, to signify the origin of the call. It was the precursor of those old-fashioned telephone switchboards which remained in use until well after the Second World War. But, as would often be the case, Hatry was ahead of his times. His invention did not work. Either the shutters failed to drop and 'Upstairs' grew increasingly infuriated by jabbing vainly at the bell-push or else all the shutters dropped at once, so that the equally infuriated 'Downstairs' had to go scurrying around the large house to find the summoner.

Through a chance encounter on the front at Brighton, he next went into the re-insurance market, followed by a system he created for the matching of guarantors. (When he was in a rare sombre mood, one of his favourite sayings was, 'Every man has one friend but few have two.') By the age of twenty-one, already married, he had made his first million. (The equivalent today would be over £50 million.) During the ten years after the First World War, he made and lost fortunes with equal facility. He had a large private house in Stanhope Gate off Park Lane, where at enormous expense he built an indoor swimming pool, one of the first such in London, a string of racehorses, including the winner of the Lincolnshire Handicap, and a yacht in which he raced against George V at Cowes. The list of important companies that passed through his hands or which he helped to merge is impressive – Debenham's, London Transport (then several privately run bus companies), United Glass, Leyland Motors (much later to become the main part of the nationalised British Motor Corporation), Swan & Edgar, Jute Industries and Allied Ironfounders amongst them.

The Leyland episode is typical of Clarence Hatry's mercurial nature. In the early 1920s, the company was probably the leading manufacturer of lorries and buses in the country, having prospered greatly through the wartime demand for heavy transport. The man who had built it up from scratch died and left the business to his two sons, who spent their time arguing bitterly over how it should continue to be run. At length, the only thing they could agree on was that the company must be sold before their continual feuding ruined it.

They approached Hatry, who studied the balance sheets and offered them a fair price – £500,000. They agreed; contracts were drawn up and signed. Shortly after they had left and while the papers and the latest balance sheets were still on Hatry's desk, a friend of his, another City financier named Gerard Lee Bevan, called on him. (Bevan was later to acquire some brief notoriety when, wanted for fraud, he attempted to flee the country, dressed as a woman.) According to CCH, he had two special qualities – great nerve and the ability to read a balance sheet upside down.

Unashamed, he cast an eye over the figures and remarked that they looked interesting. 'How much do you want?' he asked.

Hatry demurred, saying he had only just bought the company and intended to operate it himself. But the more he protested, the greater became Bevan's appetite to acquire Leyland. Finally, after much argument, he came up with £750,000 as a firm offer. Hatry accepted. Within one hour, he had cleared £250,000 in sheer profit, equivalent to over £7 million today. And that was long before the imposition of profits tax or capital gains tax.

His great weakness – and I am aware of the implication – was that he tended to surround himself with second-rate yes-men. By nature ebullient and optimistic, he disliked seeing long faces or listening to words of caution. He wanted to believe the best in people – and that the best was yet to be for himself. Several times during his switchback career, he was to be brought down with a crash through being too trusting. The worst occasion occurred in 1929.

One of his associates was a man named Daniels. Hatry prided himself on his flair as a graphologist and, when he had first seen a sample of Daniels's handwriting, he had said, 'Sack him.' But he had quickly been persuaded that the order was unjust. Before long, by always being the first to arrive at the Austin Friars Trust office and the last to leave, and by carrying out his chief's slightest wish at the double, Daniels had become a valued colleague. A year or so earlier, Hatry had been approached by some senior men in the Scottish jute industry. The market was depressed and the rivalry so cut-throat that several large firms were on the brink of ruin. Through his silver tongue and a demonstration of common sense, he had induced them to save themselves by a series of corporate mergers, which he backed with his own finances and from which he made a tidy profit. A little later, he brought his special skills to bear on the iron foundries in the Midlands, which were facing similar problems, and again he achieved a successful and profitable merger.

So far, so very good – but it was to be a case of third time unlucky. A leading bank invited him to work his magic on the steel companies, which were suffering even more than the iron foundries. Unemployment and the trade slump had cut the demand for steel in the manufacturing and the construction industries. Price cutting was swiftly turning to chaos and ruin. Only a rational approach would work – and there was no time to lose. Hatry agreed and set to.

Unknown to him – for he was a man who never openly bore a grudge and who expected his business rivals to behave similarly – he had made a deadly enemy in that strange, saturnine figure, Sir Montagu Norman, Governor of the Bank of England. Before his elevation, Norman had been head of a large stockbroking firm which specialised in placing corporation loans. Hatry's Austin Friars Trust had entered that specialist market and, through a combination of nerve and skill, had undercut the more staid and complacent opposition, removing a large portion of what Norman's firm considered its private property.

The merging of the separate companies that would make up Steel Industries of Great Britain was proceeding smoothly; Austin Friars was following the custom of the times by issuing scrip that would later be redeemed as shares when the new group was launched. Hatry was within a few hundred thousand pounds of completing the deal when the general election brought a Labour government into office. The City lost confidence, financial belts were tightened. A merchant bank that had promised him a multi-million-pound loan on the strength of a handshake – the City method of business in those days – reneged on the deal. The value of shares plummeted. The Bank of England could have saved the day for Austin Friars and McKenna, the ex-Chancellor of the Exchequer, even made a plea on its behalf. But Sir Montagu sat impassively in Threadneedle Street.

There was a panic meeting on a Sunday evening at Hatry's London mansion. They were so close to successful completion – and yet so very far away. Daniels harangued the other three or four men present, urging that additional scrip should be issued to cover the gap. (Scrip is the technical term for provisional certificates issued by a bank or company, entitling the holder to the formal documents, such as share certificates, later on.) It was then a common, though strictly illegal, practice in the City to issue scrip over and above the proper limit and redeem it when the shares were taken up and paid for. He even threatened suicide if they failed to agree. In the end, Clarence Hatry, physically exhausted and emotionally spent, gave in.

He and the others were eventually arrested and appeared before Mr Justice Avory at the Old Bailey, charged with fraud. Sir Norman Birkett, QC, that golden orator who was much later promoted to the Bench, appeared for Hatry – and gave one of the few inept performances in a long and distinguished career. Avory, a hanging judge, who later, I was told, died in a brothel whence his body had to be spirited so that it could be officially discovered in the somewhat more respectable surroundings of his club, sentenced Hatry to fourteen years and his colleagues to lesser terms of imprisonment.

The story has it that CCH, before being moved from the Old Bailey cell to prison, was asked if he would like anything to eat and replied, 'Just a savoury.' That was typical of his impish sense of humour. So was the occasion many years later, after the Second World War, when he was walking along Fleet Street and saw a man, whose face was vaguely familiar, approaching him.

He stopped and asked, 'Haven't we met before?'

'Oh yes, Mr Hatry,' came the answer. 'I was one of your warders at Maidstone Gaol.'

'What are you doing now?'

'Nothing. I've retired from the prison service.'

'Well, you did a great job of keeping me in. Would you like to be my commissionaire and keep unwelcome visitors out?'

The man eagerly agreed. For many months thereafter, he stood outside the Tudor Street entrance, wearing a peaked cap and keeping a canny eye on all who entered.

With remission for good conduct, CCH served ten years of his savage sentence, latterly as librarian at Maidstone Gaol. During his time inside, he wrote a book, published by Hurst & Blackett under the title of *Light out of Darkness*. It was not, as one might imagine, a prose version of *The Ballad of*

Reading Gaol but a well-reasoned argument for mass emigration. Britain had several million unemployed in the 'hungry thirties' and the Dominions were severely underpopulated. Hatry's ingenious idea was that whole communities, including the very old and the very young, should be encouraged to emigrate *en masse*, thus avoiding the psychological problems facing individual emigrants.

After all those years locked away, he came into the light in 1939, penniless and back where he had been over thirty years earlier when his invention failed. But this time he had a thrifty and prudent wife, Dolly, who was Scottish. He told me once that when he and she were at their wealthiest, living in the Stanhope Gate mansion with its built-in swimming pool and a regiment of servants to look after their slightest whim, before going to bed at night Dolly used to go from room to room, removing the live coals from the open fireplaces and putting them aside for burning another night. Another time, he said, when he was temporarily short of liquid funds, she had gone to her Georgian desk and pulled open a drawer, which was stuffed with high-denomination banknotes, pearl necklaces and diamond rings, all of which he had given her when he was in the money. They were his for the taking, she indicated.

All those assets had long disappeared when CCH went to prison. Dolly was devoted and had stuck by him throughout the long years, as had his son Cecil and his daughter Diana. Dolly had managed to put by some modest savings; he borrowed £500 from her. He had learned something of the book trade, both as prison librarian and as an author. Within a few days of his release, he knew exactly what to do. He went in search of the Shepherd brothers, who owned Hatchards bookshop.

187 Piccadilly is a fine location, the perfect address for a shop catering to the 'carriage trade', almost opposite Albany, a mere stroll from the clubs of St James's and Pall Mall, and a neighbour of Fortnum & Mason. A gentleman could – and still can – spend a happy morning visiting his shoemaker, his hatter and his wine merchant in Lower St James's Street and his shirtmaker in Jermyn Street, rounded off with some gentle

browsing in Hatchards before enjoying a leisurely lunch at
White's or Boodles. Surely no shopkeeper could go wrong
with an address in Piccadilly?

But the Shepherd brothers could. They dearly loved a lord –
and half Debrett's, it seemed, treated Hatchards like a lending
library, except that there was no annual subscription. The
gentry strolled into the bookshop, selected and walked away
with books that took their fancy, charging them to accounts
that might never be settled. In those pre-war days, the standard
price of a novel was 7/6d (37½p) and illustrated non-fiction
books cost a pound or less. Once, the story ran, even the
Shepherds had been moved to issue a writ when a cavalry
officer, who was – at least, by title – an 'Honourable', had
run up a bill of several hundred pounds.

The irate hussar went storming into Hatchards, summoned
the elder Shepherd and shouted, 'Here, my man, this is what
I think of you and your damned writ.' He tore the document
into strips and flung it at the shopkeeper's feet. 'You'll
withdraw it at once – do you hear?' He strode out – and
the writ was duly withdrawn.

Hatry told the Shepherds what in their hearts they had long
suspected. The firm was on the verge of bankruptcy – in fact,
over the brink as the larger bills from publishers had been
unpaid for many months. He offered to buy Hatchards, debts
and all, for £5,000 and, as a telling stroke, handed over the £500
there and then, as a 10 per cent down payment. They could
stay on as joint managing directors until retirement. (I dimly
remember in the late 1940s seeing two elderly white-haired
men in black coats and pinstripe trousers greeting Sir Osbert
Sitwell with a deep bow apiece.)

Hatry set to work. He sent a letter to every aristocratic
debtor, stating that in one week's time he would remove all
the books from the Hatchards windows. In their place would
appear a typed list, showing which customers owed how much
and for how long. There were abusive phone calls and threats
of writs for libel but, as if by magic, the cheques poured in.
Within a fortnight there was enough in the till to pay the staff's
back wages and settle the agreed purchase price.

The harder task was to placate the impatient publishers.

There were some shrewd, hard-bitten men in their ranks – Stanley Unwin, Billy Collins, George and Walter Harrap, and the eccentric Walter Hutchinson. Hatry went to see them in turn and the message was always the same. 'Foreclose – and you will get a few pence in the pound. And lose a great bookselling outlet. Give me six months and continue to supply books – and I will start paying you back. In another six months, you will be paid up to date.' It says much for his charm and the force of his personality – and their acumen – that they all accepted the word of a recent gaolbird.

And then on the ill-wind principle, Hatry had a stroke of luck. The war broke out. The blackout, followed a year later by the Blitz, kept people indoors. Apart from listening to 'the wireless', the only way to pass the time was to read. And for the young men and women in the services, in billets or on lonely campsites, a book was a good companion. Hatchards thrived. Its debts were quickly paid off and bumper profits followed throughout the war years. Clarence Hatry was back in business.

In those early days, a few doors away from Hatchards, there was a nightclub called La Pigalle. At lunchtime, it served champagne and smoked-salmon sandwiches. Clarence Hatry, who disliked the pomp and ceremony that would accompany an official visit to the Werner Laurie offices, would quite often telephone me in the morning and ask politely if I had a lunch date that day. Whether I had or not, it was politic to say No, postponing any date that might have been made and meeting him at the appointed time for an hour's talk that was partly business and partly gossip. He would tell me anecdotes from his varied career – not always to his best advantage – and trot out several maxims for my education. One was, 'Always watch a short man carefully. He has something to prove – probably to himself.' (CCH was, as it happens, no more than five feet six inches tall.) Another was, 'Never have dealings with a man who displays a Bible prominently in his room. Or one who has too many family portraits on his desk.' In all my years in business, the only Bible I ever came across was in an American hotel bedside desk and, although I have been duped many times, cannot recall that the offender lavishly displayed the family photographs.

As a recent infantry officer who had latterly passed through the Staff College in Haifa, I was used to the military system of briefings and operation orders. One received concise orders from one's seniors and passed them on to one's juniors. That was the way life operated. And before the orders could be issued, the troops had to be given a thorough briefing – 'put in the picture', as the saying then went. So at one of our lunchtime meetings, I asked CCH, 'When are you going to brief me?'

'What do you mean?' he asked.

'Give me a briefing. In other words, what's the policy? What kind of books do you want me to publish? That sort of thing.'

He paused for a moment. 'That's up to you. You're the publisher, not me.'

'That's not much of a briefing.'

'Well, it's all you'll get from me.' Then he must have seen my despondent look. 'All right, I'll give you a briefing. You go ahead and publish what you like for a full year. At the end of the year, we'll look at the balance sheet. If it ends up in black ink, fine – you go on for another year. If it ends up in red ink, I'll give you the gypsy's warning but you'll still go on for another year. But if at the end of the second year, there's still red ink on the balance sheet, you're fired. You understand? Right, that's my briefing for you.'

And that was the basis on which we operated for five and a half happy years.

Hatry was something of a manipulator with a whimsical sense of humour. After I had been in charge of Werner Laurie for over a year, he and I were having one of our cosy lunches. I had not at that stage been invited to join the board of directors.

With no preamble, he said, 'We're thinking of appointing a managing director for the firm. There are two people in the running. One is yourself and the other is . . .' and he mentioned the name of a man with a solid reputation, who had been for many years with an important house. He went on, 'Now, I don't know this fellow. He was recommended by a friend. Do you know him?'

'Not well,' I said. 'We've met a few times. At publishing functions – that sort of thing.'

'I look on you as virtually one of the family, George. I trust your advice. So I want you to take him out to lunch – a good lunch, don't bother about the cost – and listen hard to what he has to say. Then I want you to tell me privately who you think would do the job better.'

'What?'

'Yes, it's either you or him. Or should I say "he"? Perfectly simple. Talk to him first. Then, if you reckon you'd do the job better, fine. Or if you reckon he's the one, equally fine. I'll accept whatever you say.'

There was a confusion of anger and incredulity inside my head. I managed to say, 'CCH, it's an impossible situation. You're asking me to be judge and jury when my own future's at stake. I can't win. If I end up recommending him as managing director, that's the same as saying I don't trust myself to do the job. And if I come back and tell you I'm the one, I could be cheating him out of a job he deserves. It's not fair. It really isn't.'

I protested in that vein for some minutes but Clarence Hatry was adamant. The quickest way to suppress one's discomfort is the knowledge that the other party is secretly enjoying it. So at length I accepted the assignment. The lunch duly took place at the old Holborn Restaurant with its marble columns and ancient staff creeping from table to table. I tried to approach the meeting with an open mind. If I was duly impressed with my guest's grasp of publishing as it might apply not to his own well-established firm but to one that needed building up and if his plans were consistent with Werner Laurie's needs, then I hoped to have enough integrity to recommend him for the managing directorship, even though it would mean putting a halt to my own career with TWL or indeed abandoning it. He might have been five or more years older than me – but close enough to keep me back for a long, long time.

I *was* impressed with him. He clearly knew most aspects of publishing from first-hand experience. He also had definite plans for reshaping Werner Laurie. But the more he described them in detail, the more I felt they differed from CCH's concept and indeed my own – which was to elevate the publishing house above the slightly squalid 'frilly knicker' department it had landed in. My guest was greatly taken with crime books, both fiction and non-fiction. (For almost twenty years after the war, the death penalty was still in force and the more sensational murder trials were instant fodder for the cheap end of the market.) His main plan was to turn the firm into a purveyor of crime books *et praeterea nihil*.

As he went on spelling out his ideas, I noticed that he used positive rather than conditional tenses. It was not 'I would want to do so-and-so', more the statement 'I shall do so-and-so.' Perhaps he had been informed by the man who put his name forward that the managing directorship was his for the taking; or perhaps the chance of a monologue, lubricated by a mellow bottle of burgundy, had raised his expectations. He also had plans to fire some of the Werner Laurie staff, senior as well as junior, and to bring in replacements from his own firm. Efficiency might well be improved but morale would inevitably suffer.

In the early post-war years, Piccadilly was a two-way street throughout its length and a Number 19 or a Number 38 bus would have transported me from the Holborn Restaurant to the front door of Hatchards. But I decided to walk back – and think as I went. CCH was due that afternoon to see his friend and fellow-investor in the group, the financier Herbert Rothbarth, who had a suite of offices in the building next door to Hatchards. I arranged to see him there.

He looked at me quizzically down the edge of that curving scimitar of a nose. There was a twinkle in the pale blue eye on the right. The other was partly obscured by his customary monocle, worn with a black silk ribbon. 'Well?' he asked.

'I've thought hard,' I said. 'I don't think he's right for the job. Honestly. I may not be ideal but I think I'd do it better. Let me explain what I mean . . .'

'You don't have to explain. I accept your verdict. That's fine. Oh – and congratulations. I'll see it goes through at the next board meeting.'

'I'm very grateful,' I said. 'But I would like you to know *why* I reached this conclusion. You see . . .'

He cut me off. 'George,' he said, 'I'm sure you have good reason. There's no need to explain. I trust your judgement implicitly. Well, I'm running late, I must be off.' The neat feet in their silken socks and hand-made shoes twinkled towards the door. Quick, effervescent, he seemed always on the move.

What he did not confide – out of his long business experience – and what I took months to realise was that my decision had made me an enemy for life. I learned later that my rival for the post of managing director had indeed been told by his backer that the job was his for the taking. When my appointment was finally announced, there could be only one reason. I must have done him down. Naturally, he never forgave me but fortunately he never had any real opportunity for retaliation. He stayed with the firm where he had started, performed his duties with competence, if not with enthusiasm, and spent many hours and telephone calls paid for by the office in playing the Stock Exchange. His investments prospered and he was a rich man when he retired.

Looking back from the present age of plenty, when possessions are only limited by one's ability to buy them with real or plastic money, it is hard to recall in detail the problems abounding in the immediate post-war years. Everything, in the jargon of the day, was 'in short supply'. And, inevitably, everything was rationed. There were coupons for food, including the daily bread, coupons for clothes, coupons for furniture, coupons for petrol. Publishers were limited to a strict quota of paper for printing, which in mid-1946, thanks to the fuel-shortage, was reduced to 60 per cent of the amount they had used in the last full year before the war. (New publishers were allowed a quota of a few tons.)

The Labour government had, it appeared, three rallying cries. No one could properly argue with the first – 'fair shares for all' – but the second, Hartley Shawcross's parliamentary taunt, 'We are the masters now' and, the third, Douglas Jay's ineffable remark, 'The gentleman in Whitehall knows better' (than the housewife), betrayed a spirit that was as mean as it was unrealistic. In practice, fair shares meant strict rationing and automatically led to those Whitehall gentlemen and ladies proliferating throughout the land in government departments and local offices, clipping coupons, when they might have been better employed in actually making things to overcome the shortages.

Wherever there are shortages, the black market will flourish, well beyond the parliamentary draughtsman's ability to control or suppress it. I was myself to be an early victim. For the first few months of my employment with Werner Laurie, my wife, our infant son and I had been living temporarily at my parents' home outside Maidstone in Kent. The long hours of work and the irregular and still blacked-out train service helped to make family life difficult, and we were desperate to find accommodation in central London. At length, we found a second-floor flat in Aberdare Gardens, that hinterland between Finchley Road and West End Lane often known as 'County Kilburn'. The whole house had been bought by a German refugee named Steiner, a fat man with expressionless eyes, for the sum of £600. When the bombing had been at its height and residents were selling up cheaply and leaving London, he had had the wit and, somehow, the money to buy up properties at knock-down prices.

The Labour government had banned the practice of paying 'key money' for the right to take a lease on a flat. But there was nothing to stop an owner from charging for 'fixtures and fittings' over and above the controlled and reasonably low rent. The flat was mine, Mr Steiner assured me, provided, of course, I was willing to pay £450 – 'in cash, please, sir' – for the fixtures and fittings. And so I went to my bank, drew out ninety of the then current large white five-pound notes – over half my gratuity for six years' army service – and walked round to the Mayfair offices of his agents, who later became one of the biggest letting firms and property developers in England. There, a swarthy young man riffled through the bundle of fivers, grinned when I innocently asked for a receipt, and handed over the keys. It was, I suppose, in his terms, a case of charging a levy. The fixtures and fittings turned out to be three bent-wire coathangers and a four-foot strip of motheaten matting. But at least the three of us now had a home of our own.

I must jump ahead a couple of years to recount a more sinister case of how government regulations, no doubt well meant in their inception, led to corruption. The Werner Laurie office comprised the complete third floor of the Hatchards building. There was a large room at the south side, which was occupied by Miss Claus, the company secretary, a royalty clerk, an invoicing clerk and several secretaries, rattling away on their manual typewriters. The din was continuous, compounded by the inevitable chattering. At length, Miss Claus gently and rightly complained. She needed quiet. As the royalty ledgers were still written in by hand, as were the invoices, I arranged in my ignorance to have a wooden partition with glass in the upper half erected to divide the room in two, separating her and the clerks from the noisy typists. Hatchards had a permanent staff of carpenters in residence and the work was swiftly completed.

I had inadvertently broken the law. Unknown to me, one of a mass of government regulations stated that all forms of new building, even simple internal structures, required prior governmental approval. Application forms, spelling out in detail the purpose, the size, the appearance, the building materials required and the approximate cost, had to be submitted – no doubt, in triplicate – and after many months, consent might or might not be given. Somehow, word of my rashness must have leaked out. 'The inspector called' – and shortly I received an unpleasant document, calling on me to justify my act, if I could.

I knew that the last thing Clarence Hatry wanted or needed was that kind of unfortunate publicity – but I had to tell him. He gave a wry smile and a typical shrug. He did not chide me, as he had good reason to, but merely told me to see Sir Thomas Moore after he had spoken to him. I was to do whatever Sir Thomas instructed – without argument.

Sir Thomas Moore was then in his early sixties, a short man with wavy grey hair and a grizzled moustache. He was a Conservative backbencher of long standing. Having

represented Ayr Burgh in Scotland since 1925, he had been
knighted pre-war and had been created a baronet for political
services shortly after the war. He held many directorships,
apart from that of Hatchards Associated Interests, the holding
company, and he had an office in the bookshop building. In
one sense, he was what used to be known as a 'guinea pig
director', a name that looked good on the official letterheading,
but he was also, as I soon learned, a fixer.

'You've got a problem here,' he said to me. 'We mustn't
have Clarence's name involved. Bad publicity. Tell me, have
you got £500 handy in the Werner Laurie account?'

I said, 'Yes.'

'Right, this is what we'll do. First, you let me have
the £500.'

'I can get a cheque back to you within ten minutes,' I said.
'Who do I make it out to?'

He looked at me pityingly. 'Not a cheque. Definitely not a
cheque. It must be in cash.'

£500 then would be worth about £8,000 today. The company's accounts were, as I well knew, audited every year and
it would be difficult to 'lose' that amount of money. So I asked
him, 'Do I get a receipt?'

He looked at me again with a mixture of pity and private
amusement. 'No,' he said, 'you don't.'

'But you must at least tell me where it's going,' I pleaded.
'After all, I've got to account for it – somehow.'

'Well, you shouldn't have gone building partitions without
a licence! All right, I'll tell you – but this must go no further,
you understand?'

I nodded.

'It's for Nye.'

I must have looked as shaken as I felt. One had been brought
up in the belief that our rulers, whatever their political beliefs,
were men of substance and good conscience. And Aneurin
Bevan above all, that man from the mines of Tredegar, the
tribune of the people, the defender of the oppressed and
the downtrodden, now our Minister of Health, under whose
mantle for some arcane reason building applications fell. It is
true that Churchill had called him a 'squalid nuisance' during

a stormy wartime debate – but Churchill always had a rough tongue for his opponents. I was almost convinced that Sir Thomas was having me on. But I drew the money from the bank, handed it to him and heard nothing further until, a few weeks later, I was informed that retrospective permission had been granted.

As the months and indeed the years went by, I still could not fully accept that Aneurin Bevan of all men could act so corruptly. True, there was the Lynskey Tribunal in which a junior Labour minister named Belcher was found to have accepted bribes from a spiv, Sidney Stanley, who promptly fled to newly founded Israel. But surely not Bevan, an orator whose eloquent tongue defended the poor from whom he came and lashed the rich upper classes for sticking to their privileges? I began to think that either I had completely misheard Sir Thomas' remark or, if I had heard him correctly, he must have been indulging in a perverse sense of humour.

Bevan had been the member for Ebbw Vale since 1929. As such, he would have earned £1,000 a year or less. He was a Cabinet Minister for about six years from 1945, first as Minister of Health and then Minister of Labour and National Service, after which he returned to the back benches. In the Cabinet, he would have received £3,000 a year – but at a time of high direct taxation. He did some occasional journalism, mainly for the *Tribune*, which paid only modest fees. Many years later, we learned from Richard Crossman's diaries that Bevan had made £2,500 in tax-free damages from committing perjury as a plaintiff at a *Spectator* libel trial, along with Morgan Phillips and Crossman himself, who benefited similarly from lying under oath.

Nye may have despised the rich but he liked living in their style. He drank a great deal of champagne and was a regular frequenter of the White Tower, an excellent restaurant which has always been one of the more expensive in London.

He died in 1960 at the age of sixty-two. His estate, which included a substantial farm in fertile Buckinghamshire, was valued at £60,000 – the present equivalent would be over £700,000. When I read the details, the episode of the partition, overlaid by more than a decade of other happenings, came vividly back to mind. Had it indeed been one of many untaxed contributions that had helped to build that fortune? Over thirty years later, we shall probably never know – but I do not recall any convincing explanation of 'wealth accumulates and men decay' in the official biography.

Hindsight has the happy knack of highlighting the successes and hiding the failures. It was my good fortune to enter the publishing world when the boom in book sales, created by wartime conditions, still had a few years to run. After hostilities ended, there were many thousands of sailors, soldiers and airmen – and women – awaiting demobilisation and with few alternatives to book-reading to alleviate their boredom. On the home front, austerity and the general drabness of life encouraged people to 'get away from it all' through the pages of an exciting book. And there were more outlets to cope with the demand. Apart from bookshops and public libraries, there were numerous commercial outlets, ranging from Boots Libraries at the top end with their green-shield lending tags to the local newsagent's, with a couple of shelves of popular fiction to be borrowed at 3d or 6d a time. Clarence Hatry had in fact bought the Argosy & Sundial Libraries chain, then managed by the pompous Cyril Edgeley, who later ran the Times Bookshop in Wigmore Street and who became a pundit in the columns of *The Bookseller*.

So it was little wonder that Tom Brown, the Werner Laurie sales manager, could sell a complete edition of a new book, amounting to 3,000 or more copies, in three or four telephone calls. If I had had more experience or perhaps more sense, I should have realised that the good times do not go on forever. The quick and easy profits could have been used to improve the sales force and its coverage against the day when sales would be so much harder to achieve. The abrupt end of paper rationing in March 1949, almost nine years to the day since its inception, was, strangely enough, one factor in the downturn of sales. On reflection, it was not perhaps so strange; throughout the austere days, items 'in short supply' often attracted would-be buyers because of their scarcity. There were many stories of

queues increasing merely because those at the far end of the
queue hoped for an attractive purchase of whatever it might
be, once they reached the buying point. (Clarence Hatry's
impeccable sense of timing deserted him for once. He bought
on Werner Laurie's behalf a greeting-cards manufacturer,
Todd Publishing, which had a large paper quota to spare,
for £30,000 – then a small fortune – just two or three weeks
before rationing was abandoned.)

Once hardcover editions were no longer selling out within a
few weeks of their publication, the trade reverted to its pre-war
practice. 3,500 copies, say, of a modestly saleable book might
be printed but only 2,000 bound up. The published price might
be 10/6d (52½p). Six months later, the publisher would bind up
another 1,000 copies which, together with any surplus copies
from the full-price edition, he would proudly announce as '*BY
PUBLIC DEMAND! THE FIRST FANTASTIC CHEAP
EDITION!*'; the copies would be re-subscribed and put
on sale at 5/- (25p). Then, another six months afterwards,
the residue of sheets would be bound up and, along with
the last stocks of the cheap edition, they would quietly be
remaindered at 6d (2½p) per copy.

The firm of Hutchinson, with all its subsidiary firms like
Jarrolds, Hurst & Blackett, Rich & Cowan and Popular
Dogs, was adept at this practice and employed it with
almost military precision. But so vast and varied was the
group's output that on one occasion at least it came to
grief. Barry Rowland, who was briefly in charge of the
Hutchinson remainder department before he moved to the
heights of advertising manager, muddled up one of the
multitude of orders landing on his desk – and remaindered
his allocation of one title a week before the trade department
officially published it. Not that the megalomaniac Walter
Hutchinson probably ever noticed it. Irrespective of the
actual sales, he would demand that the dustjacket of a novel
carried the legend – 'Author of XYZ (120 Thousand Copies
Sold)'. On one occasion at least, an author whose previous
novel had sold less than a tenth of the numbers claimed on
the new dustjacket, wrote after a drunken party to Walter
Hutchinson, threatening to sue him for the missing royalties

on the surplus copies, and the story goes that Walter settled up without demur.

Hardcover cheap editions did not long survive. They were killed off by the growing power of the paperback market. Penguin had prospered throughout the war years and into the peace; Pan Books were started in 1947 and Transworld/Corgi, an offshoot of Bantam Books of New York, some three years later. By the mid-1950s, there were half a dozen and more flourishing paperback firms. Very few readers would spend 5/- on a hardcover book when they could buy as good or better novels for 2/-. And the paperback houses, who were spending increasing sums to license cheap rights for publication one year after the original publication, would not tolerate a cheap hardcover edition being interposed a few months before their own publication.

But the remainder market, like the poor, was continually with us. We became quickly accustomed to the sight of a slim young man, almost a boy, with his pale face and slight lisp and ready chuckle – and equally ready ability to mop up the results of our over-optimism. His name was Paul Hamlyn. He glided through the murky waters of a tough trade like an eel or, perhaps, a young shark and, as he was to show throughout his career, he knew exactly what he was doing. A little later, one marvelled at his *chutzpah* when he arranged to place one of his remainder stalls within Selfridges and outside its book department. His eventual great strength as a publisher – and yet some would consider it a strange weakness – was that to him, apparently, there was nothing mysterious or intrinsically exciting about a book. Like a tin of beans or a bottle of beer, it was a product: something to be acquired cheaply, such as a remainder or with a new book by buying the copyright for a small fixed sum from the author; something to be produced at knock-down prices, such as printing in Czechoslovakia where prices were subsidised in the quest for hard currency; and something to be mass-marketed, such as selling the complete edition to Woolworth or Marks & Spencer at large discounts which could be afforded through the savings on royalties and production costs. It was a simple and brilliant formula, and it earned him the first or second of several large fortunes. What connection it has with 'the precious life blood of a master spirit' is for the reader to decide.

Around the same time but in very different circumstances, I met another young man who was to have a lengthy and interesting connection with the book world. In 1951, Tom Brown and I were invited to the opening ceremony for the new Simpkin Marshall premises in Marylebone Road. Simpkin Marshall was a long-established and famous wholesale house. In spite of the boom in books during wartime, it had gone through a difficult period and had largely been supported by several of the bigger publishing houses. But now it was 'under entirely new management'.

The building was large and the layout impressive. There were long corridors of metal strip racking, like a form of adult Meccano, with shelves laden with mint copies. There were even electrically driven forklift trucks available to shift loads of books from their shelves to the packing bays. Familiar faces and the leading names of the publishing world were there to greet this demonstration of the last word in wholesaling; William Collins, Mark Longman, the brothers George and Walter Harrap, Dr Desmond Flower from Cassell's – the very cream of the publishing trade. Punctuating the hum of conversation were the subdued reports of yet more bottles of champagne being opened. And the climax was the rousing speech from the young man who had ignited the phoenix. His impeccable English vowels, the result one would have argued of centuries of breeding in the shires, assorted strangely with the Middle European appearance, the glossy, slicked-back black hair, the elliptical, dark clown's eyebrows and the brooding, unfathomable eyes. He was Captain Robert Maxwell, late of Lange, Springer & Maxwell, the importer and exporter of mainly German books.

At the end of the party, Tom Brown and I left in a champagne-induced glow. As we wove our way along the Marylebone Road, I asked Tom, 'What credit do we give Simpkin's?'

He thought for a moment. 'About £400.'

I said, 'Cut it to £200.'

He stopped short on the pavement. 'Well, I like that! That's gratitude for you. We go to a smashing party, almost bathe in free champagne – and all you can think of is cutting their credit. If it's meant to be a joke, I don't get it.'

'No joke,' I said. 'Sorry, Tom. Maybe this isn't the right moment. We'll talk about it in the office tomorrow. But the credit's got to be cut – in half.'

Luckily, we had walked as far as the Baker Street Underground station, which would take me to Finchley Road, and we parted company. I can still see the disgusted look on Tom Brown's owl-like features. 'Man's ingratitude', he must have been thinking. Drink their champagne, eat their canapés – and then go away and hit them below the belt.

Perhaps my Staff College training was to blame. The party itself was neither here nor there. A few hundred pounds can always be written off and the expense had helped to show that Simpkin Marshall was up and running again. My fears ran deeper. The ground-floor space was enormous and the rents in West One would be high, far higher than in the suburbs. The cost of all that metal racking and shelving and the forklift trucks puttering around must have been great. Mr Minshull, who had run Simpkin Marshall on a tight rein for many years, was no longer in charge.

And what was the profit margin? A mere 5 per cent. True, some loyal publishers were giving the wholesaler for old times' sake 10 per cent but their numbers were swiftly decreasing. The average price of a published book was then about 15/-. The retail discount was one-third – in other words, bookshops paid 10/- per book. For bulk orders which were then distributed to the shops, Simpkin's received an additional 5 per cent – 6d per copy. About, or somewhat under, 30,000 new titles a year were then being published. If one allowed a sale of 3,000 copies per title, which would be highly optimistic, of which two-thirds would be sold in the home market and one-third for export, that would amount to ninety million books, with a turnover of £45 million. And if Simpkin Marshall distributed one-third of the total, which would be unlikely in view of the superior wholesaling abilities of W.H. Smith and John Menzies, its 'take' – at 5 per cent – would be £750,000.

That is to paint the picture in the rosiest hues. More

realistically, the likely turnover would have been £600,000, perhaps as low as £500,000. When one deducts the high rental charges, depreciation on the expensive fixtures and fittings, staff costs, insurance, transport and postages, an allowance for bad debts, the servicing of bank loans and the other inevitable overheads, the profit margin would vary from slim to invisible.

As indeed it turned out. Within a matter of months, Simpkin Marshall crashed, owing large sums to its major suppliers – £18,000 to Longmans and £15,000 to Collins, among many others. (One would need to multiply by a factor of fourteen to get the modern cash equivalent.) Werner Laurie, as I recall, was in for about £180. (Tom Brown, usually loquacious, had no comment to make.) Captain Maxwell was fortunate enough to walk away without a scratch. The auditors, when conducting the post-mortem, had some scathing remarks to make but, as was to be proved on at least one later occasion, hard words bounce off a moving target.

The end of paper rationing in 1949 and the contemporary, perhaps consequent, end of the book sales boom started the decline in Clarence Hatry's fortunes. Throughout his business life, he had been a brilliant opportunist. In fact, a simile he often used with his juniors was that of the Underground station. You stood on the platform and waited. Sooner or later, a train came thundering along and stopped. The doors slid back with a swish. After a few seconds, they closed with another hydraulic sigh and then the train moved off again.

'There is no such thing as luck,' he would declare. 'Everyone gets opportunities in life, just like the passengers waiting for the tube train. But the smart man is the one who sees it coming and positions himself near where the doors will open. And he jumps aboard as soon as they do. Others may get left behind but he is on the move.'

Hatry was one of the first asset-strippers back in the 1920s but never as ruthless as men like Charles Clore and the Slater Walker bright young men almost half a century later. He read balance sheets in the way most of us read murder-stories and he spotted clues that detectives would miss. A family firm, where the first two generations had prudently written down stocks and assets which the pampered and over-educated third generation would fail to understand, was the perfect prey. Exercising charm and an intellectual legerdemain, Hatry would buy the company at its balance-sheet value with, say, a quarter of the price down and the rest in six months. He would then sell off a large part of the concealed assets and thus use the company's own money to fund most of the purchase. Over one such deal, where a family printing firm was involved – this was in the days when the hot-metal linotype printing process was prevalent – he spotted from the balance sheet that the company owned many tons of lead, heavily written down in value and surplus to requirements. Hatry ended up by buying the firm almost entirely out of its own assets.

He was an early apostle of 'vertical integration'. The mini-conglomerate, Hatchards Associated Interests, included two printing works, a publishing house, the bookshop in Piccadilly, a chain of lending libraries and even a remainder firm; all it lacked to top or tail the vertex was a papermaking firm. The idea, simple but grand, was that the publishing house, Werner Laurie, would select good and saleable books, one of the printers would produce them, Hatchards and the lending libraries would sell them and any small mistakes would eventually be decently interred by the remainder outfit. Naturally, it didn't work. The printers, knowing that Werner Laurie had to deal with them, did not offer competitive costings or delivery dates. On the other hand, there was no point in Hatchards or the libraries ordering more copies than they could reasonably use. So the publishing end was squeezed on both sides.

Even a big and highly efficient group like William Collins – in the pre-Murdoch days – could not make vertical integration work. Fontana, the in-house paperback firm, could not make sufficient profits from exploiting the Collins hardcover titles alone and the printing works in Glasgow had to woo outside publishers for their paperback printing.

The rickety structure might have endured longer if Clarence Hatry had possessed the ability to pick good subordinates. Ebullient and quick-witted, he liked to surround himself with men who amused him and who tended to agree with him. He should never, for example, have left the Shepherd brothers in charge of Hatchards for five minutes and when he did come to make a change, he installed an old colleague, who had stood in the dock with him at the fraud trial some fifteen years earlier. Mr Tabor was a decent and intelligent man who knew nothing about bookselling and only learned as he went along. By the same token, Hatry should never have appointed me, almost straight out of the army and wholly ignorant of publishing, to run Werner Laurie. An experienced editor-*cum*-manager would not have committed the errors of omission and commission that I did through sheer lack of knowledge.

The opportunism that produced so many successful business coups also contributed largely to his downfall. At one of our informal meetings around 1950, he told me he had been lucky enough to acquire a wonderful new colleague with impeccable qualifications, who had brought the chance of acquiring a revolutionary machine – the Brehmer stitching machine. It was a German invention but the patent could be acquired cheaply through the Custodian of Enemy Property. Apparently, where hitherto the stitching-together of a book's 'signatures' before the covers were attached had been done manually or by some laborious contraption, the Brehmer machine, which had proved itself in the war years in Germany, would do the job more quickly, cheaply and efficiently. Moreover, this brilliant new colleague had arrived with the highest possible references from his previous two employers, an important printing trust and a famous firm of printers. The man ran his own consulting firm and Hatry at once agreed to give it free space inside the valuable Tudor Street head office. He also made his new friend a director of the main board with the right to sign cheques.

In the hope, no doubt, that some of his brilliance might reflect back on me, Clarence Hatry suggested – he was always silky in his approach but I knew it was more of an order than a suggestion – that I should meet the new director as soon as possible. I arranged a meeting. He put me in mind of Alec Guinness's study of Fagin in the film of *Oliver Twist*; not in his dress, for he wore a tailor-made suit, but in his visage and mannerisms. There was an oily sibilance about him that I distrusted at first sight.

At our next get-together soon afterwards, Hatry asked me what I thought.

I said, 'I think he's a crook.'

I then received a sharp lecture on jumping to conclusions and the need for complete loyalty between comrades and colleagues. Jealousy should not come into play, just because a man was older, more experienced and much, much more of a business success than oneself. If I had not been a friend of the family, my career in the group might well have been abruptly terminated.

I was not a particularly shrewd judge of character. Smarter men than me had spotted long before that the man was an utter fraud. There should, indeed, be a law against giving someone who leaves under a cloud a fulsome testimonial. Both the printing trust and the famous firm of printers, his previous two employers, had, it turned out, got rid of him but, instead of calling in the Fraud Squad, which at least one of them should have done, they each let him loose on an unsuspecting world, waving the signed references in the faces of the gullible.

A year or so later, over a smoked salmon sandwich and a glass of champagne, Clarence Hatry ruefully admitted that my first reaction had been right. The trusted colleague had quietly been making out holding-company cheques to his small private concern, which was offering no services in return, and was using his signing rights to round off the one-way transaction. At a time when it was increasingly short of money because, for all the efforts and capital poured into it, the British (as it was now called) Brehmer printing machine was still not functioning properly, he had defrauded HAI of £30,000 – about £450,000 in today's terms.

'You're going to prosecute him,' I said. It was more of a statement than a question.

Clarence smiled and shrugged. 'No,' he said. 'With my record, I can't afford the bad publicity. I've written it off – to experience.'

I tried to argue but he was adamant. He was not going to stand up in court and give evidence in a case of fraud when defence counsel was bound to belittle his testimony through the 'Et tu, Brute?' gambit. So the crooked colleague went his merry way unscathed, although, thanks to a for once just providence, he did not long enjoy his ill-gotten gains. Within a year or two, I learned, he was cut down by a fatal heart attack.

Clarence Hatry had an endearing – as it turned out for me – characteristic. He always promised every investor in one of his many companies that he would buy back the shares at the price paid, even if their value had since fallen. This may have been partly due to vanity but I like to think it was redolent of the man's bigness, his feeling that faith and trust are more important than mere money. Indeed, he was never greatly interested in money as such. Cash or bank credits were just the essential playing cards. It was how you played the hand and the tricks you won that mattered.

The buying back of his friends' investments at par had one large adverse factor, as several of his pre-war contemporaries have pointed out to me. In a general slump when share prices are continually falling, it denuded him of ready money either to make advantageous purchases at bargain prices or to prop up his own stretched resources. In fact, had he not been so quixotic, there is a chance that he could have bridged the financial gap over the shares of Allied Ironfounders and thus never have been persuaded to issue forged scrip – for which he ultimately sacrificed ten years of his life.

From my army gratuity and the royalties from a fairly successful novel, Desert Episode, I had about £1,500 to spare when I joined Werner Laurie at the beginning of 1947. As a form of thanks and an act of faith, I bought £1,000-worth of HAI five per cent preference shares. My wife, baby son and I were living in a rented flat in West Hampstead with a seven-year lease. Towards the end of 1951, the chance arose to buy a freehold house with a garden on the edge of Hampstead Heath. Apart from the mortgage, I needed to put down £1,600 out of my own resources, which meant selling my HAI shares at par, to Clarence, following his personal promise.

It must have been the worst possible moment for him. I knew that British Brehmer was still siphoning in loans from other companies in the group, as Werner Laurie itself had contributed more than once. But I was not aware that the group itself was insecure, only propped up by advances from the Countess of Seafield, the largest shareholder and one of the richest women in the kingdom, and from Clarence himself out of his private resources. But he never demurred. Not by the twitch of an eyebrow, a sigh or a grimace did he betray the fact that my request could not have come at a worse time and that he was almost searching the linings of his pockets to find the (in his general terms) paltry amount of £1,000. He wrote out a personal cheque, signed it with the flourishing loops of the initials 'CCH' and handed it to me with a smile and a word of thanks. The pressure was great – but the grace was greater.

A few months later, in the early summer of 1952, he succumbed to nervous exhaustion and effectively gave up control of the HAI group, handing his power of attorney to a City figure, Samuel Hogg of Hogg Bullimore, the insurance brokers. Another friend, Herbert Rothbarth, the financier, took over effective control of the group.

After some months, Clarence Hatry recovered sufficiently to run some moderately prosperous Scottish companies, although he suffered from periodic bouts of angina. We kept in touch until his death a decade later and met from time to time to discuss my writing his biography, which proved abortive, although I have some thirty or forty pages with curling edges tucked away in a drawer somewhere in the house. It was typical of CCH. He did not want to discourage my enthusiasm for the task but, more to the point, he was determined to preserve his own privacy. So with charm and wit and the enjoyment of telling stories against himself, he would disclose enough threads at our meetings to keep me spinning a kind of Penelope's web.

At his funeral service, a line of poetry kept running through my mind. 'After life's fitful fever, he sleeps well.' CCH's buccaneering forays through the City made him many enemies but he paid with ten good years for his failings. He had a generous heart and a sense of fun. I owe him a lot.

3

THE APPRENTICE

Thomas Werner Laurie, the son of a Scot who had married a German woman, founded his publishing house in 1904. He had learned his trade at T. Fisher Unwin, which later produced that dean of twentieth-century publishing, Sir Stanley Unwin. Werner Laurie was a friend and at first a close rival of William Heinemann, who had started his firm fourteen years earlier. When Heinemann rejected Upton Sinclair's *The Jungle* on the grounds that it was too alien for British tastes and the author was a strident socialist, Laurie jumped in and had an enormous and continuing success with the book, which was rarely out of print for the next fifty years.

In these days, when authors will swiftly pursue the largest cheque that is waved in front of them, it is refreshing to recall that Upton Sinclair stayed with the same modest-sized publisher for the rest of his life. He so much admired Britain's lone stand in 1940, and deplored the physical and financial problems besetting the inhabitants, that he refused to accept advances for his books and demanded to be paid a flat ten per cent royalty, when he could have commanded large down payments and double that royalty rate. Long after the end of the war, he insisted on the same modest terms.

Laurie had also been the first British publisher to issue a

collected edition of Colette in the English language and a new translation of Guy de Maupassant's major works. But in his last ten or fifteen years – he died towards the end of the war – his list became far less distinguished. He made a good deal of money out of 'frilly knicker' books, novels that were not openly sexual – in which case, they would have been charged under the Obscene Publications Act, like *The Well of Loneliness* and, over thirty years later, *Lady Chatterley's Lover* – but which hinted at 'delicious depravity'. They included Maurice Dekobra's *Madonna of the Sleeping Cars*, Norman Lindsay's *The Cautious Amorist* and the American novels of Donald Henderson Clarke.

Clarence Hatry had bought the firm about a year before I came on the scene. His daughter Diana had kept an eye on things but, with the boom in book sales continuing briskly after the end of the war, Werner Laurie ran on largely through its own momentum. It still published several worthy writers such as Upton Sinclair but the general reputation was poor. A new policy had to be found and the list cleaned up quickly. That kind of cheap and titillating fiction was liable to attract the wrong kind of author to the firm and stop agents from offering their better clients. And my patron deserved a list of which he could be proud, not ashamed.

It was essential, I soon realised, to attract the more important literary agents, let them realise I had a list to build and money to spend. I failed to appreciate that those same sensible agents would first show their better wares to the publishers who would, they knew from experience, publish the book successfully. The newcomer was only likely to be shown the marginal typescripts or the ones the agent was offering at well above their market value. But even that was better than being ignored. A then common saying in the trade was, 'You never lose money on a book you don't publish.' The corollary is equally valid. You don't make any money on a book you don't publish.

My first excursion into the agency world met with a rebuff. I called on Clarence Paget, who was then the assistant to A.D. Peters; after a later spell at Cassell's, where he handled subsidiary rights, he was to become editor at Pan Books and to play a leading role in that paperback house's success. The Peters firm had considerable prestige. It numbered Evelyn Waugh, Arthur Koestler, Terence Rattigan and V.S. Pritchett among its clients. I was having an enjoyable discussion with Clarence, telling him the policies I hoped to adopt to – in the modern phrase – 'improve the Werner Laurie image', when the owner himself walked into the room. Clarence sprang to his feet and said, 'Oh, Mr Peters, I'd like you to meet George Greenfield. He's taken over the running of Werner Laurie.'

'I have no wish to meet anyone connected with Werner Laurie,' was the abrupt reply and the great man stalked out of the room.

An Old Etonian whose manners were exquisite, Clarence went red with embarrassment. The snub was quite uncalled-for; whatever Werner Laurie's past shortcomings, I, as a tyro of several weeks, could hardly be held responsible. Indeed, within a short period, he made up for it by selling me a serious historical work on the French Revolution by J.B. Morton, who in his lighter role was 'Beachcomber' of the *Daily Express*. I also acquired from him a book that was to become a bestseller – *Cricket Prints* by R.C. Robertson-Glasgow, one of the two or three best writers on cricket this century. (The author, who wrote a regular column for the *Observer*, was known throughout the cricketing world as 'Crusoe'. Years before, as an undergraduate playing for Oxford in the Parks, he had bowled out a tough old pro, who on returning to the pavilion and being asked who had got him out, flung down his bat and grunted, 'Some bugger called Robinson Crusoe!')

And as it usually does in the book world, the wheel eventually came at least half circle. Ten years after the rebuff, when commercial television was about to start transmitting, A.D. Peters joined his friend and client, Norman Collins, in a firm named High Definition Studios. Their object was to produce short films for television with the emphasis on the children's market. Enid Blyton's Noddy was then by far the most popular character in that market – and I just happened to be Enid Blyton's agent. Peters wrote me a letter, asking me to call at his office. Childishly, I replied saying I was prepared to see him provided he came to *my* office in Red Lion Square. Which he did.

His opening remark was, 'I think we've met before.'

'Very briefly,' I said.

He had the grace to blush.

Apart from Peters' firm, there were four other large and important agencies in the immediate post-war years – Curtis Brown, A.M. Heath, Pearn, Pollinger & Higham, and A.P. Watt. (Significantly, those five still retain much of their power, forty-five years later. Indeed, the five have become seven, because not long after Nancy Pearn died, David Higham split away from Laurence Pollinger, whose son Murray quickly set up his own separate firm.) Watt is the oldest literary agency in the world, having been founded in the 1870s. Seventy years later, it was still very much a family firm, with three closely related Watts – W.P., R.P. and P.F. (Peter) – running things.

It seemed to exist in a sunny Edwardian era of its own. Every letter offering a typescript or book was couched in the most formal terms and always ended up with the sentence: 'We trust you will make us what the author will consider to be a satisfactory offer for his work.' The then office in Arundel Street contained a dusty filing room with shelf after shelf of green metal boxes with, stencilled in white paint, the names of the great dead on them – Rudyard Kipling, A.E.W. Mason, John Galsworthy. The youngest of the Watts, Peter, a wit and successful short-story writer, chafed at the restraints. His uncle and older cousin might believe that longevity and a fine reputation were ample assets to attract good new authors but Peter sensed they were not enough.

In about 1949, I had arranged to meet an author in the Long Bar at the Café Royal. Throughout the *fin de siècle* and the first thirty years of the century, it had been famous, notorious even, as a meeting place of bohemian artists and writers. Augustus John had been a frequent visitor, as had Oscar Wilde, Bernard Shaw, Sickert and Epstein. But after the war and until Charles Forte wrought his transformation, both the Long Bar and the Café Royal itself had become unfashionable. Because so few customers turned up, the Long Bar was an ideal place for a quiet and serious talk, accompanied by a drink. On that occasion, I arrived early – my office in Piccadilly was only a hundred yards away – and saw a solitary figure propping up one corner of the bar. It was Peter Watt. He was gingerly holding a small, tulip-shaped glass of sherry in one hand and looking thoroughly morose.

I asked him if he was waiting for a guest. He shook his head. I next asked if I could buy him a drink and again he shook his head. Then the sad story came tumbling out. The Watts held a 'prayer meeting' at the start of business each morning, when they perused the incoming letters and discussed 'policy'. On a recent occasion, Peter had happened to mention that no worthwhile new author had come to the firm for quite a few weeks. One of the two older men pronounced that the Long Bar of the Café Royal was the best place to meet good authors. It was agreed that Peter, as the youngest, would draw a few shillings from the petty cash – just enough to buy himself one drink and another for the genius who might tumble into his outstretched arms – and, for three mornings every week from noon to lunch-time, stand in wait at the Long Bar. Alas for the older Watts' hopes, the futile exercise was soon abandoned. Authors join agencies for all manner of esoteric reasons – George MacDonald Fraser submitted the first Flashman script to John Farquharson Ltd because the firm had 'a good Scottish name' – and sometimes for no reason at all. But one might as well stand at the corner of Piccadilly Circus as at the bar of a restaurant in the expectation of attracting new talent.

Peter Watt had a debonair personality and a real flair for the job which, after his two relations retired, quickly proved itself. One of his spectacular coups occurred with John le Carré's *The Spy Who Came in from the Cold*. Le Carré had written two interesting but modestly selling novels which, through the firm of A.P. Watt, had been published by Gollancz in Britain and by Walker & Co. in the USA. Then came *The Spy* and Peter at once realised its potential. Jack Geoghegan, who had learned his trade as a Doubleday salesman on the West Coast, had recently been appointed to run Coward McCann in New York; one of his first moves had been to invite Lena Wickman, a close friend of Peter's, to act as his London scout. She read the script before anyone else and enthused Jack who made a pre-emptive bid for American rights. It was the perfect case of hungry publisher meeting ambitious author. *The Spy* was – and is – a splendid novel and it came at just the right moment in the Cold War, not long after the Cuban Missile Crisis. It was also a realistic antidote to Ian Fleming's sexual fantasies and schoolboy smut in the James Bond novels. But it was Jack Geoghegan's drive and hunger for success that made the novel an outstanding bestseller. With a bigger, more established house, it might have been launched as the fifth or sixth 'lead' of that season and have fared moderately well. Where he or she has the scope, an agent's *nous* is revealed through placing the right book with the right publisher – as Peter did so signally with *The Spy*.

He died tragically young from a cerebral haemorrhage. Beneath the stylish exterior – the double-breasted waistcoats with their small lapels and the handmade shirts – he was a great worrier who usually became almost too close to and fond of his clients. (An agent ought to be friendly with the writers he represents but they need him to maintain a certain reserve, a sense of objectivity, when it comes to guiding their careers.) On one occasion, he telephoned me towards the end of my publishing days to seek my advice about a novelist I had published, who had left his previous agent and now wanted Peter to take over.

I said, 'For God's sake, don't touch him! The man's a walking disaster. And anyway, he didn't leave Curtis Brown – they kicked him out. He's loaded with talent, sure enough, but he spends most of his time in the French pub, talking away his best plots. He's always months late in delivering – and then it's never the plot he described to you when you bought the bloody book. What's more, he has the neat trick of sending his wife round to your office in floods of tears, trying to borrow money and saying she's had to pawn her mink coat to pay the telephone bill before it's cut off – and threatening suicide if you don't cough up. The man's a menace, I tell you. His books weren't earning out by miles and I had to let him go. I just couldn't take it any longer. My advice is – don't touch him, dear boy.'

He thanked me for my advice and said he would take it to

heart. A month later, I happened to glance through a copy of the latest A.P. Watt client list and saw the dreaded name on it. Poor Peter was like the good woman who marries a drunk because, deep inside, she feels she alone can reform him.

The only really unpleasant agent I met in those early post-war years was David Higham, then of Pearn, Pollinger & Higham. During hostilities, he had been some kind of chairborne warrior and still looked the military man, with his grey-white hair cropped *en brosse*, in the style of an old-fashioned lavatory brush, his horn-rimmed spectacles, pink complexion and grey moustache. Indeed, he resembled a minor Prussian dignitary, a veritable captain from Köpenick, which was ironic as his family name had originally been Hyam. With a beginner like me, he employed a brand of unctuous brutality, which at first was quite convincing.

It was his practice, every few months, to write a sharp letter to a new young publisher, criticising him severely for the way he was treating a Higham client. On one such occasion, he catalogued my shortcomings vis-à-vis Ruth Manning Sanders, an authority on circuses, one of whose books I had published a few weeks earlier. I was wholly neglectful, I ignored her completely, I lacked the grace even to write her an occasional letter to tell her how her book was selling, the production was shoddy and she couldn't find a single copy in Hatchards of all places when she last called there. It was fairly certain, his letter concluded, that as a result of my callous treatment, the unhappy Mrs Sanders would expect him to look for a new publisher for her next book.

I read his letter with complete surprise. A few days earlier, Ruth Manning Sanders, who lived in Cornwall, had paid one of her rare visits to London. She had called at my office and I had taken her down to the bookshop to meet Mr Gilbey, the head buyer of Hatchards. After a pleasant chat, she had autographed several copies of her book for him and had paused to admire the display of it in the shop. She and I had then lunched at The Caprice in a most friendly atmosphere. There had not been a breath of criticism from her throughout the two or three jolly hours we had spent together. I could only conclude she must be a consummate hypocrite.

I wrote to her at once, asking her to tell me bluntly if she had any qualms or unhappiness over the way her book had been published. Her letter in reply said she could not have been happier with the treatment she had received; she was indeed somewhat perplexed that I could ever have imagined anything else.

I sent copies of the correspondence to David Higham. If I had hoped for a contrite apology, I should have remembered that old Irish saying – 'What do you expect from a pig but a grunt?' His reply castigated me for writing to his client behind his back.

Agents often use the truth like a sponge. Sometimes they squeeze it tight and sometimes they expand it by soaking up the distillations of hyperbole. One should not really say, 'I am giving you the first exclusive option' to more than, perhaps, three or four publishers in turn. And one should always be careful to shake the book or typescript vigorously before making another submission and so ensure that the previous publisher has not left the offer letter in it as a bookmark. On one occasion with a Higham script, I found no less than five earlier offer letters at intervals between the pages. It was indeed interesting to note the tolerance of my more favoured rivals. One had given up around page 15, another had struggled on to about page 25, two had stalled in the low fifties and only one had had the perseverance to press beyond page 100. All the offer letters, including mine – the sixth – referred to granting 'first offer'. I wrote, 'No, thanks' across the bottom of the one addressed to me, clipped all six together and returned them to him along with the typescript.

One worthy script which David Higham sent me was the autobiography of Wing-Commander Huskisson. He had been blinded in the Blitz but with indomitable courage had refused to let his handicap interfere with the war effort. He had indeed invented a kind of spiked wheel, which a sighted person could trace along the lines of a plan or diagram. By turning it over and feeling the indentations with his fingertips, he was able to envisage the details of the plan. In this way, he had worked with great success in the Ministry of Aircraft Production under

Lord Beaverbrook and had made a considerable contribution to the war effort.

After reading the script and admiring the author's courage, I told David Higham that I definitely wanted to make an offer but would first like to meet the wing-commander. He was not going to let a little handicap like blindness interfere with his way of life. Aided by his devoted wife, he had evolved a series of special procedures for coping with everyday life. For example, when his lunch was placed before him, she would have deftly cut up the meat and set out the plate so that the vegetables occupied the 'northern' section, the potatoes filled the 'south-west' part and the slices of meat were in the 'south-east'.

He could pick up his knife and fork, unerringly stab a piece of meat, add a portion of potato and vegetable to the back of the fork and, without pausing in his conversational flow, transfer the helping to his mouth. Again, in his flat, the furniture was arranged in a set pattern, as were his pipe rack and tobacco box on the mantelpiece behind him. He would stand up, thread his way between two armchairs, reach unhesitatingly for one particular pipe from the rack, open the lid of his tobacco box and proceed to fill the pipe and then light it with a match from the specially sited box. He did all this with such customary ease that, more than once when leaving him, I would stretch out my hand to shake his – and then suddenly realise he could not see my gesture.

I asked Tom Brown, the sales manager, to read the type-script. He admired it as I did but struck a cautionary note. He knew from long and tough experience that books about one of the two taboo subjects – cancer and blindness – almost never sell well, as they represent the potential reader's most secret fears for himself. If I wanted to make an offer, he said, for Gawd's sake, keep it low.

In those remote days, when there was some sense as well as sensibility in the publishing trade, an advance offered to an author was indeed 'an advance on account of royalties'. It had two purposes; one was to help the author financially over the eighteen-month or longer period between the time his book was accepted and the moment when he began to earn royalties from the actual sales; the other was to give concrete evidence of the publisher's confidence in his purchase. Royalties for new or not yet successful authors were fairly standard, most often 10 per cent of the published price on the first 3,000 copies sold in the home market, $12\frac{1}{2}$ per cent of the published price on the next 3,000 copies sold and 15 per cent thereafter. The royalty on copies sold for export was usually a flat 10 per cent of the net amount received.

So the publisher had a simple calculation to make. The sales manager – there were no 'marketing orientated executives' in those days – would guess that he could sell, say, 3,000 copies, two-thirds in the home market and the other third for export. The production manager would do some quick costings and reckon that the published price should be 15/- (75p in today's money). If both estimates were close to the mark, the author would earn a little under £200. The advance was usually set at no more than three-quarters of the likely earnings, to allow a safety margin for error. In the case of an existing typescript, half the advance would be paid on signing the agreement and the other half on the date of first publication.

When our sums had been done, I wrote to David Higham, expressing my great admiration for the wing-commander's story and offering him £150 advance against standard royalties. He pooh-poohed the offer, saying that his client was expecting at least £500. (The present equivalent would be over £8,000.) I said in that case I had better return the script at once. He asked me not to be hasty; he would try to persuade his client to reduce his expectations. A week went by and then Higham telephoned me to say that, after much discussion and persuasion on his part, Huskisson would now accept £350.

With a touch of asperity, I replied that he had not taken my message on board. I was not bluffing. £150 was my first and last offer. If that was not good enough, I would be very sorry for I genuinely admired the man and his book, but I was not going to raise the sum by a penny. He said, 'Leave it with me' and rang off.

Another week went by and then there was a repetition of the charade, except that Higham had now 'persuaded' his client down to £250. Again, I said that £150 was still my best offer.

Then several more days elapsed until he called me to say his client very grudgingly accepted my terms. He even added a short lecture on how novice publishers should not risk the ill will of authors by being stingy.

After the agreement had been signed and the first part of the advance had been paid, I had a celebratory drink with the wing-commander. I had already learned not to trust Higham but I did have lingering doubts over whether the bargaining might have upset his client.

So I said, 'I hope that rumpus over the terms didn't put you off.'

'What rumpus was that?' he asked.

'Oh, I thought you were holding out for more than I felt able to pay.'

'Good God, no! Right at the beginning, when you first said you liked the book, my agent told me you were offering £150. I said that was marvellous and told him to grab it before you changed your mind! In fact, I got quite worried as the weeks went by and I didn't hear anything further.'

'So he never mentioned £250 or £350 – or even more? And you didn't mention anything like that to him?'

'Not a whisper,' he said firmly.

I was relieved but I did feel like giving Higham a small lecture. The gist of it would have been: if an agent is going to tell a publisher blatant lies, which thrust the blame on his client's greed, he should first make sure the author knows and, if pressed, will repeat the same fictitious story.

The experience ended happily. Wing-Commander Huskisson's book had very good and widespread reviews, and sold well enough to earn out the advance by a comfortable margin – but still well short of the lowest figure Higham had plucked out of his imagination.

The biggest London literary agency in the 1940s, and still the biggest more than forty years on, is Curtis Brown. Albert Curtis Brown, the founder, was an American who came to London in 1888, representing the *New York Press*. His duties included selling British rights in articles first published in the *Press* and he soon got to know London newspaper editors and book publishers. By the close of the century, he was head of the

International Publishing Bureau in Henrietta Street, Covent Garden, and in 1905 he was running it under his own name. The firm prospered and expanded. Albert, it seems, was a good delegator who gave the younger agents working under him a fairly free rein.

It had been his intention to make his elder son his successor but, when the young man died untimely, he turned to his second son, Spencer, who, in 1935, was a comparative novice. The appointment irked the three senior non-family agents, any one of whom might have hoped to succeed. On a fateful Friday, they walked out – or at least two of them did, Nancy Pearn and Laurence Pollinger, to be followed shortly by David Higham – and took many of the firm's clients with them. The *coup* was enough to sour the most magnanimous of men – but magnanimity was not one of Spencer's special attributes. Somehow, he overcame the defections: the advent of war and the resulting boom in books helped the firm of Curtis Brown to regain and maintain its premier position. Yet the bitterness went on into the second and even third generations. For years, the formation of an agents' association had been mooted but all efforts had failed because no representative of Curtis Brown would willingly sit in the same room with someone from Pearn, Pollinger & Higham – and *vice versa*. In the early 1950s, Nancy Pearn having died, the Pollingers and David Higham split up with apparent acrimony; now there were three powerful firms who were not prepared to sit down together. The Association of Authors' Agents eventually came into being but, even as late as 1986, the senior agents at Curtis Brown, most of whom had not even been born when the original walk-out occurred and none of whom was related to the founder, refused to join.

Spencer Curtis Brown was in his early forties when I first met him. A rumour current in the 'booksy' world for many years credited him with three simultaneous mistresses among his female staff, each unaware that the other two were involved. I found it hard to accept. Apart from the sheer nerve, the acting skill, the extraordinary memory and the stamina required for such Stakhanovite loving, how on earth would he have found time to run a large and efficient business?

Besides, Spencer was not the most physically prepossessing
man one might meet. He had thick pebble glasses, a straggly
moustache and acne pitmarks on his cheeks and chin. Nor was
he a snappy dresser. There would be egg-stains on his tie, holes
in the old cardigan he wore instead of a waistcoat – which
was considered *de rigueur* in the 40s and 50s – and buttons
missing off his shirts. His famous clients, such as A.A. Milne,
C.S. Lewis and Daphne du Maurier, must have seen through
the scruffy exterior to the high and incisive intelligence of the
man beneath – and to the genuine kindliness in his nature.

Although he firmly believed in W.C. Fields's motto –
'Never give a sucker an even break' – and oversold his
wares to naive young publishers like me, he did it in a
friendly, avuncular way. When I left publishing to enter the
shark-infested seas of agenting, several of the agents who had
previously been friends, as I thought, then cold-shouldered me
as a new potential rival. In any case, I was no longer a potential
buyer of their goods. But not Spencer, who went out of his way
to maintain our friendship. During the summer, he would ring
me two or three times a month and say, 'You very busy?'

If I said No, he would go on to suggest we met at Lord's
for a beer and a sandwich, watch a couple of hours' cricket
and then return to our respective offices. Almost invariably,
I would accept and enjoy the inconsequential chat as we sat
in the sun and watched the white figures flickering across the
smooth turf.

The one time I refused, to my everlasting regret, was in
June 1953. It was the final day of the Lord's Test match. The
Australians were in an almost impregnable position. Several
hundred runs ahead, they had ripped through the leading
English batsmen in their second innings on the previous
afternoon and there were only a few wickets to fall before
the Poms were crushed into abject defeat. When Spencer rang
me to meet him there, I said it would be pointless to go. The
match might well be over by the time we arrived and, even if
our countrymen were still lingering in their death-throes, the
obsequies could hardly last far into the afternoon.

So Spencer went to Lord's on his own and was one of the
few spectators to watch a gallant rearguard action to match

the Battle of Rorke's Drift. Watson and Bailey pushed and prodded throughout the morning and into the afternoon. When Watson scored his great century and eventually fell through the sheer fatigue from such total concentration, the bluff figure of Freddie Brown came in to deliver some hefty blows and the tail end did its stuff. Honour was saved – just. And I had missed the heroic drama through underrating my countrymen. I should have listened to a man smarter than myself.

Spencer Curtis Brown had a daughter who married a bright and handsome young man named Colin Young. He had already established himself as a first-rate agent inside the firm and, with added experience, would have made an able successor, when he was diagnosed as having cancer of the jaw. He underwent several operations which sadly ruined his appearance and made it difficult to understand his speech, but he bravely went on at his job until shortly before his grievously premature death. His going must have disheartened Spencer who in his early sixties sold Curtis Brown Limited to the small merchant bank, Dawnay Day, for a reputed figure of over £600,000, which in today's terms would be more than £5 million. He retired not long afterwards and Sir Peter Parker became chairman. In his other capacity as chairman of British Rail, he was unable to match the late Signor Mussolini by making the trains run on time and he showed a similar inability to keep the agency making full steam ahead. Indeed, rather more than a decade later, its balance sheet was so rickety that I decided to make an offer to buy it cheaply. But that is another story.

An interesting small agency in the immediate post-war years was run by E.P.S. Lewin. A man of property, he operated from a smart address on Chelsea Embankment. In the early years of the century, literary agents had advertised widely, but by the end of the war the practice had virtually ceased. It was generally felt that the expense of advertising in literary periodicals would only attract hordes of yellowing typescripts with curling pages – a final plea from the damned – and that the added effort of scrutinising them and the cost of return postage would far outweigh the value of the very occasional publishable script that might emerge. But Lewin advertised regularly in the *New Statesman & Nation* – and acquired some good clients thereby. One such was J.F. Burke, whose novel *Swift Summer* won an Atlantic Award; I published it with pleasure and some profit.

Peter Lewin told me one day that Sir John Squire was a client of his and was about to write his autobiography. I agreed at once to pay an advance of £200 down – and then marvelled at my good fortune. Sir John had not only been a Georgian poet of some note but, as a literary man about town and then the editor of the *London Mercury*, he had been an intimate of all the great names of Bloomsbury and beyond over the first half of the twentieth century. And what touched my heart even more, he had been the captain of that wonderfully eccentric cricket team satirised in A.G. Macdonell's *England, Their England*. In the twilight of his career, he was then chief reader for Macmillan. When the ink on the contract was dry, I asked Lewin if I might invite his – now my – author out to lunch. I wanted to drink deep from the Pierian spring.

The lunch was to be at Kempinski's, then a rather smart restaurant in Swallow Street, off Piccadilly. I arrived early and sat nervously fingering a small glass of dry sherry. When my special guest turned up, he could have stepped out of the pages of the *Pickwick Papers*. He was wearing a black coat, green with age when the sun's rays caught it, and formal pinstripe trousers. He had a cataract of white hair and small round spectacles far down on a red nose. He greeted me with considerable courtesy.

I offered him a pre-lunch drink. He asked for a large scotch, no water. ('Rocks' were then unheard-of.) We chatted briefly and then I asked if he would like another drink before we went into lunch. He had another large scotch. When we reached the dining table, he confessed that he never ate lunch. 'You go ahead, my boy,' he said, 'and order yourself some food. If I may, I'll have another large scotch.'

It is unnerving in any event for an inexperienced publisher to take lunch with a distinguished guest more than twice his age;

doubly so when the guest just drinks his scotch and watches each mouthful on its way from the plate to the host's mouth. So that he would not feel out of things, I ordered him another large scotch and yet another. And, alas, somewhere between the fourth and the sixth large scotch, his eyelids began to droop and his voice became slurred. By the end of my solitary meal, he could still stand up and with a little elbow-gripping make stately, if erratic, progress out of the restaurant. But the Pierian spring had turned out to be dark brown in colour and tangy to the taste.

I did rescue one conversational gem from the pre-lunch part of the disaster. Somewhat fatuously, I had remarked on the great difficulty there must be for the chief reader in such a large and august house as Macmillan in deciding what books to recommend and what to reject.

'Nonsense,' he said firmly. 'It is an easy task. There are only four kinds of book. There are good books that do sell and good books that don't sell; bad books that do sell and bad books that don't sell. All you have to do is put the book in its proper category. My masters would not, I hope, want to publish the bad books, even the ones liable to sell. As to the others, it's up to them.'

It is a useful maxim. My only problem over the years has been to tell a good book from a bad one.*

---

* Sir John died in 1958. He never did deliver his memoirs and I had to write off the £200 advance, which would be over £3,000 in today's currency. Publishers need a touch of the philosopher if they wish to enjoy a peaceful night's sleep. I was consoled by the thought that the payment represented perhaps 2,000 large scotches at the then going rate and so lent a rosy glow to the gathering shadows of his final years.

4

FROM THE AIR TO THE PAGE

During the war and for seven years afterwards, radio or, as we then called it, 'the wireless' was the main form of home entertainment. BBC Television had closed down 'for the duration' and was still a minor attraction, comparable perhaps with Morris dancing and playing Real Tennis, until the screening in 1953 of the Coronation with its unctuous yet authoritative commentary by Richard Dimbleby and in 1957 by the arrival of commercial television. But at the height of its popularity, BBC radio enjoyed larger audiences than the most popular TV programmes would attract forty years later. 'ITMA' ('It's That Man Again'), featuring Tommy Handley, Wilfred Pickles' 'Have A Go' and 'Take It From Here' with Jimmy Edwards and Dick Bentley, would have listener ratings well in excess of ten million per programme. So would 'Band Waggon' with Arthur Askey and Richard Murdoch. Their catch-phrases – 'It's being so cheerful as keeps me going' or 'Can I do you now, sir?' or 'Give 'im the munny, Barney' – became common usage.

Apart from his great merits in keeping the public laughing in gloomy days, Tommy Handley was responsible for a change in the tax laws. After his widely lamented death in January 1949, he was found to have left an enormous sum of money.

Everyone, not least the Inland Revenue, was surprised in view of the penal rates of taxation then in force. It turned out that he had conveniently forgotten to declare his numerous repeat fees from the BBC and, apparently, not a few of the original fees as well. Following the Revenue investigation, the loophole was closed through the passing of an act whereby the payer – in this case, the BBC – was responsible for declaring annually to the tax authorities all sums paid to individuals in excess of £15. The responsibility was extended to include publishers, newspapers and indeed all organisations liable to pay fees to freelance contributors. One man's excessive greed had queered the pitch for innumerable minor offenders.

Juliet O'Hea, a director of Curtis Brown and one of the outstanding post-war agents, offered me early in 1949 the chance of publishing the memoirs of Wilfred Pickles under the title of *Between You and Me*, which was one of his catch-phrases. His weekly radio programme, 'Have A Go', was basically a quiz show with modest cash payments to the winners but its appeal lay in the way in which Pickles selected 'characters' from his live audience and drew funny anecdotes out of them. He was the essence of Yorkshire-ness, fairly short and thin, with sandy hair and a sharp-pointed nose. His public persona was that of the slightly cocky, no-nonsense man from the dales, smart and quick on the uptake but laughing with you, not at you. For several years, he was one of the two or three most popular entertainers in the country and by 1949, 'Have A Go', which had started three years earlier, had many millions of regular listeners.

Up to that stage, no radio personality had published his or her autobiography in book form and so there was no guide to potential sales. A serial version in a popular newspaper might well attract many readers – but would the majority, who were probably not frequent book-buyers, still be attracted by a hardcover version at the then stiff price of 10/6d (52½ pence)? As I recall, Juliet O'Hea was asking for an advance of £1,500, which would require sales of close on 30,000 copies to cover it. There was the added question of whether publishing a light entertainer's story might risk taking the Werner Laurie list 'down market' (though we did not then use that phrase) and to some extent negate my efforts to lift it.

In the end, I took a deep breath and plunged in. I need not have worried. *Between You and Me* was an instant success. The reviews were at the least kind and at the best encouraging. The crowds flocked into the shops, particularly at the big stores where Wilfred Pickles carried out signing sessions. At Bentall's in Kingston, for example, he autographed and sold well over 300 copies in an hour and a half. We had to reprint and reprint again and in a few weeks the total sales exceeded 50,000 copies.

I went to most of the signing sessions. It was at Bentall's, indeed, that I first witnessed the fine art of 'gifting', as performed by a master. Pickles was accompanied everywhere by his wife Mabel, a large bosomy lady with a hard eye. We arrived outside the store in a hired Daimler. Cheering crowds were being held back by the police as we made a triumphal entry, to be greeted by the Bentall's manager, all smiles and bows. (For the first time in my life, I realised what it must be like to be an equerry to royalty.) As we passed through the electrical-appliances department, Mabel paused and indicated with an imperious, gloved finger the most expensive brand of dry shaver.

'Wilf,' she exclaimed, 'look! A Remington shaver. You've always wanted one of those.'

'Goodness me, Mabel,' said Wilfred, with the beatific expression of a Kalgoorlie miner who had just felt a solid gold nugget with the tip of his pick, 'an electric razor. Just the job!'

'So useful when you have a quick change between shows,' Mabel murmured. 'Oh, you really ought to have one, Wilf.'

By now, the manager had caught the drift. Still smiling – but through clenched teeth – he said, 'Perhaps . . . with the compliments of Bentall's . . .?'

It was enough. The counter assistant gift-wrapped the shaver in its box, the parcel disappeared into Mabel's capacious hand-bag and the stately progress continued. In her heyday, Queen Mary was held to be the scourge of the antique dealers' annual fair at Grosvenor House for nominating expensive items of

furniture that she would deign to accept; but on a lower scale
Wilfred and Mabel Pickles probably outdid her for the variety
and volume of the gifts they would drop heavy hints to acquire.
Many of the 'trophies' were on display in their luxurious flat in
New Cavendish Street, a few yards from Broadcasting House.
The man of the people had left his people a long way behind,
yet he never lost the common touch.

Nor did he lose his quick wit. One of my many *faux pas*
was to arrange a book-signing session for him at Hatchards.
I should have realised that Pickles was not a name to attract
readers from Mayfair – and no one turned up. Nothing is more
embarrassing for an author, particularly one used to adoring
crowds, than to sit behind a table with a fountain pen at the
ready and piles of books just waiting to lose their virginity
through the flourish of a bold signature, and nobody comes
forward to get his copy signed. The minutes grind by, small
talk falters and then dies, the author's impatience grows until
it turns to anger. Disaster looms.

Then I had a small brainwave. Asking Wilfred to excuse me
for a moment, I rushed up to the third floor, corralled all the
publishing staff, told them to put on their coats and hats – men
and women in those days wore hats – grab a copy of *Between
You and Me* and go downstairs, entering the bookshop from
the street as though they were passers-by. They did so and
formed a queue in front of the signing table. Wilfred duly
obliged and then each of the staff went out through the main
door, re-entered by the side door and took the lift back to
their respective offices. There had at least been the makings of
a crowd but unfortunately no outsiders had been attracted.

So there was another embarrassing pause. And again I
excused myself and rushed upstairs once more to enlist the
aid of my now slightly less loyal staff. I was banking on the
fact that an author, busy signing a copy of his book, hardly
notices the person pushing it across the table. Thus, when there
was another lull, I summoned the Werner Laurie staff for yet
one more crowd scene. And when one plump junior clerk for
the third time of asking offered a new copy of the book for
his signature, Wilfred Pickles looked up with a bright eye and
said in his broadest accent, 'It's awreet, lass. Last lap!'

The most consistent policy in many publishing houses is the simple fact that one thing leads to another. At Werner Laurie, we seemed to have stumbled on a winning formula. *Raising the Laughs*, the memoirs of Ted Ray, *Take It From Me*, the life-story of Jimmy Edwards and even the memoirs of the then famous crooner, Donald Peers, followed in swift succession and each of them gained some fame, if fleeting. Jimmy Edwards had been an organ scholar at Cambridge and a wartime pilot in the RAF, where he won the DFC for gallantry in the Arnhem operation. He was of a different background and culture from the others, who were basically, as Tommy Handley had been, products of the old variety halls. Bud Flanagan and the rest of the Crazy Gang once found themselves sharing a railway compartment with Jimmy. While they guffawed and told jokes and played tricks on each other, he sat back, reading *The Times*. Flanagan leaned forward, tapped him on the knee and said, 'The trouble with you, Jimmy, is – you think you're doing the business a favour!'

With his broad red cheeks and walrus moustache, he was a marked man wherever he went in public. We were walking along Piccadilly on one occasion when a small man in a cloth cap, a complete stranger, accosted him and said, 'Say something funny.'

He replied, 'Why don't you fuck off?'

As we walked on, we saw the little man convulsed with laughter, quite convinced he had been the beneficiary of a smart epigram.

Jimmy Edwards wrote his own book, with some help in punctuation and spelling from his secretary. If there was a certain sameness in the approach and style of the others, it was because their books were secretly ghosted by Gail Pedrick, a soft-spoken, prematurely silver-haired Cornishman who had a job in the BBC Variety Department. (That supposedly private fact did not stop Donald Peers from telephoning me at home on many successive weekends and reading extracts from the forthcoming text in his mellifluous voice for half an hour at a time. He would ask my opinion of various phrases and often long sentences, as though they had come straight from his own pen. Indeed, as the writing progressed, I felt he had somehow convinced himself that he had written every word himself.)

As Brian Glanville has shown in his perceptive novel, *The Comic*, comedians who learned their patter and their timing the hard way through touring the old variety halls are usually insecure, and often morose and bitter when away from the footlights. The audience is like a wild beast out there, needing to be tamed and then wooed twice a night. It helped, of course, to have the backing of a popular radio series but, night after night, you either had to wheedle them into submission through a quickfire patter, as comics like Ted Ray and Dickie Henderson would do or club them brutally into acceptance in the manner of Jimmy Edwards. Almost alone among the top names of his day, he did not give a damn. If the audience didn't take to him, that was their fault.

He could be equally brutal to his colleagues. On one occasion, when he was heading the bill at the Strand Theatre, I called at his dressing room for a prearranged drink. Tony Hancock had his first big West End part as second lead and we could hear the beginning of his act on the tannoy system in Jimmy's room. He switched it off so that we could have an uninterrupted chat. Ten minutes later, Tony Hancock, sweating profusely, came rushing in.

'How was I, Jimmy?' he asked anxiously.

'Bloody awful,' came the reply.

'You don't mean it – honestly?'

'I just told you. Bloody awful.'

The exchange went on in that vein for several minutes and poor Tony Hancock was so crestfallen, I feared he might burst into tears. Then he suddenly realised that the tannoy was off – and had been off for some while.

'You weren't listening,' he exclaimed. 'You never heard a word of the act!'

'Better things to do,' Jimmy said. 'But I'll still bet you were bloody awful.'

One of the last showbiz books I published was *The Piddingtons*. It was an unusual story. Sidney Piddington had been a soldier in the Australian forces, who was captured by the Japanese at the fall of Singapore and who underwent with thousands of others terrible privation in Changi jail. To while away the time and amuse their comrades, he and a fellow Australian POW, Russell Braddon, developed a thought-reading act. On his eventual release and return to Australia, Piddington soon married and inducted his wife Lesley into the secret formula that lay behind the apparent mystery. (I tried very hard through casual and not-so-casual questioning to discover the secret but never succeeded. The only thing I did find out, largely through a process of elimination, was that Russell Braddon, who played a background role as their 'manager', was somehow the conduit. Although Russ and I became friends for another thirty years and more, he never would – and never did – break his vow of secrecy.)

After instant success on Australian radio and on the local music halls, the act came to London around 1950. The success here was even more dramatic. The Piddingtons topped the bill more than once at the London Palladium, which was then the Holy Grail for variety artists. Danny Kaye, Jack Benny and Bob Hope would eagerly accept an invitation from George Black, then the Palladium's supremo, to come over and play a season as top of the bill. And the Piddingtons' BBC programmes were followed intently by a vast audience each week. It was no ordinary music-hall act. On one occasion, the listeners were enthralled by the fact that Lesley Piddington, aloft in an aircraft circling over London, could – without the usual patter and codewords – unhesitatingly and accurately name objects held by her husband Sidney in the studio thousands of feet beneath and indeed recite such and such a line from a certain page out of a book apparently chosen at random.

When I took them and Russell Braddon out to lunch, they were adamant that he must write the book. He was a quiet, slightly sardonic young man of obvious intelligence, who had been at university studying law and a lawn-tennis player of Davis Cup standard when he was called up for the Australian infantry and after training sent to Singapore to reinforce the British garrison. He and his fellow countrymen had fought bravely against overwhelming odds until Braddon was captured by the Japanese on the eve of his twenty-first birthday. He was forced to dig his own grave and then sit, with his feet dangling in the hole, while his captors debated whether or not to shoot him on the spot.

Then, for no apparent reason, they decided to postpone the execution. Braddon was hustled to his feet and marched on his way to Changi jail, where he found himself in the same compound as Sidney Piddington and Ronald Searle, the artist.

All this was fascinating but it did not provide the guarantees I needed.

The book had to be published quickly. Showbiz fame can be fleeting. A tyro author might produce reams of rubbish or get bogged down in the task of writing 70,000 words against a deadline, not least when he was busy helping the other two create new radio programmes or accompanying them on a provincial tour. But the Piddingtons would not budge. Either Braddon wrote it – or there would be no book. Swallowing hard, I accepted the ultimatum.

I need not have worried. The showbiz episodes were at the least stylishly and amusingly written. What gave the book a strange imbalance was the extraordinary power of the middle section, the account of brutal imprisonment by the Japanese and the origin of the mind-reading act to take the emaciated prisoners' minds off their grim conditions. The sandwich held too much meat between the slices of bread.

I was so impressed with the middle part that I commissioned Russell Braddon before *The Piddingtons* was published – with reasonable success – to write a complete book on his experiences as a Japanese POW. Sidney and Lesley were due to return to Australia at the end of their tour but he had decided to remain in England. He set to with a will and quickly produced a script whose working title, taken from a contemporary speech by Winston Churchill, was *Boasted Fortress*. It was soon retitled *The Naked Island*, a quotation from the same speech. ('I saw before me the spectre of the almost naked island.') Ronald Searle, a friend of Braddon's and, as already mentioned, a fellow-prisoner in Changi jail, had produced some expressive line drawings in the prison camp; they were used as illustrations on the dustjacket and inside the

book. I had been deeply moved in my reading of the text, at
the crass stupidity and complacency of the higher command
which, imagining that Singapore could only be assaulted by a
naval taskforce, had sited the big fortress guns to fire seawards
only, at the brutal lack of logic and sheer inhumanity of the
Japanese guards and the stubborn endurance of the prisoners,
many of whom died through starvation or disease brought on
by lack of vitamins and medical care, and the rest survived
until the Japanese surrender in 1945 as mere bags of bones,
hardly more than half their normal fighting weight.

It was a grim and yet somehow exhilarating account, which
proved the indestructibility of the human spirit. If I ever
had to justify my six years of publishing by citing just one
book for which I was personally responsible, it would be
The Naked Island.

There is a pathetic fallacy to which most publishers are
prone. It can be condensed into one sentence: 'This is a good
book; therefore, it will sell.' Even if the publisher is correct
in his assessment, the second half of the sentence does not
logically follow the first half. As Sir John Squire had put it to
me some years earlier, 'There are good books that do sell and
good books that don't sell.' And the early signs pointed to a
lack of sales. The boom in war books that was soon to provide
The Wooden Horse, *Escape from Colditz* and *The Dambusters*
still lay ahead. Besides, as our travellers were quick to point
out, no one wanted a gloomy book about prisoners of war
who didn't escape. 'Sad stuff', in George III's phrase, was
out. Even loyal Hatchards only ordered a few copies.

With just a handful of pre-publication sales, my last hope was
for warm and widespread reviews when the book appeared.
And then the worst happened. It was published on the first
Thursday of February 1952, the very day when the death of
King George VI was announced. There was only one review
– by Guy Ramsey in the *Daily Telegraph*.

In the 1930s Arnold Bennett could make a book succeed
through praising it in his *Evening Standard* column. Nowadays, no reviewer has that power, but for some years after
the war Desmond McCarthy and Ralph Straus, who looked
after non-fiction and fiction respectively for the *Sunday Times*

(and later Cyril Connolly for the same newspaper), and Guy Ramsey, the chief non-fiction reviewer of the *Telegraph*, inherited something of that ability. His praise for *The Naked Island* was forthright and enthusiastic; he devoted most of his double column to it.

I had hoped for a first printing of 10,000 copies but, as the negative sales reports had come flooding in, the print order was reduced and reduced to a level of 3,000. Even then, there were ample stocks in the warehouse on publication day – more than ample, we felt, when the news of the king's death swept other events out of the newspapers. And suddenly, triggered, no doubt, by Guy Ramsey's praise, to be followed by that mysterious magic, word-of-mouth recommendation, orders for *The Naked Island* came trickling and then streaming and, finally, flooding in. By the middle of the week following publication, there were orders for 5,000 more copies. We rushed a reprint of 10,000 but before it was delivered to the warehouse, another 10,000 orders came in – and another 10,000 and yet another. By the end of March, seven weeks after publication, total sales exceeded 70,000 copies, of which we had managed to supply about 50,000. By the end of the summer, we had caught up with the demand and over 100,000 copies had been sold in the trade.

Pan Books bought the paperback rights and went on selling the book, year in, year out, until at length Russell Braddon qualified for a Golden Pan when the millionth copy was sold. That was over twenty years ago – and still the book soldiers on. He stayed on in England, writing a score of popular novels and non-fiction books, appearing frequently on BBC Radio's perennial 'Any Questions?' programme and becoming the Foyle's Lecture Agency's leading client.

An all-round and deserved success: but I suspect that, if asked point-blank, he might agree that the acme of his career was reached over forty years ago with *The Naked Island*.

5

CITING SHAKESPEARE

With Clarence Hatry's departure, my working life changed completely. Hitherto, I had been my own boss, working on that free and easy understanding with him that if Werner Laurie's balance sheet stayed in the black, I could go my unsupervised way for the next financial year. More through luck and an easy market than judgement, I had survived nearly six years on that basis. Now the board of directors was to be stiffened – the choice of verb is deliberate – by bringing in Herbert Rothbarth, the financier, the Countess of Seafield's London lawyer, her accountant, another accountant representing Hatchards Associated Interests, the parent company, and the second Mrs Laurie, much younger than her late husband and rumoured to have been a barmaid who had consoled him in his bereavement. None of these people actually read books, of course; they were far too busy. So the plan was that we would meet every Wednesday afternoon and I would give them an oral synopsis of the titles I wished to acquire. They would then have a discussion, after which I would be told what I could or could not buy.

The system might work in the case of an established thriller writer or romantic novelist, where one could say that the new offering was typical of X's work which usually sold about

5,000 copies and earned his or her regular advance. Again, it would work with a well-known sportsman or radio celebrity, of whom most of them might have heard. But where there was an unusual first novel by a writer of talent or a travel book that depended more on the quality of the observation and the description than the excitement of the adventures *en route*, a recitation by me of the plot – and it is difficult indeed to keep up one's enthusiasm in the face of a bored and boring audience – would do scant justice. After a month or so, I was growing more and more sulky, partly from the wound to my self-esteem and partly at their boorish rejection of one or two choice novels that I badly wanted to publish.

One Wednesday afternoon after an especially good lunch at The Caprice, I felt a rebellious surge when I looked down the long table at the dull faces, like a row of cows in the byre awaiting milking. I said, 'Ladies and gentlemen, I have just one subject to discuss with you this afternoon. It is only fair to warn you in advance that the theme could be considered controversial.'

They nodded gravely. The general feeling of 'Oh dear, what's he up to now?' was almost palpable. I cleared my throat and delivered the usual synopsis. There was this general who commanded the forces in Cyprus. He was a splendid man, powerful, assured, a fine commander. He happened to be a negro but he was married to a lovely white woman. She was completely honourable and as faithful to him as the day was long but she had the unfortunate habit of dropping her handkerchief. A scheming lieutenant picked it up and managed to persuade the jealous commander that she was having an affair with one of his white officers on the island. So, to cut a long story short, the general strangled her and then stabbed himself to death over her corpse.

For once, my account left the audience animated – but not in favour of the story I had told. It was dreadful stuff, the black–white controversy, unpleasant characters, a downbeat ending – they could see no saving feature. It was bound to be a disastrous flop.

When the condemning voices quietened down, I said, 'Ladies and gentlemen, I have just told you – very badly,

I admit – the plot of *Othello* by William Shakespeare. It has enjoyed quite a success on the stage for almost 350 years.'

The following afternoon, I was summoned to a meeting with Herbert Rothbarth. My lucky star must have been twinkling above the skyline because lunch had been arranged that day with Innes Rose, who ran the small but well-respected John Farquharson agency. His office was in Red Lion Square and mine had previously moved, as a cost-cutting measure, from Hatchards in Piccadilly to Number One, Doughty Street, a few hundred yards from his. We met at that long-gone but then noted haunt of businessmen, the Holborn Restaurant.

Innes had a dry wit and he loved a gossip. So, as a joke and with no ulterior motive, I told him the *Othello* anecdote. His laugh was gratifyingly loud but brief. Then he said, 'Look, I can't imagine you'll be long in that job. Got any plans?'

I told him I had just signed a new seven-year contract as managing director of Werner Laurie but, certainly, my position did seem untenable. And in any case I was not prepared to spend my publishing days in spelling out plots and storylines to a bunch of philistines.

He said his firm was doing well but that he and his wife Pauline, who looked after their short-story department, were both fully stretched. They had already begun to consider taking on a junior partner. Would I be interested?

Having acquired several of his clients, including the Australian Jon Cleary whose fine novel, *The Sundowners*, I had recently published and the witty but much underrated New Zealander, John Guthrie, I knew Innes to be totally honest, always ready to fight the good fight for his clients but with an objective common sense and the guts to tell them if he thought they were ever in the wrong. He was eight years my senior; we had both served in the infantry during the war – he in the King's Own Scottish Borderers and I in The Buffs – and we once worked out that at one stage of the Battle of Alamein, we must have been unknowingly within 200 yards of each other.

I drank some more wine, took a deep breath and said, 'Yes.'

That afternoon, I told Herbert Rothbarth about my lunch-time encounter. Quite properly, he said that I could be held to working out the six years and many months remaining of my recent contract but because of my apparent views on the rest of my boardroom colleagues – and certainly their adverse opinion of me – he was prepared to release me, provided that I first found a suitable replacement and stayed long enough to effect a smooth handover. It was then September 1952 and when I phoned Innes Rose with the news, he was prepared to wait till the end of the year but not much longer, he hoped.

I began to cast around. In those far-off days of forty years ago, people who went into publishing usually stayed with the same firm for many years, if not for the whole of their working life. The feverish hirings and firings that have characterised the late 1980s and the early 1990s did not exist. And the power of management lay with the man whose name was over the door. One could not imagine William Collins, Michael Joseph, Hamish Hamilton, Noel Evans, Colonel Murray, Mark Longman, Walter Hutchinson or Robert Hale – even if I had known any of them well enough to make an approach – leaving his own prosperous domain to run a problematical Werner Laurie.

Now for a detour in this already twisting path. I had joined the Authors' Club in Whitehall Court for three reasons: it was cheap, there might (I thought in my ignorance) be a good author or two knocking around, looking for a publisher, and it was easy of access. You could walk down Doughty Street and then John Street and catch a tram – yes, a real clanking tram that ran on lines along Theobalds Road where, at the intersection with Southampton Row, it plunged downhill and rattled on a subterranean course until it emerged on the Embankment, close to where the Howard Hotel is now situated. It proceeded westwards and there was a tram stop at the bottom of Northumberland Avenue, not a hundred yards from Whitehall Court. After lunch, one caught another tram in the opposite direction. The journey took ten or twelve minutes in all. Today, with the advancement of science and technology, a cab would take up to half an hour on the southerly journey and could hardly achieve the return journey at all, since it would not be allowed to turn right from Southampton Row into Theobalds Road.

Graham Greene described the Authors' Club in those days so well, if savagely, in *The End of the Affair* that I would not presume to give my detailed version. Lunch usually consisted of overcooked meat, watery vegetables and boiled potatoes with black plague spots on them, followed by syrup pudding or spotted dick. Fortunately, the drink more than compensated. Most of the members seemed to be parsons who had each published a pamphlet, probably at his own expense. (Graham Greene once wrote in the Suggestions Book that it was surely high time the club lived up to its name and persuaded a few real authors to join.) The qualification for membership was that one had to be a published writer.

Apart from Greene himself, who was there frequently and who looked around with a bilious eye, the stars were his then fellow-directors at Eyre & Spottiswoode, the cold and snobbish Douglas Jerrold, Sir Charles Petrie, a jovial round man with a black Van Dyck beard, and Frank Morley, their American literary advisor. Another habitué was Hugh Kingsmill, a sad and decrepit figure, who would sidle up with the implausible excuse that he had left his wallet at home and could one kindly lend him a ten-shilling note – much more than a fiver in today's currency. I was caught twice but on the second occasion he was careless enough to make only a half-turn, so that I had a glimpse of the missing wallet as he tucked the note away. He never, of course, repaid his debts.

Several years later, Innes Rose told me that a young man, the son of one of Pauline's friends, had written the biography of Hugh Kingsmill, then dead. Innes had read the script and thought it rather well written. What did I think? Simple, I said. Kingsmill had been a fringe literary figure, a drinker and, in my view, a bit of a crook. Forget it. And that, in fact, is how the Farquharson agency failed to take on Michael Holroyd as a client. It was a good lesson to have learned, when I finally realised my error. Never condemn a biography unread, even if – especially if – one knows or knew the subject quite well.

A youngish, dark-haired Cornishman with glowing eyes named Waveney Girvan was a member of the Authors' Club. He was a publisher, in charge of a small firm named Westaway

Books, owned by the then Duke of Bedford, father of the present incumbent. He was, according to Girvan, wildly eccentric
and although enormously wealthy – he owned most of the area
between Tottenham Court Road and Southampton Row, apart
from his vast family seat at Woburn – he was parsimonious,
insisting on keeping a close, almost daily, watch on his
publishing venture, even though it accounted for a minute part
of his income. The Cornish are themselves a strange breed, as I
know from having had a Cornish grandmother, and Waveney
Girvan, I soon discovered, believed in UFOs and visitations
from other planets. But he had more than met his match in
His Grace, *le patron*, whose ideas for likely publications were
far weirder than his own. In short, he was fed up.

Luckily for me, he unburdened himself over a bottle of wine
at the club just as I had come to a cul-de-sac in my thoughts
for a successor. I tried not to paint too rosy a picture of life at
Number One, Doughty Street – I was fond of my colleagues
and of many authors I would be leaving behind – but I may
have glossed over the amount of interference he was likely
to get from the other watchdog directors. At least, none of
them was, in the modern jargon, barking mad, like his present
owner. ('Pray tell me, sir, whose dog are you?')

And so it came to pass. His *curriculum vitae* impressed
Herbert Rothbarth, and the other directors of Werner Laurie
took to him at the following interview. I absented myself,
having an interest to declare, but it must have been so, as
they promptly offered him the succession. He was able to
serve out his notice at Westaway Books and spend a few
days taking over in time for me – after six years to the very
day – to say goodbye to publishing and jump over the fence
into the new world of ten per cent.

John Farquharson himself had retired soon after the war but
his spirit lingered on. I had met him once in his retirement,
when he called at my office above Hatchards to make a
bitter complaint. He had been a reviewer for the in-house
monthly magazine, *Books of Today*, getting 10/- (50p) per
review plus the chance of selling the review copy to Foyle's

at half price – perhaps, another 5/- (25p). When John Brodie, the magazine's editor, left, Hatry asked me to find a successor and I appointed Nancy Spain. She dropped most of the existing reviewers, including Farquharson, and brought in her friends like Hermione Gingold. (Nancy's extravagance and slaphappy methods soon killed off *Books of Today* but not before it had given her some prominence and her own column, first with the *Daily Express* and eventually with the *News of the World*.) The old Aberdonian, who reminded me in size and appearance of Sir Harry Lauder, was, I later discovered, a rich man with a large house and estate in Surrey and a villa in the South of France but he made it clear that he deeply resented losing his monthly reviewing stipend.

He was the archetypal canny Scot. Not marrying until he was in his fifties, he used his bachelor-flat at Halsey House, Red Lion Square, as his office as well. He kept a large and vicious-looking Alsatian in the compact top-floor flat and the animal accompanied him on his visits to publishers. The late Robert Hale, who knew him well, once told me that if a publisher argued too strenuously over an advance or the royalty scale, 'old Farky' had trained the dog on a secret signal to growl and bare its sharp teeth.

His lack of imagination was matched only by his meanness. Innes Rose had joined him as a junior in 1932 and had worked hard at low pay for nine years until his call-up for the Forces. He enlisted in the infantry and saw service in the Western Desert and in Germany, spending more than half of those five years overseas, away from his wife, Pauline. Demobilised early in 1946 and due several months of paid leave, he thought it only courteous on his first day in London to pay his respects to the boss before enjoying a prolonged second honeymoon.

They shook hands. Farquharson said, 'Innes, my boy, I'm proud of you. You have served your country well – and you need a break. Why don't you take the rest of the morning off – and not report for work before two o'clock?'

And such was the man's utter conviction that Innes found himself meekly agreeing.

Farquharson had instituted the rule, which was still in force when I joined years later, that nothing was to be wasted.

At that time, there were no jiffy-bags or Sellotape. When a publisher returned a typescript, it was wrapped in brown paper and secured with string. The string was never to be cut. Every single knot had to be unpicked, then the string was to be rewound and used again. As for the brown paper, it was merely turned inside out and used for wrapping another parcel. It was the firm's proud boast that it never had to buy wrapping paper.

Most authors sent in their scripts either in loose pages inside a typing-paper box or in ring binders or in those dreaded spring-binder files, which had a neat trick of suddenly disgorging the pages, usually unnumbered, which shot in a cascade across one's desk and on to the floor. It would then take hours to get the pages in consecutive order by matching grammatically the last line of one sheet with the first line of another. But, however the typescripts may have arrived, their appearance when sent on to a publisher had to be uniform. Before the Second World War, Farquharson had bought very cheaply some items from a fire-damage sale, notably several hundred sheets of strong paper in alternating shades of brown. One had to cut the paper with a large pair of shears to match the size of the script after ensuring that the pages were in their proper order and that no edges protruded – a flat wooden tapper ensured the latter process. Then, if there were no holes already punched in the margins of the pages, an awl was used to bore them, after which string was threaded in and out, and secured in a neat knot at the back. For my clumsy, untrained fingers and thumbs, a valuable hour could fly past and I would still be gouging the holes or creasing the antique brown paper or having to moisten the end of the string with my tongue to thread it through the pages.

When I joined, the Farquharson firm was a partnership, not a limited company. Its commission income in the previous year had been £5,000. The staff consisted of Innes himself, his wife Pauline and a secretary who also acted as receptionist. The rent at Halsey House would have been a few hundred pounds a year and a secretary would consider herself lucky to earn more than £750. So, allowing for entertaining and some travelling, the overheads would amount to around £2,000 annually, leaving

Innes and Pauline £3,000 as their income before tax. (The present-day equivalent would be at least fifteen times as much.) My salary at Werner Laurie had been £1,500 but I agreed to drop it to £1,000 on joining Farquharson, provided I also received a quarter of the commission income I earned for the firm. In the event, it was such a useful proviso – useful to me, that is – that after a year or two I became an equal partner and went on a straight salary matching Innes's.

But long before then, I had worked out that unpicking string and binding up typescripts in an arcane manner – quite apart from typing my own letters, which I did for the first year or two – was taking up at least three hours a week of my time, say 130 hours per year. That was nearly ten per cent of my working life, and was costing the firm over £150 a year in salary and lost commission. When it was put to him like that, Innes at once saw the point and we soon employed an old-age pensioner to do up the scripts and pack the parcels for a few pounds a week.

Before the First World War, John Farquharson had been manager of the English Books Department at Curtis Brown. He had become a long-distance friend of Paul R. Reynolds, the first ever New York literary agent, who had founded his firm in 1893. Reynolds had a distinguished list of clients, including Henry James and his philosopher-brother William, Scott Fitzgerald and, from across the Atlantic, Bernard Shaw and Winston Churchill. Farquharson told Reynolds that, if he survived the war, he intended to set up his own literary agency and would be delighted to act as the Paul R. Reynolds British representative. In other unexpressed words, he would cut out Curtis Brown and take over one of their more important American clients. And so it happened. When I joined the Farquharson agency over thirty years later, the bulk of its earnings derived either from Reynolds clients or New York agencies recommended by Paul Reynolds Junior, such as Littauer & Wilkinson and Rogers Terrill.

As the man said, wisely if ungrammatically, 'It isn't what you know – but who you know.' Many agents find themselves with a self-appointed benefactor, someone who out of the goodness of his or her heart recommends new clients with no thought of personal gain. Over the years, I had several such: Alan Mitchell who introduced me to Sir Edmund Hillary, Sir Harold Gillies, the great plastic surgeon, and Dr (later Sir) Vivian Fuchs, among many others; or Ron Roberts, cricket writer for the *Daily Telegraph*, who offered Richie Benaud, Bobby Simpson, Neil Harvey, Sir Frank Worrell, Sir Garfield Sobers and E.W.('Jim') Swanton, to name a selection; David Ascoli of Cassell's with Pat Smythe and Peter May. John Farquharson, in the 1920s, had an elderly lady as his benefactor. She was continually trying to land him with aspiring young poets or new novelists who had not digested the truth that the best way to convey a message is by Western Union. Her ploy, which he soon spotted, was to invite him to afternoon tea and then, as a captive audience, invite him to meet her latest prodigy.

Farquharson was a keen golfer, who usually played once a week on Sunday afternoons. One Sunday morning after breakfast, when it was raining hard, the telephone rang in his Halsey House flat. It was his benefactress, inviting him to tea that afternoon. He declined on the grounds of a previous engagement. Before lunch, she telephoned again. It was still raining stair-rods and again he declined. About two o'clock, she rang him yet again and said, 'Look, Mr Farquharson, I know you're hoping to play golf this afternoon but the weather is impossible. You'll be drenched before you reach the first tee. Now, no excuses, please. Do come to tea at four o'clock. I promise you won't regret it.'

Trapped, he could only murmur an acceptance. With ill grace, he arrived at her Kensington home and the maid, after taking his wet raincoat, ushered him into the drawing room. There was his hostess talking to a young, dark-haired man in his early twenties, clearly very nervous. He was clutching a parcel in his left hand.

'Oh, I'm so glad you could come, Mr Farquharson,' murmured the old lady. 'Do let me introduce my young friend, who has a great career ahead of him. Mr James Hilton!'

Random Harvest, Lost Horizon, Goodbye, Mr Chips – the titles still ring down the years. They were worldwide bestsellers, the Hollywood studios fought over the movie rights, stars like Ronald Colman, Greer Garson and Robert Donat played the leading roles. Even in recent years, *Goodbye, Mr Chips* has been a successful musical. It is fair to say that John Farquharson, the man, lived off James Hilton for close on a quarter of a century. And it might never have happened if the weather had been fine that Sunday morning.

6

THE FAMOUS ONE

In my first week as an agent, there had been a telephone call from Enid Blyton. She wanted to know if I would act for her. The question excited but did not wholly surprise me. I had been crafty enough, before leaving Werner Laurie, to write a careful letter to the more important authors, warmly recommending my successor, Waveney Girvan, telling them how much I had enjoyed working with them and wishing them all good fortune in the future. And if, of course, there was any way in which I could be of help, they could always get me at Number 8, Halsey House, Red Lion Square. Apart from Enid herself, Russell Braddon and Brian Glanville responded in that same week and stayed with me for nearly thirty-five years until my retirement.

Enid Blyton had first come to my notice in 1948, when Tom Brown, the sales manager, told me that his friend, Mr Ray, the head book buyer at Boots, wanted to sell a Blyton Christmas annual and had suggested we got in touch with her. I knew nothing of her and apparently asked, 'What's so special about Enid Blyton?' – to Tom's evident disgust. There was perhaps some excuse for my ignorance. She had not reached her full stride when I was a small boy in the 1920s. Besides, my father, a middle-grade civil servant, was a discriminating yet wide-ranging reader, who brought me up on *Pilgrim's Progress* and Defoe's *Robinson Crusoe*. (In his last years, he reread the whole of Gibbon's *Decline and Fall*.) So the trumpets of cadenced prose sounded for me on this side and I never fell for the weekly lure of *Sunny Stories*, which Newnes began to publish when I was nine years of age.

Then came senior school, followed by three years in the thin cold air of Eng. Lit. Crit. under the snipey gaze of Dr F.R. Leavis at Downing College. D.H. Lawrence was dead, James Joyce had retired to Trieste and the only practising novelists he might have grudgingly approved were Djuna Barnes and John Dos Passos. Then there were six years of war service before I was flung back into Civvy Street, a stranger to the endearing, now middle-aged, charms of Enid Blyton.

By the time I first met her in 1948, she had already been an established children's writer of twenty-five years' standing. In 1925, she had earned £1,200 – more than £35,000 today. Ten years later, she brought out eight different titles in the one year and in 1940 eleven titles under her own name and two by 'Mary Pollock', the surname being that of her first husband, a director of Newnes. Werner Laurie became her *seventeenth* regular publisher and, although we fed off the scraps, reprinting the Mary Pollock books under her own name, and putting together odds and ends from *Sunny Stories* and various out-of-print pieces to make up the Boots Christmas annuals, it was a comfortable, risk-free enterprise.

Where her publishers were concerned, Enid was a professional to her fingertips, friendly – when things went well – and as tough as dried pemmican underneath it all. She had four simple conditions that had to be included in every publishing agreement: 1. She would not take an advance but 2. the publisher had to guarantee a first printing of at least 25,000 copies; 3. she was to receive a straight 15 per cent royalty on the published price of all home sales. (At that time and even today, a children's author would normally receive half that percentage.) And her fourth stipulation was that she had to approve the dustjacket design and lettering. Very often, she insisted that her friend, Eileen Soper, should be the artist.

Yet it behoved her publishers to follow her instructions to

the letter. She knew exactly what she was doing. She told me once that she deliberately wrote for children of every age from three or four to fourteen and fifteen. Her idea was to catch them young and keep them enthralled as they grew older. The prose style might be pre-digested, the stories themselves simple and the morality old-fashioned but they were narrated with gusto and complete confidence.

When she was reaching puberty, as the Edwardian period was giving way to the Georgian, Enid Blyton's father had run away 'with another woman'. She had felt particularly close to him and his defection must have seemed like a rejection of her as well. There was also in those stricter times the shame of the gossip and scandal in the lower-middle-class, lace-curtained neighbourhood where the family lived. A psychiatric theory has evolved which claims that her emotions were permanently frozen by this trauma, so that she remained a child-woman for the rest of her life. The theory gathers some credence through the apparent fact that when, after her first marriage, she had difficulty in conceiving, tests showed that she had an immature uterus.

Oddly enough, part of her continuing appeal to young readers – almost a quarter of a century since her death, her books still sell four million copies a year in the United Kingdom and about ten million worldwide – must be the period flavour. The middle-class families live in nice detached houses, where there is usually a gardener to look after the hollyhocks, an upstairs maid, probably a cook and a chauffeur, when required. The children have dormitory feasts at their boarding schools and, in the holidays, muck about with boats, and have exciting adventures on rugged islands or ancient haunted houses. The lower orders, even adults, know how to keep their place and their distance: the police are properly subservient to the young master and mistress. There is a warm feeling of plenty inside the homes – second helpings for the greedy ones and constant hot water in the baths to wash away the mud and the bruises from the genteel horseplay. That sense of 'And is there honey still for tea?', that never-never land where the comic villains always got their comeuppance and virtue always prevailed in the end, must be highly endearing to a youthful audience in these rougher, tougher times.

In her political and social outlook, Enid Blyton was very much part of that between-the-wars middle class which believed foreigners were either untrustworthy or funny or sometimes both, that 'lesser breeds' would always let you down when it came to the crunch – in short, that wogs begin at Calais. (My own mother was typical. On a short army leave in June 1940, I found her full of smiles. 'We're in the final now,' she declared. 'I never did trust those French.') In his acute and witty study of the adventure and detective-story writers of that period, names like Dorothy L. Sayers and the now forgotten 'Sapper', Colin Watson in *Snobbery with Violence* shows the currents of racism and anti-Semitism that flowed through their novels. Class also played a part. If not every amateur detective could be a lord like the dreadful Peter Wimsey, he could at least be a a member of a good club – and never, never wear black socks with brown shoes.

Enid was not knowingly a snob or a racist and she was hurt by the somewhat far-fetched attacks on her because her naughty characters were almost always black in hue – such as the wicked golliwogs in *Noddy in Toyland*. (Revanchist editing, mistaken in my view, has now removed them in a good-taste purge.) A trendy archdeacon once castigated her for upsetting immigrant families and giving the false impression that to be black was automatically to be bad. I replied on her behalf, asking if he would care to apply the same criteria to the parable of the black sheep in the bible and let me know his conclusions. I heard nothing further. All one can really say is that Enid's attitudes and beliefs were moulded in the golden years before the Great War, when the sun did not set on the British Empire and Britannia in fact ruled the waves. She was a storyteller, not a philosopher, and, if she lived a blinkered life, she was not alone.

At our first meeting, she would have been about fifty years of age. She wore her hair in an old-fashioned bob, with clusters of tight curls on either side of her face. She had a high complexion which increased to brick-red if she was at all nervous or excited, fine dark eyes and a prominent, somewhat bulbous, nose. No one could have classified her as beautiful or even good-looking, but in her prime there was an attractive sense of coiled energy about her. She had a chirruping quality in her voice and a strange way of eliding vowel sounds.

In public, she could be stiff and awkward or overly gushing, but in the context of Green Hedges she was in every sense at home. Less than a mile north of the Beaconsfield roundabout, on the Penn Road, the house stood back behind a high ever-green hedge and a semi-circular gravel drive. Small statuettes of Noddy and Big Ears and Mr Plod were planted in the borders on either side of the front door. The house itself was typical 'stockbroker Tudor' with mullioned lead windows and a red-brick façade. On the north side there were outhouses and a large garage for the cars. To the east and behind the house was the three-and-a-half-acre garden, immaculately laid out with a large vegetable plot, and elsewhere rows of shrubs and rose bushes. There must have been at least one full-time gardener employed, because although Enid and Kenneth were both knowledgeable, the pressure of her work and the inhibiting factor of his arthritis would have rendered them spectators more than performers.

With each visit I paid to Green Hedges while she was still mentally alert, I had the increased impression that she was living sealed off, going round and round like those blindfolded donkeys in Middle Eastern countries, drawing up water from a deep well as they tramped in circles, imagining they were making progress. In the late 1950s, Enid sent me the typescript of a new Noddy story. He had done a good turn to a Toyland character and Mr Plod had given him a penny in gratitude. The rest of the story was concerned with Noddy's efforts 'to spend a penny'. I telephoned Enid to say the script was splendid but there was – ahem – a small problem. She enquired brightly what that might be. Blundering along, I said that there was a double meaning to the phrase 'spending a penny'.

'Really, George,' she said. 'What's that?'

So I began to explain that if one went to a public lavatory, it was necessary to put a penny in the slot before the door could open. Thus the euphemism had developed that 'spending a penny' meant 'going to the lavatory'.

'How fascinating,' she exclaimed. 'I never knew that. Well, really! I'll have to change it.'

And she did.

She was indefatigable. She not only kept in touch with her seventeen publishers (and with me) by return post through hand-scribbled but extremely legible postcards but she also corresponded with countless children in the same way. And this on top of writing – typing, in fact – anything up to 10,000 words a day of whatever book she was then working on. I once telephoned her on a Friday and said I hoped to see her the following week, as there were some fairly urgent points to talk over.

'Not next week, if you don't mind, George,' she answered. 'Unless it's terribly urgent. You see, I'm going to start a new Famous Five on Monday and I have to finish by lunch on Friday, as Kenneth wants to play golf that afternoon.'

A Famous Five book would be about 50,000 words long. Most authors, even under the spur of inspiration, would be unable to write or type 1,000 publishable words in an hour. To average ten times as much in a day and to keep up the momentum for nearly five days on end would seem physically impossible; not least because Enid used to sit on a veranda on the south side of Green Hedges, with a shawl around her shoulders and a plank across her knees. On it she would place an ancient manual typewriter that clanked like a threshing machine. Her scripts were clean-typed by a professional typist before they went to the publishers but I knew from inspection that the originals were impeccable, for spelling, punctuation and grammar, with hardly a crossing out. She claimed – and less successful authors, often with a green-eyed glint, scoffed at her – that once she hit on a dramatic opening sentence for a new story, her conscious mind switched off and the overdrive of the sub-conscious took over. In any event, she really did complete that Famous Five book on the following Friday, in time for golf.

Enid's career was bound by a strange and sad irony. She commanded the affectionate loyalty of literally millions of children and, as a Froebel-trained teacher in her youth, could restore order with an inflection of her voice, as I experienced once at an unruly autographing party at Hatchards where, arriving some minutes late to find the six- and seven-year-olds crawling over the furniture and squabbling shrilly, she went straight on to the platform and said in a crisp tone, 'Now then, children, sit down and keep quiet. I'm Enid Blyton and I'm going to tell you a story.'

The young audience sat down. There was a magical hush.

But her forte was for children at a distance – either through the separating medium of the classroom or the lecture platform, or through the pages of a book, or a handwritten postcard. Children up close, at hand, under one's feet, were another matter. She sent her two daughters away to boarding school and, according to a rather sour biography published a few years ago by her daughter Imogen, the warm embrace, the impulsive hug and kiss, the snuggling up to Mummy were signally missing. When Mother was working on a book – and when was she not? – one had to keep very quiet and tiptoe around the work area. It could not have been an ideal atmosphere to grow up in.

There is a story which I have known about for a very long time but have never been able to verify. Now it is too late, as both the protagonists are long dead. Apparently, around 1950, Agatha Christie and Enid Blyton met for afternoon tea at the Ritz. The real point of the meeting, beneath the polite chitchat, was to decide which of them enjoyed the larger writing income. Enid Blyton had written ten or twenty times as many books but, unlike Christie, had not as yet had the benefit of film sales and stage plays. According to the legend, the two formidable women agreed a dead heat over the cucumber sandwiches. Each was earning about £150,000 every year. At today's purchasing values, that would equal almost £2.5 million.

Another story which I take to be true, as Kenneth, her second husband, told it to me, was that one evening in the 1940s there was a ring on the front-door bell at Green Hedges. When the door was opened, the visitor announced that he was from the Inland Revenue. It had come to his department's notice that Miss Enid Blyton had been a successful writer for at least twenty years but did not appear ever to have submitted

an annual return of her literary earnings. He assumed that their
records must be in error and that she had filed her returns
in another district or under a different name, since every
author of great experience must have been aware of the legal
requirement to render accurate statements of writing income
and to pay the statutory tax thereon.

Had there been a close in or near Green Hedges there would
have been a breathless hush in it that night. Whatever the
reason, she had failed to submit any Schedule-D tax returns
and presumably owed the Revenue tens, if not hundreds, of
thousands of pounds. This was several years before I became
her agent and I never discovered what manœuvring took place
with the taxmen. One excuse might have been that up to 1941,
when they divorced, she thought her first husband, Hugh,
had incorporated her earnings with his own and that from
1943 onwards, when she married Kenneth Darrell Waters,
the same method had been employed. (Although a German
shell-burst at the Battle of Jutland in the Great War had
made him permanently deaf – he was then a junior naval
medical officer – Kenneth had through great determination
successfully overcome the handicap and was a senior surgeon
at St Stephen's Hospital in Chelsea when he retired in 1957.)

At any rate, an expert team was quickly assembled to limit
the damage, do a deal with the Inland Revenue and, most
important of all, keep the news quiet. The Famous Five and
the Secret Seven were wholly committed to upholding law
and order; it would never have done for their creator to be
widely known as a defaulter – through ignorance, no doubt
– in rendering Caesar's dues. There was John Basden, an
accountant who looked after Sir Laurence Olivier's and
Ralph Richardson's tax affairs, among other well-known
actors. There was Arnold Thirlby of the firm of West
End solicitors, J.D. Langton & Passmore. (On the 'small
world' principle, I record in passing that Stanley Passmore,
who founded the firm, had in the 1920s acted as Clarence
Hatry's lawyer and had been cut in – to his great advantage
– on forthcoming share issues. When Hatry was arrested for
fraud near the end of the decade, Passmore had wriggled out of
the relationship, claiming that his erstwhile benefactor needed

a lawyer versed in criminal matters.) And there was Eric Rogers, 'Wing-Commander Rogers', as he continued to call himself in peacetime, although he had only been a 'penguin' in the Second World War. A company was soon formed, to be known as Darrell Waters Limited, and all Enid's past, present and future copyrights were assigned in full to it.

Enid may have fallen down on her tax returns but she possessed an incisive mind, a phenomenal memory and, of course, through many years' experience, comprehensive knowledge of the children's market. We spoke on the telephone at least two or three times a week. She never kept copies of her handwritten cards and letters sent to me and, as she had no secretary to file her incoming correspondence, I suspect she just flung it into a box or a drawer somewhere in the house. And yet she would regularly amaze me by referring to the third paragraph on the second page of a letter I had written to her more than six months earlier and ask if anything further had happened to the point I then raised. I once said to her – and it was not meant as an empty compliment – that if she had not been Enid Blyton, she could well have been managing-director of Selfridges.

On her home ground, she had the surest of touches. Early in 1954, she rang me and asked, 'George, do you think I could write a children's pantomime?'

I replied – and I meant it sincerely – 'If you put your mind to it, Enid, I reckon you could write almost anything.'

She sounded pleased and soon rang off. Two or three weeks later, she sent me the completed book and lyrics of the *Noddy in Toyland* pantomime. When it was staged at the huge Stoll Theatre in Kingsway that Christmas, where every performance was fully sold out, neither the producer, B.A. Meyer, nor the stage director, André van Gyseghen, had changed it to any great extent.

Bertie Meyer was in his seventies when I introduced him to Enid and Kenneth as the potential producer. Tall, with luxuriant white hair, a Roman nose and a clipped moustache, he was a commanding and courteous figure. He had been involved in the West End theatre for over fifty years; soon after the turn of the century, Sir Henry Irving had been one of his leading actors.

After the meeting, when Bertie had left us, Kenneth Darrell Waters said in his bleating falsetto, 'He's far too old. He'll drop dead on us in the middle of a run – and then we'll be stuck.'

I told Kenneth that I had already discussed this delicate point with Bertie Meyer, who had a clean bill of health from his Harley Street doctor and who was quite prepared to undergo any further tests Kenneth might care to suggest. Luckily, his aider and abetter, Eric Rogers, was not present. Enid said firmly that she liked and trusted Mr Meyer, and wanted to appoint him as the pantomime's producer. Still grumbling, Kenneth half-heartedly assented. In the event, Bertie Meyer produced *Noddy in Toyland* for the next five or six years until the demand did not warrant a West End production. Kenneth died in 1967 and Enid the following year. Bertie Meyer, then close on ninety, though naturally frail, still had all his wits about him.

There is an interesting thesis to be researched and written on the subject of the husbands of successful women writers. The sensible ones, like Dr Mallowan, get on with their own life's work and maintain their self-respect by establishing a reputation in a separate field. The idiots – J. Middleton Murry, Leonard Woolf, Dorothy L. Sayers' husband and several present-day examples whose names are protected through my fear of an expensive appearance at Court 13 in the Strand – end up as page-turners and candle-lighters at the shrine. Most agents know them all too well. Lacking intimate knowledge of the publishing trade and its current conditions, they interfere with contracts, get between the author and her editor, create problems that need never have existed and generally drop tintacks on what should be the smooth road of progress. And sadly enough, very often they have done so from the best of motives, out of pride for their wife's achievements and their wish to enhance her success.

I had a case once where a husband, who had virtually deserted his wife for many months on end while she was a struggling writer, decided to move back to the apartment when her first long novel rose rapidly up the bestseller list. He appointed himself her 'business manager' and, although he was barely literate and knew nothing about publishing, the supervisor of all her contracts. In late January one year, he sent me a chiding letter. Her British publisher accounted every six months, at the end of June and December respectively. It was now three weeks after the end of December – why had they not paid up? Why was I so lax in failing to pursue them? In my reply, I pointed out – tactfully, I trust – that if he read on to the end of the accounting clause in the contract, he would see that the publisher 'rendered and settled' the account four months after each of those closing dates. No payment would be due until the end of April.

Kenneth Darrell Waters was just such an interferer. He may have been an incisive slicer of human flesh as a surgeon but, away from the scalpel and the germ-free smock, he was one of the most stupid and philistine men I have met. Art, the theatre, good music, literature – over fifteen years and many conversations, I never heard him once refer to anything of the mind or the spirit. He enjoyed the large garden that Enid's success had brought him, although in his latter years, increasing arthritis in his neck and hips prevented him from doing any gardening. He enjoyed golf – with the same reservation – and he liked to go horseracing with his friend, Eric Rogers. He would smoke an occasional large Havana cigar and, as a connoisseur of claret, he laid down many delectable bottles of Châteaux Latour and Lafite. But when it came to the nuances of publishing and the subtle details that those in the know accepted automatically, his simplistic mind and innate suspicions, augmented by his profound deafness, made the explaining of a contract to him like playing catch with a hedgehog.

In Kenneth's company, especially if Eric Rogers was also present, when it came to discussing business matters, Enid used to play the role of the silly schoolgirl, vintage 1920. 'You men,' she would simper, 'always talking business. That's right over my head. You'll have to go more slowly if you want me to understand.'

It was fascinating to watch. Her quick mind was a long way

ahead of them and she knew much, much more than they ever would about book rights and publishers – not least the fact that, if you constantly grind your publisher's face in the dirt, he will lose that extra brio for promoting your sales. But after all, business was a man's prerogative; a woman should not worry her pretty little head over it. Eric Rogers lunched every day at a corner table in the Savoy Hotel restaurant, no doubt at the expense of Darrell Waters Limited. Each week or so, the court would assemble, Eric as host, Enid and Kenneth as the guests of honour, Thirlby and Basden and quite often myself as equerries. Champagne would be ceremoniously drunk in the anteroom at the foot of the stairs leading to the restaurant. There followed a three-course lunch, accompanied by fine wines and rounded off with cigars, port or cognac. The men would talk across and, in their assumption, over Enid's head. She gallantly played her part – the schoolgirl niece allowed out to lunch with her favourite uncles.

Just as some unimaginative publishers occasionally forget that without authors they would cease to exist, so the band of advisors too often failed to appreciate that the past, present and future of Darrell Waters Limited depended entirely on Enid's creative flair. It was after one of those stuffy lunches that I realised why she had invited me to become her agent. She was fully capable of looking after her own affairs, apart from handling tax returns, as she had proved again and again over the previous quarter of a century. I was her one act of rebellion, someone who knew the trade from the inside and whom she could talk to straight, with no need to bolster the audience's confidence by putting on the simpering-little-girl role.

One of the most fertile and inventive minds in post-war publishing belonged to the late Gordon Landsborough. He was the creator of *Weekend Novel*, the reprint of a popular novel in tabloid newspaper form with advertisements and line drawings. When it collapsed through insufficient funding, he joined Panther Books and swung that paperback house editorially away from 'frilly knicker' books to good fiction – sufficiently well to attract the puritan taste and the deep

purse of Sidney Bernstein. He then started Four Square
Books, a division of Godfrey Phillips, the tobacco company,
and developed it into a substantial firm. Somehow, he also
found time to write successful war and adventure novels at
the rate of one every year or so. He was a bluff man from the
dales who spoke his mind bluntly yet, as quite often happens,
was somewhat thin-skinned himself. His quick mind made him
impatient with the slower-witted: all in all, a man ill-suited to
be an employee but without the funds to be an employer.

Early in 1960, he and I were lunching at a fish restaurant off
Leicester Square. He said, 'There's a revolution taking place.'

I looked up from my plate and he went on, 'When you and
I were kids, what was your pocket money? Penny a week,
if you were lucky. After the war, what was it? Sixpence a
week, maybe. Children's books then cost at least five bob.
So what happened? The parents bought 'em at birthdays and
Christmas. It was the parents' choice, not the child's.'

'What about public – and the commercial – libraries?'

'Oh sure. But that's only *borrowing* the book for a week
at a time. Kids like collecting books, the ones they've chosen
themselves.'

'Okay, I accept that. But so what?'

'So this. For the first time ever, youngsters get at least half
a crown a week pocket money these days. In the better-off
families, they get five bob. Don't argue – I've done the
research. So now they can afford to buy their own books.
In paperback. But Pan and Panther and Four Square and the
others don't have juvenile lists.'

I was beginning to get the idea – and I liked it. 'What's
your plan?'

'I'm gonna start a paperback firm, exclusively for children.
Armada Books – how about that? With the picture of a galleon
on every copy. I'm all set to go – apart from one thing.'

'Which is?'

'Enid Blyton. I must have Enid. I start off with a batch of her
titles, there's no stopping me. Why do you think I'm buying
you this lunch? You're her agent. Introduce me to her.'

Within a week or so I did. When I spoke to her on
the telephone that afternoon, she saw the merit in the

concept at once and realised it could open up a big new 'buyers' market' for her books. The following week, I drove Gordon Landsborough to Beaconsfield to have lunch with her and Kenneth. Before he could voice any objections in that piping treble, she asserted herself for once, declaring she was completely taken with the idea. Her hardcover publishers controlled the paperback rights of all her titles in print but she agreed to get on to them and make it clear she wanted Mr Landsborough to have every opportunity; she would be most unhappy if she felt they were driving too hard a bargain with him.

For a year or two, Armada flourished. Indeed, its very success caused problems because, being badly under-capitalised, Landsborough quickly found himself caught in that vice that has squeezed so many small publishers to financial death. It is the non-equation that the larger bookshops and chains demand ninety days' credit, whereas most printers, when dealing with a new outfit, require payment either 'on the nail' or, at the best, within thirty days. He might well find himself with orders for 100,000 or more copies but with no cash in hand to get them printed. And even if he went into hock to get the printing done, yet more orders would flood in during the three months he had to wait before the bookshops paid him. It finally reached the point where he had to sell a majority interest in Armada Books to his biggest printer-creditor. The printer in turn eventually sold the company to Collins, which already had a flourishing adult paperback list in Fontana.

Through its Glasgow office, Collins had for a long time published children's books in hard covers, several of Enid Blyton's among them. The purchase of Armada Books was therefore something of a coup, not least because it would bring in many sorely needed long runs for the under-used printing capacity at the Collins works in Glasgow. Vertical integration had been leaning at a growing angle to the perpendicular.

Enid and her Tweedledum and Tweedledee advisors, Kenneth and Eric Rogers, wanted to meet the new publisher who would be taking over from Landsborough. I arranged to take Ian Chapman, managing director at the Collins London office, to Beaconsfield for lunch. Although an outstandingly shrewd publisher, Ian Chapman was – and is – quiet and apparently unassuming. Taking this manner to be shyness or weakness and on being told that Ian had served in the RAF towards the end of the war, Eric Rogers put on his 'wing-commander' act and, no doubt to impress his host and hostess, began questioning Ian in a tone that veered from the patronising to the bullying. His target took it all with a good grace.

Enid and Kenneth were both keen golfers and, ostensibly as an investment, Darrell Waters Ltd had bought Studland Bay golf course. (Enid disliked 'abroad' and always took her holidays at a hotel in Studland Bay.) The Eric Rogers barrage was lifted during the first half of lunch while Kenneth, in his querulous falsetto, recounted the last round he had played there, stroke by agonising stroke, from the first tee to the eighteenth green. As he droned on, I could not lie back and think of England, so I sat up and thought of Bordeaux, warming a very drinkable glass of Château Latour vintage 1947 in my hands.

When the recital at last ended, Eric Rogers returned to the attack in his best 'Stand to attention when you speak to an officer' voice. He barked at Ian, 'Know anything about golf?'

Ian answered mildly, 'A bit.'

'Could you follow what Mr Darrell Waters was saying?'

'Yes. Most interesting it was.'

Eric said, 'He's a very good player, you know. Plays off a handicap of fourteen. What's yours?'

'Oh, I don't really rate a handicap nowadays. Don't play enough.'

Eric must have thought the quarry was beginning to squirm. He said, 'That sounds strange. Did you have a proper handicap when you did play regularly?'

'Yes.'

'May I ask what it was?'

'It was quite a while ago.'

'You can hardly have forgotten it, Mr Chapman?'

'No.'

Now for the kill. The rest of us round the table were

alert, leaning forward. Eric said silkily, 'Then perhaps, Mr Chapman, you'd kindly tell us what it was?'

Ian Chapman had been looking down at his plate throughout the inquisition. Now his head came up and he stared at Eric Rogers.

'I was never better than scratch,' he said.

Eric's red face went even redder.

The *Noddy in Toyland* pantomime evolved its own pleasant little tradition. Because it appealed to very young children, there were two daily performances, the first in early and the second in mid-afternoon, usually ending at around five o'clock. After the final performance on the last day of the run, Bertie Meyer would book a large hall in the neighbourhood and the whole cast, adults as well as children, would assemble for a party. Enid would be the guest of honour, the cast would present her with flowers and a speech, often from the young actor playing Noddy, and she would respond, thanking them for all their efforts and looking forward to next year. The party was always an hour after the last curtain came down, to give the cast time to change and wipe off the greasepaint.

Enid had her own box at the theatre. During a run of *Noddy in Toyland*, she would attend at least three or four performances a week and watch everything with a sharp gaze. If any of the adult actors, Mr Plod the policeman or the Saucepan Man, put in too many bits of 'business' or overdid milking the young audience – 'Oh yes, I did!', 'Oh no, you didn't!' – Enid would be on to it at once and would make sure through the director that the culprit was told firmly of his errors. And of course, she always attended the final performance.

On this occasion, for some reason Kenneth had not accompanied her and she had been driven from Beaconsfield by their chauffeur. The show was on at the Scala Theatre; Bertie Meyer booked some congressional rooms in Tottenham Court Road, not a hundred yards away. There was an hour to kill. On previous occasions, I had passed the time chatting with Enid and Kenneth in their box, so that she could make an entrance at the party once we knew the whole cast was there, ready and waiting. As it happened, I had left a typescript in my office, which was about half a mile away. I wanted to read it that weekend, so, having explained things to Enid, I apologised for having to leave her and said that I would go straight back to the party and meet her there, a few minutes after six o'clock.

I arrived at the party on time and congratulated Bertie Meyer on yet another successful season. We chatted for about five minutes. There was no sign of Enid. Ten minutes went by. Still no sign of her. The child actors were beginning to get restless, as were the adults: for the young ones, dishes of jelly or trifle, iced cakes, fizzy drinks and for the adults bottles of scotch, wine and beer. It would not be proper to tuck in before the guest of honour arrived.

By half-past six, Bertie was getting concerned – and so was I. Enid was normally the most punctual of women. When I had left her, she had been sitting in the back of the Rolls Royce, about to take a short rest before the party. The car was almost in sight of the venue and the chauffeur was a reliable servant of long standing. What could have happened?

We were reluctant to get in touch with the police because of all the publicity that would ensue. As a last resort, I decided to telephone Green Hedges, in case she might have left a message. After a few rings, a voice answered. It was Enid herself. She was pleasant and polite but clearly quite surprised to be hearing from me. We had said goodbye well over an hour earlier, her tone conveyed; what possible grounds could there be for me to get in touch again so soon? I blurted out something about the party. She did not grasp the point and I decided quickly not to press it, as she would be most upset if she realised her *faux pas*.

It was as though her mind or her memory had slipped a cog and then gone on working with its usual high efficiency. The journey from the centre of London to Beaconsfield thirty or more years ago would have taken the best part of an hour, even in a chauffeur-driven Rolls. There were many fewer cars on the roads in those days but Westway and the M40 did not then exist. So Enid must have told her driver to take her home within a few minutes of my leaving her. At that moment, she had been in high spirits, happy with the success of the pantomime and the resounding cheers that greeted the finale. Equally, when I spoke to her on the telephone an hour and a half later, she had sounded stable and serene. Had there been some massive distraction to make her forget temporarily that she was shortly to be guest of honour at the farewell party, she would surely have mentioned it on the phone.

In 1960, one had not heard of Alzheimer's Disease. The layman knew that the very elderly sometimes suffered from senile dementia but it was unthinkable that Enid Blyton, then hardly in her mid-sixties, might qualify. Enid Blyton of all people – the most famous and successful of living children's authors with her enormous energy and computer-like memory. But over the next five years, her memory-lapses became increasingly frequent. To my knowledge, they did not cause her any personal anguish or even discomfort; she was apparently either unaware of them or unconcerned. For instance, on several occasions after lunch at Green Hedges, when she, Kenneth and I were sitting in their drawing room, she would mention one of her books and go out to the library across the hall to fetch a copy. A few minutes would go by and then she would return with a puzzled look and say, 'What actually was I supposed to fetch?' One of us would remind her and she would then go and get it without further problems.

Fortunately, she was surrounded at home with devoted affection. Kenneth, who had retired from surgical duties in 1957, doted on her and shielded her from the difficulties of public contact. Doris, who had been her maid for many years, was also a stalwart helper. As her condition deteriorated inevitably, her creative spirit, alas, did not keep pace. Although she was unable to write a new story, as she could not then recall the first half of a sentence, she was still able to take a story or even a book of hers and type it out afresh. On a good day, she would ring me up and tell me she was sending a brand-new story she had just finished. On the first few occasions, I was thrilled to think she had overcome her illness but, after more than ten years as her agent, I had some acquaintance with her backlist. Either the characters or the events or both would sound familiar. An hour's detective work in my files would usually track down the source. I would write her a letter of grateful thanks and then quietly file the typed copy. Once or twice, if I could not be absolutely certain and the script was one of a series, I would invoke the relevant publisher with an excuse – 'I have come across the enclosed in a Blyton file and just wondered whether it might be an unpublished work.' It never was.

Long before we knew she was losing her memory, Enid told me a weird tale. Macmillan had published her 'Adventure' series with conspicuous success. There were half a dozen titles and each included the word in the title – *The Ship of Adventure*, *The Island of Adventure* and so on. The children's editor at Macmillan had become a close friend of hers and of Kenneth's and quite often stayed at Studland and played golf with them. The time came for him to retire and, shortly afterwards, Enid, finding a gap in her writing programme, decided to tackle another 'Adventure' novel.

When I first became her agent, we agreed that she would continue to deal directly with the publishers of her existing series. The interposing of an agent might risk upsetting cordial relationships. She had therefore sent the script straight to Macmillan, she told me, and, not knowing the name of her friend's successor, addressed it to the firm. Two or three weeks later, it had been returned – with a rejection slip. Some bright young thing, perhaps a Leavisite with a Cambridge degree in Eng. Lit., presumably did not recognise the potency of the Blyton name and so threw away a pearl 'richer than all his tribe'.

In fairness, it has to be added that the spurned typescript never turned up among Enid's papers after her death nor in the archives of one of her publishers. All of us tend to embroider stories in the frequent retelling – and Enid was not immune. But I never knew her to invent an oral tale, even an ingenious or a harmless one. Perhaps, unknown to all, she had begun to suffer spasmodically from the disease three or four years before it was detected – and the Macmillan story was just a symptom of that.

As I have mentioned earlier, apart from his profound deafness, Kenneth Darrell Waters also suffered from severe arthritis in the neck and the hips. In his latter years, he wore constantly a leather-covered neck support and used lightweight crutches. His driving, erratic enough through his deafness and bad temper, exacerbated by continual pain, became a threat to fellow drivers and pedestrians alike. On one occasion when his two step-daughters were at Benenden School, and he and Enid had driven down for the annual Speech Day, the headmistress stood up on the platform and said, 'Before we commence the prize-giving, I have an announcement to make. Would the owner of a black Rolls Royce report to the car park at once. He or she has locked the doors but left the engine running.'

To alleviate the nagging pains and to keep his kidneys flushed out, Kenneth apparently took a mixture of drugs in increasing doses, as his system grew inured. Genuinely loving Enid, he fell under greater stress and strain as her condition worsened. By the summer of 1967, a dying man, he booked himself into a private room at St Stephen's Hospital, Fulham Road, his old stamping ground. Enid, overwrought by his absence from Green Hedges, was put into a nursing home south of the river, where she could be looked after day and night.

When I visited him late one afternoon, he had not heard of or from Enid for a day or two and was extremely worried. Till then, I had not known of her move to the nursing home. My car was in the hospital car park and it would be a short drive to go and see her and bring back a message. So off I went. Edgar Allan Poe would have recognised that nursing home with a knowing leer. The gravel drive was bracketed by thick, dark green and dripping hedges, interspersed with gloomy monkey-puzzle trees that stretched their awkward arms as if to trap the visitor. The front door of the low red-brick building was oak, reinforced with iron strips and knobs. I banged on the heavy knocker.

After some minutes, a surly porter in a white coat opened the door. When I said that I wanted to see Miss Blyton, he asked me if I was a close relative.

I said, 'No – but I am a close friend. And I've come on behalf of her husband.'

He left me standing outside the half-open door while he went to seek advice. After several minutes, a stout woman in nurse's uniform, whose cold little pig's eyes made me think of concentration camp guards, came to the door and repeated the formula. *Raus, raus* – unless you were a close relative.

She blocked the doorway and was impervious to argument. She did not look very bright; I decided to try a bluff. To have to go back to Kenneth without actually seeing Enid was unthinkable. So I told the nursing sister that I was an advisor to the editor of the *Daily Mail*. That was stretching the truth paper-thin. I had briefly been the man's agent some years before he became editor and was then a New York correspondent. The *Mail* had recently run a series about the shortcomings of National Health hospitals under the dead hand of Labour bureaucracy.

I said, 'A word from me – and he could be looking into private nursing homes. What they've got to hide. Why they refuse entry to legitimate visitors. That sort of thing.'

It was a swift collapse. She stood back and let me in. I followed her waddling shape along polished wooden floors where her rubber-soled shoes squeaked and sucked. There was a pervading smell of lavatory cleaner and waxy floor polish. We turned a corner and, a few yards along the next passage, came to a door. Without knocking, she pushed it open and let me enter.

There was Enid, sitting up in bed, looking lost and forlorn. Her cheeks were strangely withered inwards and there were creases around her mouth I had never seen before. The nursing staff had removed her upper and lower sets of false teeth, presumably in case she became violent and bit herself to death. She was staring about her wildly and did not at first recognise me. Gradually, she came to and perked up when I mentioned having just come from seeing Kenneth. Her powers of concentration, at that stage of her life spasmodic at the best, had been further reduced by the spell in that cold, unloving place. But after perhaps half an hour of persuasion and cajoling, which ended up with my virtually dictating the words, she managed to write a little note on the lines of 'Dear

Kenneth, I love you and hope you are getting better. I am getting on well. Your loving Enid.'

I drove back with the note and handed it to him in his private room. When I left him, he was lying back against the heaped-up pillows, a contented smile on his face and the note firmly clutched in his right hand.

He died some weeks later, in the early autumn. I had feared that the shock of his death, added to all the previous emotional hurts, would separate her entirely from reality. But it was not so. Perhaps Alzheimer's Disease, with its fleeting memory span, had the counter-advantage of absorbing or, more accurately, deflecting the impact of pain and sorrow. I used to drive to Green Hedges to have lunch with her once a month. On some occasions, she would not recognise me throughout my stay and would chat inconsequentially, as she might to a stranger who happened to share the same railway compartment. On others, she might be lucid but fantasising. Once she was clearly under the impression that Kenneth was very much alive but was her infant son. She told me with Ophelia-like simplicity how he had had a nightmare and had crept into her bed, and how she had cuddled and comforted him and driven the nasty goblins away.

As you went through the front door at Green Hedges and stood in the capacious hall, the dining room was on your left and beyond it the kitchen. I arrived one lunchtime and, as I stood in the hall, the most fragrant aroma came wafting from the direction of the kitchen.

I said, 'Oh, Enid, what a delicious smell! Is there something special for lunch?'

She said, 'Oh no, it's burgundy beef. But, you know, Doris came across a lot of old bottles of wine down in the cellar. All dusty they were and cobwebby. So we're using them up in the cooking.'

They were old bottles of wine, all right. Some Château Latour and Château Lafite, first growths, 1952 vintage – even then in those pre-inflationary days worth close on £100 a bottle; the younger and lesser-known Margaux and Pauillac growths were still worthy of a connoisseur's nod of approval. Kenneth had possessed both the money and the taste to pick his wine with loving shrewdness. And here it was, bubbling away in a pan on the gas-stove, suckling the morsels of beef and boiling away on the desert air. I did not have the nerve to suggest to Enid that, if she really wanted to get rid of the dusty old bottles, I would happily put a case or two on to the back seat of my car.

Latterly, when she needed continual medical care, she was moved into a nursing home in Belsize Park, north London. I visited her twice in the few weeks she was there but her mind had slipped away along with her memory. I preferred to remember the vital, positive Enid Blyton I had first met twenty years earlier rather than the withered husk that remained. Her death on 28 November 1968 must indeed have been a release for her.

It is sad to record that of her important publishers, men whose companies had made millions of pounds from her books over the years, only a very few had the good grace or the gratitude to visit her in the year between Kenneth's death and her own. Many flocked to her memorial service at St James's Church, Piccadilly, and fell over themselves in offering to give addresses in her honour but merely a small minority could be bothered to make the twenty-five mile journey to Beaconsfield once during that time. Some did take the trouble to telephone me and ask how she was getting along. But, I suppose, there is no point in putting oneself out when the goose has stopped laying and one already has a large share of the golden eggs.

Green Hedges should have been maintained as a shrine to Enid Blyton and a source of pleasure to countless children. It could have contained exhibitions, a complete library of all her books in every edition, a range of toys and, latterly, a video room. With rides and seesaws and games for the younger children in the capacious grounds, it could have been self-supporting; if there had been a financial gap, no doubt several of her publishers would have contributed an annual grant for the sake of the ever-spreading publicity as each new generation of children discovered the great storyteller. For Enid Blyton's books to be selling four million copies a year in the United Kingdom, a quarter of a century after her death, is proof enough of a durable popularity.

But it was not to be. Eric Rogers, who had been in unfettered charge of Darrell Waters Ltd since Kenneth's final illness, had Green Hedges demolished, and the large mature garden cropped and cleared. The empty site was sold for building development. Within months, Green Hedges and its smiling environs had become a miniature Carthage. When I first heard the news, I wondered whether it might have been an act of spiteful revenge, whether behind his benevolent chuckles and soft-voiced adulation, Eric had somehow been jealous of Enid's huge success or resentful of Kenneth's obvious admiration of her. But then I discarded the fanciful theory and decided that it was just the financier's adding machine of a mind at work. Tear it down, sell it off, make some quick bucks and then – close the ledger. There's no percentage in sentiment.

My abiding memory of Enid Blyton comes from her latter days, on one of the last few times I visited her at Green Hedges. We happened to be standing in the dining room, which doubled as a library. The two side walls contained glass-fronted bookcases which held an almost comprehensive sample of her multi-hundred different titles. She was in a lucid period and had been telling me how much she missed Kenneth, and how she would often look up from a newspaper or magazine and quote some interesting point, imagining that he was still sitting in the armchair opposite. To comfort her, I made a fatuous remark about how fortunate she was to have her own children, her two grown-up daughters, each with a family coming along.

'Children?' said Enid. She opened her arms wide, half-turning as if to embrace the bookcases on the wall behind. 'These are my children.'

7

POLE POSITION

The status of literary agents has changed considerably in the past forty years. In the early 1950s, they were very much second-class citizens. That odd and at times, it seemed, anti-Semitic club, the Garrick, would not accept an agent for membership. The so-called grounds were that, if literary agents were admitted, theatrical agents would force the thin end of the wedge and then the club table would be sprinkled with contracts for signature. More than ten years later, Peter Watt, whose lineage was far more distinguished than that of jumped-up publishers like X or Y, who, thanks to the laws of libel, must remain anonymous, became the first agent-member.

Newspapers like the *Sunday Times* and *The Times*, then completely unrelated, refused to deal with agents. The *Sunday Times* was owned by the pompous Lord Kemsley. As one of the Berry brothers, Welsh boyos on the make under the tutelage of a notorious 'financier', Jimmy White, he had sailed right up against the financial wind, but by then had bought respectability and a peerage. As Humbert Wolfe neatly put it:

The House of Lords is waiting for
The newspaper proprietor.
Soap, attention! Listen, Beer!
Glory to the new-made peer.
Hark, the Herald's College sings,
As it fakes his quarterings.

H.V. Hodson, then the editor of the *Sunday Times*, invited Sir Harold Gillies, the doyen of plastic surgeons, to write an article on the subject. 'Giles', as he was known to friends and colleagues, had already asked me to represent him, so I telephoned Hodson, who refused to speak to me. I then wrote him a letter, to which he replied tersely that he did not deal with agents. Giles in a rage rang him and threatened to sue for restraint of trade. Shortly afterwards, I received a brief letter from Hodson, agreeing terms for the article. One up – but there were many more to go.

The Paternosters was – and still is, I believe – a lunching club that met on the first Thursday of each month at the Connaught Rooms in Great Queen Street. An author or well-known figure in the book world would be invited to give a post-lunch talk. On one occasion in 1955, the speaker-guest was Duncan Carse. An Antarctic explorer, he was famous to the general public as 'Dick Barton' in the hugely popular BBC radio series of that name. He told his audience that a major expedition was to take place the following year – 'the last great journey on earth' – which would be the first ever crossing of the Antarctic continent via the South Pole. The crossing party would be British but a New Zealand team would establish a base on the far side at Scott Sound and would lay depots for the second half of the journey. Carse added that either he or a Dr Vivian Fuchs was likely to be chosen as leader.

The publishing house of George G. Harrap & Co., then a powerful, privately owned firm, more or less ran the Paternosters Club and I knew through trade gossip that they had already signed up Duncan Carse for any book he might care to write – which made everything neat and simple. In a two-horse race, if you cannot back the favourite, you can only back the outsider.

My friend, Alan Mitchell, was in charge of the New Zealand

Press Association at 85 Fleet Street. He had already proved his help by introducing me to Ed Hillary, whose graphic account of climbing Mount Everest, *High Adventure*, had been published in 1954. Hodder & Stoughton, his publishers, had omitted to tie up serial rights in their contract with him. I was fortunate enough to sell those rights to *John Bull*, then a literary high-circulation weekly magazine, for the sum of £7,500 – over £100,000 in today's terms.

Alan made some enquiries and located Dr Fuchs at a small government office in Queen Anne's Mansions. He also told me privily that Hillary was almost certain to be invited to lead the New Zealand team, which was a bonus for me. Using the number he had discovered, I telephoned Fuchs's office, spoke to his secretary and made an appointment – without disclosing the nature of my visit.

Fuchs was immensely impressive, the kind of man with whom you would go tiger-hunting in the jungle without a qualm. A little above average height, square and powerful in build and with enormous muscular hands, he had greying hair, almost level gaze under tufty eyebrows and a fresh complexion. He always thought before he spoke and in countless meetings over the next thirty-five years and more, I have never heard his voice raised. At first sight, he exuded a sense of controlled strength and indeed wisdom.

After a few minutes of polite chitchat, he asked me what I wanted.

I said, 'I think you are going to be appointed leader of this great Antarctic expedition. I would like to help.'

For once, even the impassive doctor blinked. The expedition was supposedly top secret. The Eden government had decided to back it to the tune of £500,000, and the New Zealand government half as much again in cash and kind. British Petroleum wanted to become a sponsor by supplying the oil needs and paying for the colour film that was to be shot during the crossing. All this I learned a little later from Fuchs himself. But his surprise at the advent of a brash stranger airily breaking the secret was understandable; all the more, because in the last day or two the leadership had fallen to him and not to Duncan Carse.

He asked how I knew and I explained about the literary luncheon and Carse's announcement, which it was now clear to me he should never have made. Then he wanted to know how I thought I could help. I mounted my hobbyhorse and rode briskly round the ring. This was to be a great Commonwealth venture, the first ever attempted crossing of a virtually unknown and inviolate continent. The newspaper rights during the course of the expedition and the subsequent volume rights should be placed in every possible civilised country in the world, both for the prestige and also for the substantial copyright income; the more money at the expedition's disposal, the more scientific experiments could be undertaken. But it needed an expert – me – to supervise the placing of rights to the best advantage, reporting back to the leader or his committee of management.

I went on to tell him that, thanks to Guy Ramsey of the *Daily Telegraph*, I had been called in to act for the British North Greenland Expedition, led by Commander C.J.W. Simpson, but far too late in the day. The expedition was on the point of packing up and returning home from Greenland. I had been able to place book rights with Chatto & Windus, and a long feature article with *John O'London's Weekly* but far more could have been achieved if I had been involved from the start – indeed, long before the actual start. Newspapers and book publishers deal in 'futures'. Something that has not yet happened is always more exciting, more glamorous, than a recorded fact, even in the immediate past. Now was not too soon to be sounding out the potential market.

He was at once receptive. He had, it turned out, already been thinking along these very lines. He was aware of the problems encountered by the BNGE and had heard of my last-minute efforts. His expedition, he told me in confidence, was to be carried out in two phases. Later that year, an advance party would go down to the Antarctic and winter over at Shackleton Base. The following year, the main party would follow, spend the Antarctic winter (our summer) in the huts prepared by the advance party and then start the crossing in the autumn of 1957 into the spring of 1958. The Prime Minister was due to announce the details of the expedition in the House of

Commons in a few weeks' time and then it would be 'action stations'.

We had several more meetings in the next fortnight. We discovered that we were both enthusiastic performers at squash. Indeed, we worked out that some sixteen years earlier, when he was playing for his county, Cambridgeshire, as third string and I was representing the university at fourth string, we had occupied next-door courts at Portugal Place, the university squash centre, without actually meeting. He invited me, on behalf of the Farquharson Agency, to look after the Commonwealth Trans-Antarctic Expedition (CTAE).

To jump five years ahead, after the successful conclusion of the expedition and his immediate knighthood, 'Bunny' (as he was always known to his friends) took charge of the British Antarctic Survey and had to spend his weekdays in London, away from his home and garden in Cambridge. Twice a week in the early evenings, we used to play squash at the Lansdowne Club throughout the next decade. With scoring confined to the player 'in hand', a slight superiority over one's opponent will be magnified in the eventual score-card, and when a player opposes the same partner over a long period and gets to know his scoring points all too well, one of them usually gains a long-running dominance. But throughout that time, Bunny and I could never tell in advance which of us would win. I had the advantage of age, being ten years younger, and was perhaps a more naturally talented player but he was very fit and in a quiet way very, very determined. If I did not win in three straight games – and most often I did not – I knew that he would grind me down until my breath was gone and my legs a-tremble with fatigue. At the end of 1971, I tore an Achilles tendon and was advised by an orthopaedic specialist to give up the game. I did. Fuchs, then close on sixty-five, went on playing with other opponents for at least another five years.

Sir Anthony Eden made the official announcement and soon afterwards the Committee of Management held its first meeting under the chairmanship of Marshal of the Royal Air Force Sir John Slessor. Apart from myself, the great and the good held sway. There was Sir Edwin Herbert, later to become Lord Tingay, the senior partner of Slaughter &

May, the City solicitors; Patrick Pirie-Gordon of Glynn Mills Bank, which had helped finance many famous expeditions; Sir Miles Clifford, an ex-governor of the Falkland Islands, who had personally 'seen off' an attempted Argentinian invasion; General Sir James Marshall-Cornwall, president of the Royal Geographical Society, and, of course, Fuchs himself and his one-time patron, Sir James Wordie, a distinguished Antarctic explorer in his youth and then the master of a Cambridge college. Add in Sir John Hunt, the Mount Everest leader, and the Bishop of Norwich, Lancelot Fleming, another 'snow and ice' man in the past. A worthy gathering.

The meeting was about to begin with a short message of welcome from Sir John Slessor, when Sir James Marshall-Cornwall cleared his throat and said, 'On a point of order, Mr Chairman. In its long and distinguished history, the Royal Geographical Society, which is very much part of this enterprise, has never seen fit to employ an agent. As president, I can vouchsafe that it does not wish to be associated with an agent on this special occasion. I therefore propose that Greenfield be asked to leave the room at once.'

There was an embarrassed silence. I could only look down at the papers on the table in front of me and wonder why this foxy-faced little man with his military cropped moustache had seen fit to drop his bombshell.

Then Fuchs spoke, quietly but very clearly. 'Mr Chairman, I invited George Greenfield to act on behalf of the expedition. If he has to leave the room, then I shall have to follow him.'

'Jack' Slessor grinned and said breezily, 'Well, General, I reckon that answers your point of order. Right, gentlemen, let's get down to the agenda. We've a lot to go through.'

It was a brave gesture for Bunny Fuchs to have made – and one I shall always be grateful for. Although he then had a high reputation in polar circles, he was in no position to dictate and, as I subsequently learned, some of the supposed polar experts were strongly against the whole concept of the CTAE. He stuck to his word and fortunately all ended well on the agenting side.

In fairness, I have to add that when the expedition returned triumphant and was given a 'welcome home' lunch at the

Guildhall, General Marshall-Cornwall came over, shook hands
and thanked me for my efforts. And I was touched when, over
thirty years later, he published his memoirs in his mid-nineties
and invited me to the launch party at Brooks's. I was, alas, too
tactful to ask him on that occasion whether he had employed
an agent to help sell the rights.

One other institution, equally valued among 'top people',
vied with the Royal Geographical Society for *droits de
seigneur* over important expeditions. That was *The Times*.
It had recently covered the first successful ascent of Everest
by Sir John Hunt's team; Jan (then James) Morris' eloquent
despatches from the mountain had caused the coffee and toast
on numerous breakfast tables to go cold. But right back to the
turn of the century, it had backed Captain Scott and, later,
Mallory, and indeed all the previous Everest attempts by a
British party.

The first ever attempted crossing of the desolate and icy
sub-continent touched the imagination of Arthur Wareham,
then the editor of the *Daily Mail*. He offered me £20,000 for
the exclusive United Kingdom newspaper rights plus 50 per
cent of all syndication proceeds. ('Syndication' is the selling-on
to overseas newspapers and periodicals of the same exclusive
text and photographs in their respective territories.)

The CTAE committee of management had spawned a
finance sub-committee to deal with all offers. It promptly
turned down the *Daily Mail* proposal. Far too popular, don't
you know? The word 'prestigious' was not then in vogue but
the 'top people' on the sub-committee felt that only *The Times*
had that elusive quality. Its offer was £10,000 and 50 per cent
of syndication proceeds – with the added twist that all such
proceeds should be retained by the newspaper until a total
of £10,000 had been reached. From then on, the expedition
would receive its half-share. I tried to explain to the team of
clever and experienced lawyers, bankers and men of affairs
gathered round the table that, if the offer were to be accepted,
The Times would get the news and feature rights for nothing;
in fact, for less than nothing, because, once the down-payment
had been earned out, the newspaper would make a profit over
its continuing half-share of syndication moneys. In vain. I was

courteously made to realise that there were certain immutable facts in the expedition world. Only one newspaper had the cachet for supporting and reporting important expeditions – and it was not the *Daily Mail*, irrespective of its much larger offer.

I tried to explain things to Arthur Wareham, the editor, but suspected that he and his thwarted colleagues would attempt their revenge – as indeed they did. The American authorities had set up a permanent subterranean base at the South Pole, under the command of Admiral Dufek, one of their polar experts. From time to time, they flew large aircraft direct to the Pole from a base in South America, taking fresh teams to relieve the group of scientists at the Pole. The *Mail* managed to arrange for Noel Barber, its roving reporter, to accompany one of those incoming flights and be present at the South Pole when Fuchs and his crossing party arrived. The newspaper even, I believe, ran a competition in which the first prize was a trip to the South Pole; anything to make it look as though any idiot could get to the southernmost point in the world if he wanted to – and thus knock the rugged endeavours of the land party, crossing hundreds of miles of deep crevasses and enduring blizzards and white-outs in its thousand-mile journey from Shackleton Base.

In those days, *The Times* was in Queen Victoria Street, quite close to Blackfriars Bridge. It had a large forecourt containing the famous iron symbol with its inscription, 'Time was – Time is – Time will be'. The building was a maze of corridors with cubbyholes of rooms lurking off them. To get from one floor to another, you had to take a narrow, mahogany-lined lift – like a vertical coffin – in which a uniformed flunkey hauled you up by pulling on a rope, which set the ancient machinery clanking. On the upper east side, there was a dining room where special guests were fawned on by waiters in cut-away coats, knee breeches and stockings, and then seduced by the hosts' flattery and ample helpings of vintage port into agreements that were probably not in their best interests.

A short while before, Sir William Haley had left the running of the BBC to become editor. (Until about 1970, the post was perhaps one of the leading half-dozen in the country

– equivalent to that of the Archbishop of Canterbury or
the Lord Chief Justice or the Vice-Chancellor of Cambridge
University.) Over a period, he made a point of visiting every
one of the myriad rooms in the building to see what was
going on. At last, he came across a room in a dusty corner
of the basement. Being a courteous man, he knocked and then
walked in. There was a wooden table, a chair, a gas-ring against
one wall and a large old-fashioned safe on the opposite wall.
Making himself a cup of tea was an elderly retainer with a
shock of white hair, wearing a green baize apron.

'What's your job?' Sir William asked.

'I look after the guineas, sir.'

'The guineas?'

'Yes, sir. They're all there, I tell you. Here, you can count
them for yourself.' The old fellow took a bunch of keys off
his belt, unlocked the massive safe door and swung it open.
The only item it contained on a shelf was a chamois leather
bag. The keeper loosened the strings and poured the glittering
coins on to the table. 'There you are, sir. Seventy of 'em. And
'ere's the note I signed.'

He pulled a creased and crumpled piece of paper from a
pocket in his apron and thrust it almost defiantly at his boss,
who picked it up and managed to decipher that the date on
the form was over thirty years earlier.

He patiently questioned the old man and a strange story
came out. In Victorian days a special correspondent of *The
Times* was able to hire a private train to run him to Dover
to catch the packet boat for the Continent. In 1870, the Siege
of Paris had begun on a Saturday. With the banks closed, the
foreign correspondent was unable to draw any money and so
could not pay for the train, thus failing to arrive in Paris until
the following week and losing a scoop. After that débâcle,
the editor of the day decreed that there should always be a
sufficiency of guineas held in a safe at *The Times* building, in
case of a similar emergency.

And so, through the Boer War, the death of Queen Victoria,
the Delhi Durbar, the Great War, the rise of the dictators
and the Second World War, the chamois leather bag of
guineas had remained in its safe, awaiting some catastrophe

outside banking hours. Day in, day out, for all that time, a faithful retainer sat patiently in his basement room, making innumerable cups of tea but always ready for the call. As he grew old and withered into retirement, he would hand over the responsibility to a successor – one likes to think perhaps his son, who would carry on the family tradition. *The Thunderer* thundered, editors came and went, Geoffrey Dawson licked the shiny boots of Hitler and Mussolini, leader writers wrote leaders, Graham Greene contemplated suicide – and no one for eighty-five years gave a thought to the guardian in the basement. Had Sir William Haley been less inquisitive, a faithful grey-haired servant might still be there in Fortress Wapping, clutching his bag of guineas among the word-processors and the VDUs.

The general manager of *The Times* was a genial rogue named Francis Mathew. Plump, pink-faced with horn-rimmed spectacles, he was descended from a dynasty of bishops, colonial administrators and intellectuals – a veritable Basil Seal of the newspaper world. Once, when arrested as drunk in charge of a vehicle, he had apparently both abused and struck the arresting officer, and was subsequently heavily fined in the magistrates' court. But such was his influence in Fleet Street, along with the then benign policy of 'dog don't eat dog', that not a single national newspaper reported the incident.

He employed an ingenious trick on those whose services *The Times* required. His expressed view was 'gentlemen don't need legal contracts' with all that jargon about the party of the first part and 'not withstanding anything to the contrary contained herein'. No, gentlemen exchanged letters which set out the deal in simple English. So – and this happened on at least three occasions with the CTAE – he would send, say, a three-page letter. The first and the third pages would set out the agreed terms correctly but there would be a glaring error in the middle of page two. When that was pointed out to Mathew, he would sigh, gaze at the ceiling and blame his incompetent secretary. He would then have all three pages of the document retyped and sent round by messenger for urgent signature and return. He was banking on the fact that most people would look closely at page two, where the mistake had been properly rectified, and then express approval by signing the duplicate copy without checking the other two pages. But he would have subtly reworded the odd paragraph to *The Times'* advantage on one or both of the other pages. If caught in the act, he would naturally blame that useless secretary. He must have been a good and long-suffering man, like his ancestor, Bishop Mathew, to have continued employing such a markedly inefficient woman.

My dealings on the book-publishing side were far more straight forward and congenial. Bryen Gentry, second in command at Cassell & Company, then one of the two or three leading houses in London, had invited me to lunch at Quaglino's, a delectable restaurant in Bury Street, St James's. It was a leisurely, gossipy lunch, well lubricated with introductory dry martinis, a good bottle of wine and a *marc* or two with the coffee, to aid the digestion. I knew that the firm was still preoccupied with publishing the great Churchill memoirs and, guessing quite wrongly that there would be little room left for other big books, I decided not to display my wares.

As we were getting up to leave, Bryen asked me casually if I didn't have a book to sell him. Equally casually, I mentioned the forthcoming *The Crossing of Antarctica*, as Fuchs had decided to call it. (Not for him glory-words like 'Conquest'.)

Bryen stopped dead and said, 'Sounds great. How much do you want?'

I said, '£30,000 advance. And top royalties.' (The modern equivalent of that £30,000 would be in excess of £400,000. And there was no guarantee that the expedition would succeed.)

Bryen said, 'Would you leave it with me till tomorrow morning?'

I nodded. As it turned out, he called me before the end of the afternoon, having talked with Dr Desmond Flower, the senior director, and accepted the offer.

Most agents will confirm that a deal that starts smoothly and happily most often continues in that vein; again, a deal that begins with huffing and puffing usually gets worse as it jerks along. Cassell's experience with *The Crossing of Antarctica* fell nicely into the former camp. Their hardcover editions sold over 130,000 copies, which cleared the advance, and the paperback editions brought them in a pleasant bonus. They could not have been more assiduous in helping with the editing of the text and preparing the many colour illustrations.

Almost forty years ago in the publishing world, there was no such thing as a rights auction. Scott Meredith, the New York agent, has a good claim to having invented the practice around 1949 but it took a long time to cross the Atlantic and flourish on this side. In London in the 1950s – and well into the 1960s – an agent offered book rights to one publisher at a time and then waited on his answer. It was only if the publisher wavered for well over a month and failed to reach his decision even after several promptings from the agent that the latter tried elsewhere. Thus I was breaking no golden rules through dealing solely with Cassell's.

But when Billy (later Sir William) Collins got wind of the deal, he telephoned me in anger and threatened to 'make your name mud' with my distinguished committee. Billy, the scion of a longish line of publishers, was a fierce competitor. Well into old age, he would bowl all the afternoon at the annual Collins v. Authors cricket match and then round off his day with three or four hard sets of tennis. He also possessed that Scottish Calvinist feeling of total rectitude, even when descending, as he did, to venal tricks. (He was the one who replied, when told that a well-known Collins author had died, 'Dead? And after all I've done for him!')

He did, in fact, stir things up and at the next committee meeting, I was asked by my old sparring partner, General Sir James Marshall-Cornwall, why I had ignored the splendid house of Collins in my quest for a book publisher. I had managed to anticipate the query. Collins had just published Richard Aldington's provocative biography of T.E. Lawrence. Realising the general had known the desert hero during and after the Great War, I assumed a doleful countenance and mentioned Aldington's book, adding that – at least, in my view – any publisher who knowingly denigrated such remarkable achievements could hardly be fit to represent future great deeds in a desert of snow and ice. One could sense the

Establishment closing ranks. Cassell published the heroic Churchill; Collins published a book that belittled Churchill's friend. So – down with Collins. It was vastly unfair – but Billy had started the skirmish.

I shall not attempt to detail the successful crossing, which Sir Vivian Fuchs covered so well in the official story and, over thirty years later, in a more personal vein in his *Of Ice and Men*. Before leaving Shackleton Base, he forecast that his crossing party in their Sno-Cats would reach the South Pole in 100 days and, in spite of blizzards and treacherous deep crevasses ranging over many miles, it took ninety-nine days to do so. Sir Edmund Hillary's New Zealand support party had laid depots over the second half of the journey to Scott Base, where on arrival Fuchs was awarded an immediate knighthood. In the course of the long journey, Dr Marsh and a comrade broke the then world record for a dog-sledge trek of over 3,000 miles, while Wing-Commander John Lewis carried out a superb feat of endurance flying and navigation by piloting the single-engined expedition aircraft non-stop across the whole of the Antarctic continent from Shackleton to Scott Base, a distance of some 1,600 miles. And Ed Hillary added to his Everest laurels (and exceeded his instructions) by leading his team of converted farm tractors across the high plateau to the Pole itself.

There was a great rush to get the book out that same year, 1958, and several of us converged on the Fuchs home in Barton Road, Cambridge, to help with typing, cross-checking references and the rest of the editorial nitty-gritty. It was then I learned that Bunny and his wife Joyce shared a surrealistic sense of humour. The lunch was cold meat and salad. He sat at one end of the long table and she at the other. Close to his napkin, there was a cucumber on a dish with a sharp knife alongside. Half-way through the lunch, Joyce called down the table, 'Oh, Bunny, I could do with a slice of cucumber.' She held up her right hand, palm outwards, like a policeman halting a vehicle.

Bunny picked up the cucumber in his left hand, holding it parallel to the table. He grasped the knife firmly in his right hand and struck the end of the cucumber a slicing blow. The piece flew the length of the table and landed with a plonk in the middle of Joyce's palm, which she closed to capture it. She smiled and nodded. He smiled back and went on with his lunch.

More than a dozen foreign countries, from Norway and Sweden to Greece and Turkey, acquired their respective translation rights in the book. G.P. Putnam's Sons in New York snapped up the American rights. Usually, Sir Edwin Herbert or one of the senior members of the committee was deputed to sign contracts, once I had checked them, but on that occasion, as I was to be in New York on other business, I was paid the honour of being the proxy signatory. The redoubtable Walter Minton then owned Putnam's. A believer in 'creative friction', he liked to make his editors compete with each other. One autumn, three different Putnam editors *and* Jack Geoghegan, who ran the subsidiary firm of Coward McCann, arrived in London in the same fortnight, all of them pursuing the same titles from publishers and agents. Walter always wore thick white woollen socks and spent most of his time with his chair tilted back, and his shoes and socks propped up on the vast desk in front. He had a habit of gnawing his thumb to a point where he had to bandage it with Elastoplast.

He had the reputation of eating agents for elevenses and spitting out the husks before going to lunch. He had offered such a large advance for American book rights – $75,000, as I recall, which would be worth at least ten times as much today – that the committee had agreed to his taking a 10 per cent override on all such income as book-club and paperback rights. Like almost all New York publishers, Putnam's had their own standard printed contract – what was known locally as the 'boilerplate'. There were several points that needed to be either deleted or added. For example, Cassell's in London had already acquired Canadian volume rights under their contract and so Putnam's could only claim the United States territory, not North America. And we had to find suitable wording to cover the 10 per cent 'cut' which my committee was to allow Putnam's to receive. There were at least six closely printed pages in the contract. Once Walter and I had hammered out a point – he would have been at home in a school for divines, arguing just how many angels could dance on the point of a needle – his hapless secretary would take that page away and type in the agreed changes. Old pages were being scrapped, new pages were being added to the bundle, there were amendments within amendments, changes countermanding other changes. My eyes were hypnotised by the small print and, whenever I looked up for relief, my gaze was drawn as if by a magnet to Walter's white woollen socks.

At last, all was in order. I uncapped my fountain pen and initialled the foot of every page up to the last. My pen was poised over the space beneath the solemn words, 'IN WITNESS WHEREOF', when Walter suddenly said, 'You're sure you're happy?'

'Sure,' I said.

'No problems at all?'

'Not a one.' My pen nib began to descend, when Walter said sharply, 'Hey!'

My hand froze in mid-air. He went on, 'Take a good look at Paragraph 9 (a).'

I looked, blinked and looked again. It stated in the clearest of terms that the publisher was to receive 90 per cent of all proceeds and the proprietor (the expedition) would receive the remaining 10 per cent – the exact opposite of our agreement. That scourge of literary agents, the rough, tough Walter Minton, had saved my professional career. To have been given special authority to sign the big contract and then to have given away the expedition's birthright – or, at least, copyright – because I had failed to check the wording with due care could have led to my expulsion as agent for the CTAE. And I could only have blamed myself.

The error was quickly rectified, we signed and exchanged our copies of the contract and I shook his hand warmly. Walking up Madison Avenue, clutching the precious document, I thought of the two extremes – the suave, well-bred Francis Mathew, trapping the unwary with his letter contracts, and the plain, blunt Walter Minton, who played it straight, even to his own disadvantage. The New World had nicely redressed my balance.

When part of the earth's surface is traversed for the first

time, a special place-names committee is set up. Capes, headlands, rivers, cliffs and mountain peaks, newly discovered, are given a name. Nowadays, it must incorporate a surname, which shall not be so common as to be confused with another locale in the same area. Over a year after the end of the expedition, a cylindrical tube arrived in my office. It contained a map of one section of Antarctica, within 300 miles of the South Pole. Unrolling it, I glanced at it until my eyes fell on a closing-up of the contour lines with a peak marked at the centre. Against it were the printed words, 'Mount Greenfield'. As a friendly gesture, Sir Vivian Fuchs had given me my very own mountain.

I shall now never see it and no one has yet climbed it, although I did suggest to Chris Bonington on his last climbing trip 'down south' that it was just waiting for him. But I occasionally picture it in my mind's eye, with its sloping, permanently snow-covered shoulders, serene and icy cold. Perhaps my grandsons, or their sons, will one day make a pilgrimage to what will then be 'their' mountain.

The days of great national expeditions, largely financed through private resources, have probably gone forever. I had the good fortune to be associated with at least four of them – in chronological order, the Commonwealth Trans-Antarctic Expedition, the British Trans-Arctic Expedition, the British Everest Expedition of 1975, led by Chris Bonington, and the Transglobe Expedition. In each case, apart from the CTAE, the potential leader himself put forward the proposal. But he would hardly have time to draw his sword from its scabbard and wave it aloft before relevant members of the 'great and the good' club would be forming ranks behind him.

Having spent many hours of my life sitting at a long table with ten or more other men, each with a notepad and a sharpened pencil in front of him, I can well understand the truth behind that old saying, 'A camel is a horse designed by a committee'. But nevertheless, committees become an essential part of every major expedition. However famous the leader and however well conceived his plan, he will need the backing of experts in the same field, an experienced lawyer to keep a watchful eye on legal aspects and, above all, a banker – perhaps an accountant as well – to help fund the enterprise in its early days and ensure that the profit-and-loss account was properly run. Many likely members of a committee of management would be busy men with regular duties elsewhere, who would therefore without thought of gain be sacrificing more profitable pursuits. Several of them were also able to extend great financial help to their respective teams. The successful 1975 Everest Expedition would not have been put together so smoothly with the best of equipment and back-up if Alan Tritton, committee member and a director of Barclays Bank, had not arranged interest-free loans from the bank, running well into six figures – loans that were more than fully repaid from the big sales of Chris Bonington's book and the great public interest in the BBC film. Again, the Transglobe Expedition would not have got off the ground (literally, as well as metaphorically), if Peter Bowring, head of the long-established insurance brokers of that name, had not given Ran Fiennes free use of the *Benjamin Bowring*, a thirty-year-old boat with strengthened sides and much experience of the ice-pack.

In my experience, expedition committees tend to recreate themselves through the fertility rites of the Royal Geographical Society. Lord Hunt, a member of the CTAE, the BTAE and the Transglobe committees, was in his time president of the RGS, as was Sir Vivian Fuchs, who was on the same three committees. Rear-Admiral Sir Edmund Irving, the Hydrographer Royal, was on the BTAE committee, chairman of the Transglobe committee *and* a president of the RGS. Pat Pirie-Gordon, on the CTAE and the BTAE, was honorary treasurer of the RGS, to be followed by Alan Tritton, who was on the BTAE and the Transglobe. There was nothing unusual in any of those links. Geography and expeditions are indissoluble. It is only human nature at work when a fellow of the RGS, who is probably also a member of the Geographical Club, that select dining club limited to a little over a hundred members, nominates a colleague with the same qualifications for an expedition committee. Interestingly, I can recall no women members.

An aspiring leader gains in credibility if he can demonstrate support from authorities in his field. Wally Herbert proved himself through years of arduous service with the British Antarctic Survey, where he came to the notice of Sir Vivian Fuchs, who introduced us. He wrote a vivid account of his experiences 'down south' entitled *A World of Men*, which I sold to Eyre & Spottiswoode. Then, in the summer of 1965, he produced a striking plan – for a crossing of the frozen surface of the Arctic Ocean from Point Barrow in Alaska to north-east Greenland via the North Pole – which he submitted for the approval of the Royal Geographical Society. He had been working on the plan for some years and had modified it on Fuchs's unofficial advice. The RGS has an expeditions committee that meets periodically to examine proposals. If it does not grant approval and usually some token financial support, that would-be expedition is virtually doomed.

Wally's plan was rejected. As already mentioned, Fuchs and I played squash twice a week in the early evenings. At our next encounter, I twisted his muscular arm to put together a band of backers for Wally and his plan. Sir Miles Clifford agreed to become chairman; Colonel Andrew Croft, whose knowledge of the Arctic was almost unrivalled, joined in, as did Lord Hunt, Lord (then Sir Arthur) Porritt, Sergeant-Surgeon to the Queen and later Governor-General of his native New Zealand, and no fewer than two bankers, Patrick Pirie-Gordon of Glynn Mills and Alan Tritton of Barclays. It is perhaps no coincidence that when the modified plan for a trans-Arctic crossing was put to the RGS, approval was quite swiftly forthcoming.

A committee of management's main help to the leader and his team usually occurs in the stages leading up to departure. Apart from the overall endorsement afforded by its public association with the venture, it can offer expert advice on the plan itself, perhaps make office space and secretarial help available and often help to raise money through City contacts. Would-be sponsors or a public institution like the BBC, and even book publishers and newspaper editors, are duly impressed by a list of 'good' names on the expedition's letterheading. Planning and then putting together the myriad details of an expedition can be dreary and lonely work for the man with the initial vision. But regular meetings with his supporting committee will help him to maintain his enthusiasm and realise that he is one of a band of brothers.

Problems can and do arise once the team leaves Britain. No matter how well thought out the plan and how detailed the steps between conception and execution, sooner or later the best-organised expedition will suffer a crisis. It may be thousands of miles away from its home base, dependent upon a crackling radio link or even on runners to convey progress reports back to the London office. Committee men are busy men and a few days may elapse before a quorum can be assembled, by which time the news may be out of date. The question arises: to what extent should the committee of management back in London issue orders to the leader in the field? To my mind, the answer is 'Never – unless the leader has specifically asked for instructions.' Helping to plan the strategy of an expedition's task is very much a part of the committee's responsibilities; but only the leader, perhaps in consultation with his team, can determine the tactics on the journey itself.

The first major instance I recall occurred during the Commonwealth Trans-Antarctic Expedition. The British contingent, which was to be the crossing party, started from one end of the sub-continent and the New Zealand contingent, under the leadership of Sir Edmund Hillary, started from the other end to lay fuel depots for the crossing party over the second half of its long trek. The idea was that Hillary and his men, having laid their depots on the plateau, would halt 100 or so miles short of the South Pole, while Fuchs had the public glory of reaching the Pole and pressing on to link up with the New Zealand party at their depot.

As the episode with General Sir James Marshall-Cornwall is witness, I was very much the new boy connected with the CTAE and, certainly in the early days, felt myself to be there on sufferance. When the plan was first mooted, I did not have the nerve to stand up and express my thoughts. Apart from John Hunt and perhaps Sir Arthur Porritt, none of the others had more than a nodding acquaintance with the rugged mountaineer, whereas I had been his literary agent for two or three years and had developed a close friendship that happily remains to this day. Some of the best brains in the City and the higher reaches of academe were part of the committee of management but it was collectively naive of them to think that the first man on top of Everest would forgo the 'double' of reaching the South Pole, a feat that had not been achieved by land for many years. All the more so when Fuchs's crossing party was badly delayed through encountering a wide and heavily crevassed area; there even seemed to be some risk that the crossing itself was in jeopardy.

Fuchs and his men did in fact arrive at the Pole dead on time – to be greeted, in spite of the committee's order to the contrary, by Hillary and his adapted farm tractors. The press picked up the controversy and made play with it, which to a slight extent took the gloss off the courageous and resourceful efforts of both teams. 'The scarlet majors at the base' – except that they were generals and knights, and even a bishop – should, I felt, have known better than to tell the frontline troops when to advance and when to halt.

A decade later, a similar if potentially more critical situation occurred with Wally Herbert's British Trans-Arctic Expedition. Three of the five-man team – Herbert himself, Fritz Koerner and Allan Gill – were old comrades with many years of active 'snow and ice' experience between them. The fourth, Captain Ken Hedges, a medical officer with the SAS, was, as one might expect, a tough and determined character with a deep religious conviction but a complete ignorance of polar travel. In such a small party, there could be the built-in risk that he would find himself the odd man out. The fifth member of the team was Squadron-Leader Freddie Church, a signals expert from the RAF who would man the powerful radio at Point Barrow and act as the expedition's link with the outside world.

In the last week of February 1968, the team left Point Barrow. The early days were hazardous but, as daylight gradually increased, they were able to maintain good progress until September when Allan Gill damaged his back manhandling his heavy sledge. In such rudimentary conditions and without proper diagnostic equipment, it was virtually impossible for Ken Hedges to give a full verdict but he reckoned that Gill was suffering either from acute slipped disc or severe muscle strain.

Messages flew back and forth. Winter was approaching and with the advent of total darkness and almost unbearable outside cold in a few weeks' time, the team would have to halt on a suitably large ice-floe, erect its hut and sit tight until the following February. Herbert, Koerner and Gill himself wanted him to winter over and give his back a chance to recover. Even if, when the time came, his back had not improved, he could remain under Hedges' care until March, when some Canadian geophysicists were due to take over the hut for their observations. He and Hedges would then fly out on their returning aircraft. Meanwhile, Herbert and Koerner, the two experienced and still fit hands, would make a dash for Spitzbergen and complete the expedition with panache.

The committee was strongly opposed to the plan. The onward journey, more than 1,000 miles along the icy crust of the northern ocean, was extremely hazardous in any event. If attempted by two men on their own, no matter how tough and knowledgeable they might be, illness or an accident affecting one of them when they were still several hundred miles from land, and if weather conditions or the melting of the ice-cap made it impossible for a light aircraft to land and rescue them, could result in both their deaths.

Already, the press was having a field day over the expedition. Wally Herbert, thinking he was talking privately to Freddie Church on the radio link and feeling frustrated – as well he might – with the committee's tendency (as he had put it in a formal message back to London) to issue him 'directives' instead of 'recommendations', let off steam. Unfortunately, the public-address system was accidentally left on and Peter Dunn, the representative at Point Barrow of the *Sunday Times*, the newspaper sponsor of the BTAE, overheard Wally's remarks. He published the story and the other papers with their ability to falsify issues through stock responses – 'Arctic Hero's Lonely Battle Against Chairborne Establishment', truth sacrificed for a snappy headline – came charging in. That in turn put more pressure on the committee. If they approved the two-man plan and a major disaster followed, the press would swiftly forget that it had been Wally Herbert's initial idea. Now the London base would be the culprits. The previous instruction that Allan Gill be airlifted out for medical attention and the other three should winter over before continuing the journey was confirmed in the name of the chairman, Sir Miles Clifford.

In the event, the ice apparently broke up in the area where the Twin-Otter aircraft would have had to land, the flight was abandoned, Gill remained with the other three in their winter camp, he recovered from his back injury and the team, having reached the North Pole on 5 April the following year, completed its successful crossing of the Arctic at the end of May. 'The end crowns the work', as the saying goes – but there had been stumbles and noises off in the progress towards the throne of the first ever Arctic Ocean crossing.

A year or so later, a young woman with fair hair and bright blue eyes came to see me. Her name was Virginia Pepper and she was engaged to an ex-cavalry officer, a young baronet with the improbable name of Sir Ranulph Twistleton-Wykeham-Fiennes. He had completed a journey by jet boat towards the source of the Nile and wanted to write a book about the venture. She showed me some photographs and a synopsis. The poor girl had fallen down the escalator at Holborn Underground station and badly bruised a leg, but that had not deterred her. Working on the assumption that the man who appealed to someone of her calibre must possess at least some of her determination – and much against my better judgement – I agreed to accept him as a client. And thus began an association which was to last until my retirement nearly twenty years later and which still continues as a good friendship.

I did lay down one condition for my taking him on. As an expedition leader, author and lecturer, he would have to drop the first two 'barrels' from his name, distinguished lines of descent though they were. 'Fiennes' was difficult enough for the ordinary person to pronounce – 'Fee-ennis'?; 'Fee-ens'?; 'Fy-enns'? – instead of the recognised 'Fines'. Saddled with a title and the two other surnames, he would sound like a music-hall act to the ears of the common press and no one would take his exploration seriously. Somewhat askance and, I suspect, with some reluctance, he eventually agreed.

As I grew to know him better and to learn more of his experiences, I realised that his drive and determination were in the same rank as those of Ginnie Pepper, whom he married in 1970. After serving as an officer in the Royal Scots Greys, he had passed through the ultra-tough selection course of the SAS and had fought the Yemeni invaders while seconded to the Sultan of Oman's forces. There was an iron will beneath the affable and handsome exterior. In fairly quick succession, he organised and led an expedition that involved landing by parachute on top of a glacier in Norway and then abseiling down the ice fall, another by rubber raft through the white-water stretches of the Headless Valley in Canada, in each case writing a book about the venture, lecturing, making public appearances and gradually developing a high 'profile' as a leader of interesting and important expeditions.

In the latter part of 1972, Ginnie had a bright idea. It entailed following the Greenwich Meridian right round the world via the South and North Poles, one of the most ambitious journeys possible on the earth's surface. Ran Fiennes himself had been solely responsible for his three previous expeditions, as the cost of setting them up could be met through sales of the various rights to television, a newspaper, and a book publisher. But the Transglobe Expedition, as it soon came to be known, would be far too costly. As soon as I had digested the plan's details, I told Ran that he would need a committee of management, carefully picked from the exploring establishment, to lend him its collective credibility and to use its many contacts to find outside sponsors. And as the two Poles would have to be negotiated, his first powerful backer must be a polar expert. The outstanding name was Sir Vivian Fuchs.

Although he and I were no longer playing squash twice a week, we were still in close touch and there would be no problem in introducing Ran Fiennes to him. Which I did, after Ran and his likely team had gained 'snow and ice' experience from sledging on the Greenland ice-cap. Once Fuchs accepted him, the usual nucleus came together – Sir Miles Clifford, Colonel Andrew Croft, Alan Tritton, Fuchs himself, all under the chairmanship of the ex-Hydrographer Royal, Rear-Admiral 'Egg' Irving. There were some useful new names as well, among them Sir Alec Durie, chairman of the Automobile Association, Peter Bowring, the insurance broker, Brigadier Wingate Gray, who had been Ran's commanding officer in the SAS, and Peter Martin, a lawyer who was an authority in aviation insurance.

Colonel Croft, one of the most experienced Arctic explorers in Britain, urged that the crossing party for the two Poles should consist of three men or perhaps four but certainly not two. In his expert view, three was a good number if they all got on well together. There was just a risk that in an emergency the leader might find the other two ganging up on him but more of a likelihood, if there were four travelling, that they might split up into two cliques. But either number was vastly preferable to a twosome. In his words, 'Two men is relatively suicidal.' Ran Fiennes took his advice and chose two companions for the crossings, Oliver Shepard and Charlie Burton.

All went well on the southern half, culminating in the traverse of Antarctica in sixty-seven days by skidoo. Then a major problem arose. Oliver Shepard's wife not only missed his physical presence but was becoming increasingly anxious for his safety. Their marriage might even break up if he were to continue with the team. He decided that he must withdraw. The committee felt that a replacement should be recruited; Fiennes and Burton wanted to continue as a pair when the Arctic was reached. The debate went on from the opposite ends of the earth until Sir Edmund Irving as chairman, with Sir Vivian Fuchs and Brigadier Wingate Gray, flew out to New Zealand, hoping to influence the leader by a personal challenge. The Transglobe trade exhibition in Auckland was followed by one in Sydney, Australia, opened by Prince Charles, the Expedition's patron. Ran Fiennes was still strenuously resisting the demands for a new third member and when the patron went on board the *Benjamin Bowring* to meet the crew, it would be fair, I think, to say that Ran 'nobbled' him during a private session in the captain's cabin. If the patron agreed that a party of two would suffice for the possibly more dangerous Arctic crossing, the committee was not going to gainsay him. But Ran was left in no doubt that, if anything went wrong when they were in the field, it was on his head.

I think it is also fair to say that for the remaining eighteen months of the expedition, distrust of Ran, which almost without his knowing grew into dislike, simmered in the mind of Rear-Admiral Sir Edmund Irving. He suffered worsening pain from an arthritic leg and worries over his wife's health, neither of which contributed to a calm objectivity. Above all, he had grown up in the hierarchical society of the Royal Navy from midshipman to flag rank – a world where that old saying, 'The orders I give are orders and not a basis for discussion', was strictly relevant. A senior officer gave orders, the other ranks obeyed it. Life was that simple. The chairman of the committee was the most senior officer present, the team out in the field were the other ranks. And here was a young whippersnapper, who not only disobeyed a direct order but whispered in the ear of the royal patron to countermand it. 'A damn poor show, what?'

No one among the inner circle of the committee, not even Sir Vivian Fuchs, really understood or appreciated the enormous physical endurance and determination of Fiennes and Burton. They threaded their way through the North-West Passage in inflatable boats and trekked across Ellesmere Island up to the fringe of the Arctic Ocean. After hazardous adventures, they reached the North Pole by skidoo on 10 April 1982. Thus far, the expedition was a great success and, in spite of the sombre forecasts, two men had proved they could keep each other going through all the dangers and the pressure without the benefit of a third or fourth partner.

But the journey was not yet over. In order to complete the traverse of the Greenwich Meridian *on the earth's surface*, Fiennes and Burton would still have to link up with the *Benjamin Bowring* on the edge of the ice-pack near Spitzbergen and the ship would then have to sail back to Greenwich. Although strengthened against floating ice, she could not penetrate the heavily frozen ice-pack. So it was up to Fiennes and Burton to reach her. Their plan was to make what progress they could southwards before the midsummer sun melted the surface of the ice and brought them to a halt. Even then, they could select a suitable floe and let the prevailing current float them towards the ship and safety, and overall success.

All this time, as she had done during the Antarctic section, Ginnie Fiennes was acting as radio link between them and civilisation, stationed at Cape Nord with a powerful transmitter. Following a report on the dangerous state of the pack ice in late May, a vital committee meeting took place in London. Sir Edmund Irving was, whether he realised it or not – and he probably did – fed up with the Transglobe venture. It had been going on for close on three years and the committee had been meeting for many months before the actual departure. It had virtually completed its circuit. Besides which, there was still a grave risk that either Fiennes or Burton or indeed both could fall ill, suffer an accident or even die, which would cast a black cloud not only over the expedition in general but on the committee in particular for permitting such risks. Rallying some of the more diehard members, he swung them to vote for an instant evacuation of the team, while surface conditions would still allow a light aircraft to land. Two or three of us abstained.

To me and to those others who had been associated with the British Trans-Arctic Expedition there was a strong feeling of *déjà vu*. The batteries in Wally Herbert's radio set had been strangely weak when the order to prepare a landing strip to evacuate Allan Gill with his bad back had been transmitted, although as a *Sunday Times* journalist later pointed out, those same batteries seemed to have made a miraculous recovery the very next day. The strip was not prepared, the weather broke up, Gill stayed over to winter with the other three and remained as an active member of the successful team. History repeated itself when Ginnie was apparently unable to pass on the chairman's command to her husband. Nor did a further order get through. At last, the message was reduced to a strong recommendation to call it a day and be airlifted out to the ship – but leaving Ran to make the final decision. Oddly enough, that time the message got through loud and clear. The pair went on floating on an erratic southbound course, 'pursued by (polar) bears'. Within days, landing conditions for an aircraft had become too bad. Bits were continually breaking off their ice-floe and channels of freezing water were opening up around them. So they took to their canoes and by desperate paddling along available leads and humping the canoes across rough ice when the leads closed up, they finally reached the ship just after midnight on 4 August. They were less than a degree off the Greenwich Meridian. After a leisurely voyage to complete the final leg of the journey, the *Benjamin Bowring* steamed into the Thames on 29 August, where Prince Charles boarded her and helped steer her back to Greenwich, almost exactly three years since he had navigated her on the first few miles of her outward journey. Thousands cheered as the ship docked.

No doubt the man and woman in the street would have cheered as loudly if Ran Fiennes and Charlie Burton had been lifted off the ice-cap by light aircraft and landed alongside the ship. Few would have realised that such a move would ruin the whole point of the enterprise – to circumnavigate the world vertically but keeping to its surface throughout. But the committee, made up of men of action and leaders in other fields, should have realised it.

The horse finally won the race. But it could easily have ended up as a camel in the desert wastes.

8

A BRUSH WITH THE SPECIAL BRANCH

The voice was soft, a rustic burr with the broad vowel sounds that could have originated in Dorset or Hampshire.

'Am I speaking to Mr Greenfield? Mr George Greenfield?'

'Yes.'

'This is Superintendent Smith, sir. From the Special Branch. Colonel Scotland – we turned over his drum last night – he gave me your name and number. I need to see you urgently, sir. Shall we say – in half an hour? I will call at your office.'

He rang off before I had the chance to ask him the purpose of the visit. But I had already been briefed through a telephone call earlier that morning from a shaken Lieutenant-Colonel Scotland. An ex-officer with a distinguished war record, holder of the OBE, he was then – the year was 1955 – in his seventies with an invalid wife. Armed with a warrant, the superintendent and his team had gone to Scotland's flat in Gloucester Terrace late at night, causing a great commotion and banging on the outer door until the owner, roused from sleep, had got up to answer it. They had then proceeded to open and empty every cupboard and drawer in the place – in police parlance, 'turning over the drum' – while Scotland and his wife looked on. The object? To discover the duplicate typescript of *The London Cage*. If Smith and his team had waited long enough to ask the colonel a simple question, he would have told them, which he later did when they finally got round to it, that he had passed the spare script on to me, as his agent.

But that would have been too easy. It would not have caused gossip amongst the neighbours or given a psychological scar to an elderly patriot through being classed with sordid criminals harbouring drugs or illegal weapons or the proceeds of robbery. I knew that the Special Branch had been formed late last century from the ordinary ranks of the Metropolitan Police to combat the gangs of political terrorists that had been formed mostly in the East End of London from amongst foreign refugees arriving in England. I also knew from friends in Fleet Street that the Special Branch might occasionally cut corners when dealing with thugs who never themselves followed legal niceties to the letter. But I knew as well from the same source that a police department working in the shadows and wearing the enveloping cloak of national security can at times behave worse than the people it arrests. Superintendent Smith was notorious for breaking up a so-called homosexual ring, which included a peer of the realm, a well-known actor and other men in prominent positions. In those days, more than a decade before the Wolfenden Report was published, homosexual acts, even those between consenting adults carried out in private, were illegal and on conviction carried quite lengthy sentences.

The jolly policeman had a neat trick to play. At around six o'clock on a Saturday morning, he called at the flat of the suspect whom he thought most likely to break under pressure. If he happened to find the man in bed with a boyfriend, so much the better. In any case, Smith was banking on the fact that his target might be suffering from a hangover; even if he was not, facing a dawn raid on an empty stomach and with the sleep still in one's eyes is not the brightest prospect for victory. The victim was not allowed to get in touch with his solicitor – a blatant breach of the interrogation code – or even to use the telephone. Deliberately kept hungry and thirsty, he was alternatively bullied and cajoled until at last he broke down in tears and blurted out the names of his associates. The rest was easy. Faced with a confession that named them and their practices in considerable detail, the others had little option but to admit their membership of the ring.

Younger readers might wonder why the might of the Special Branch was brought to bear on such a trivial target. 'Who breaks a butterfly upon a wheel?' The answer, I suppose, is that, a few years earlier, Guy Burgess and Donald Maclean, both homosexuals (Maclean was bisexual as well), had caused a great furore by fleeing to Moscow. Both had been Soviet agents for many years. It was also a Foreign Office belief that a homosexual would be more prone to blackmail, as was proved a little later when a cipher clerk in the British Embassy in Moscow, a young man named Vassall, was blackmailed into becoming a spy for the KGB.

But Colonel Scotland was not a homosexual or a secret traitor. He was intensely patriotic, a man of great rectitude. The Special Branch's heavy-handed approach to him would have been farcical if it had not been sinister.

I had been put on to him by a talented young journalist-client named Wayne Mineau, who frequented the same local pub and who had heard some of his stories. Great stories they were, indeed, with the added merit of being true. Colonel Scotland, short of stature, slim, white-haired and pink-cheeked, had as a young man in the early years of this century lived in what was then German South-West Africa. German military aggression and quest for *Lebensraum*, which in 1911 was to lead to the Agadir incident, was already increasing. Scotland, working as a merchant supplying their armed forces as well as the civilian population, soon came to speak German fluently and, moreover, to have a thorough knowledge of military ranks and organisations.

He put those qualities to good use in the Great War, having by then returned to Britain. He invented a reversible uniform jacket. On one side, it was khaki with the pockets and GS buttons of the average British Tommy. Pulled inside out, it became field-grey, with the trappings and high collar of a German army *Feldwebel*. During the British retreat to Mons, he bravely stayed in hiding in a Belgian village that was certain to be overrun by the advancing German troops. Once the front had been established well down the road and the local *estaminet* had opened up again, he would emerge from hiding with the field-grey on the outside and sit quietly at a table, buying the occasional drink and listening. He quickly came to know what units were in the area and with his knowledge of staff duties would at once recall that X Infantry Regiment was always part of Y Division, which in turn was almost always part of Z Korps.

When there was a lull in the fighting, he would manage to slip through the lines, across no-man's-land and back to his own troops, with his jacket properly reversed to khaki. After a thorough de-briefing at GHQ, he would once again cross into the enemy lines and repeat the procedure. He told me that the risk of being caught as an enemy spy inside the German lines was virtually nil. His cover story was sound and, although someone from Berlin might think he had a Bavarian accent – and vice versa – his knowledge of military slang was profound. The main risk came from zealous sentries on duty in the German and the British front lines. Why he was never decorated for these repeated acts of bravery was a mystery to me and, I imagine, although he never discussed it with me, to himself as well. In the Great War, medals were supposed 'to come up with the rations'. If it were so, Scotland went hungry.

But it was in the Second World War that he performed his most important duties for the country. He became a senior interrogator at a top-secret centre known as the 'London Cage'. To it were brought captured German generals and potential war criminals. For example, there had been a mass breakout from Stalag Luft III, an RAF prisoner-of-war camp. Hitler was so enraged that he ordered every man recaptured to be shot. Fifty-two Britons died as a result. The guards from the camp, who had carried out the executions, were arrested at the end of the war and sent to the London Cage for interrogation. They came under Scotland's attention.

He had a very simple method. They were often in groups of three and he would have each man placed alone in a cell with a pencil and unlimited sheets of paper. He would then talk to them individually, saying that he was quite prepared to believe that the man he was talking to was innocent but he

would have to prove it by writing out his version of events in
detail. He knew in advance that A would incriminate B and
C and make himself appear spotless – and so on round the
trio. But by comparing one version with another, he could
spot gaps and sometimes find that B might inadvertently have
given A an alibi at one particular point. Where there were still
areas of ambiguity, he would get them to write a more detailed
version of that particular episode – and sometimes again and
again. In the end, there might prove to be one ringleader and
the others unwilling accomplices or, as happened in most cases,
three men equally guilty and condemning themselves in their
own statements.

Colonel Scotland appeared as a chief prosecution witness in
the Venice War Crimes Trials of 1947. The defendants, faced
with their own written 'confessions', had only one possible
defence: that these had been extorted from them by psychological and physical pressure amounting to torture. Scotland,
appearing for the prosecution, found himself having to justify
the results against aggressive questioning from counsel for the
accused. The court saw through the defence manœuvres and
found the German prison guards guilty, but the popular press
in Britain quickly picked up the controversy and there were
headlines in heavy black print: 'Senior British Officer Accused
of Torturing Prisoners'.

So Colonel Scotland was concerned to have his memoirs
published not so much for the money they might earn as to
clear his reputation, which he considered to be still besmirched
from the unfair cross-examinations he had undergone in
Venice seven years earlier. Working with Wayne Mineau, he
produced some sample chapters and a detailed synopsis, and
I soon obtained a satisfactory contract with Evans Brothers,
which in the 1950s developed a strong list of war books.
Naturally enough, the title selected was *The London Cage*;
work went apace and within a few months the complete
typescript was ready. Stanley Jackson, the Evans Brothers
editor responsible for the war-books list, was delighted and
a further slice of the advance was paid.

Now, in those days it was *de rigueur* for non-fiction books
dealing with one or other aspect of the 1939–45 war on land to

be submitted for clearance to the War Office. Usually, it was a mere formality. First as a publisher and then as an agent, I must have submitted at least a dozen scripts and, apart from one, they had all been nodded through. The one exception only required the deletion of a short paragraph, which mentioned a weapon still on the secret list.

It was a rude shock, therefore, to receive a crisp, formal letter from a War Office department, stating that not only was *The London Cage* banned in its entirety but the typescript was being impounded as well. I had, of course, read the text carefully and knew it contained nothing that would bring comfort to or increase the military knowledge of a potential enemy. The Edwardian and the Great War episodes were too 'long ago and far away'; the war crimes with which the story dealt – mainly, the Stalag Luft III escape and the massacre in the Ardeatine Caves – had been thoroughly reported in the press. I demanded a meeting at the War Office.

The author and his editor, Stanley Jackson, agreed it would be better for me to go on my own. For one thing, it might hurt our case if the publisher were known to be aware of the situation; and I could talk more freely, do a deal perhaps, if the author were absent. And so I was by myself when shown into a large panelled room on the ground floor of the then War Office. It must have been used as a lecture room, because there was a raised platform at one end and a trio of desks behind each one of which sat three almost identical and interchangeable senior army officers in mufti. I sat alone in the body of the hall, having to look up to the three adjudicators.

I said that the author and, I was sure, his publishers wanted to be completely reasonable. They were, after all, patriots, as indeed I was, and would never, wittingly or unwittingly, wish to harm the United Kingdom. If authority – I nearly said 'MI5' – felt that certain sentences or paragraphs unwittingly breached security, I had my client's assurance that all such references would be deleted at once. Might I, please, have an indication of what was required?

The man in the middle, presumably the senior officer, said, 'You don't seem to grasp the point, Mr Greenfield. The complete text is not to be published. That is all.'

I said, 'The complete text is over 80,000 words in length. Are you telling me that every single word is a breach of security?'

'Let me repeat the point. The book is not to be published.'

I tried to persist. 'But there must be complete chapters that have no bearing on security. His early life, for instance. And all that Great War stuff. Are you really telling me *that* would endanger national security if it is published? Won't you please point out the dangerous passages? We'll gladly have them deleted.'

One of the other men spoke. 'Pointing out the dangerous passages could itself be a breach of security. You and your friends would then be party to secret information.'

His senior colleague cut in. 'I think we have spent enough time on this matter. Thank you for calling on us, Mr Greenfield. The War Office decision is that *The London Cage* by Lieutenant-Colonel A.P. Scotland is not to be published. We are indeed impounding the typescript you submitted and I must warn you that all carbon copies and handwritten notes must be destroyed forthwith. That is all.'

Tony Greenwood, the Labour MP for Rossendale, was a client of mine, who wrote articles for various weekly magazines. I telephoned him the following day and explained what had happened to Colonel Scotland's book. The blatant censorship annoyed him and he happily agreed to raise the matter during Question Time in the House. A few days later, he called me back, not wishing to put a delicate point in writing. He had had a private conversation with Selwyn Lloyd, the Foreign Secretary, as a result of the parliamentary question. Lloyd had told him that HMG was very concerned to have a West German contingent serving in the newly formed NATO. This was not the time to publish a book by an acknowledged authority on German war crimes. A non-existent boat could hardly be rocked.

So that was it. Not for the first time – or the last – in its ignoble twentieth-century history, the Foreign Office was following the motto, 'If you ignore it, it may go away.' Expediency was all that mattered. Don't let's be beastly to the Germans; at least, not when they're raising recruits for

NATO. Pity about old Scotland – but there it is. You can't make an omelette . . . No wonder the War Office/MI5 officials had been defensive and refused to get down to details. There was absolutely nothing in the book that might enlighten the NKVD or, as it was to become, the KGB.

I was due to have a drink that evening with Elliott Macrae, president of E.P. Dutton, the New York publishers, at the Dorchester Hotel where he always stayed. Having first spoken to the colonel, who willingly agreed, I took with me the spare typescript of *The London Cage*. The War Office writ did not run outside the United Kingdom. There was nothing to stop an American publisher's bringing out the book – and I already knew Elliott Macrae welcomed a challenge. Indeed, when I explained the background, he seemed quite interested and I left the script with him.

For all his secret work during the war, Colonel Scotland could be strangely naive. Like many a canny Scot beforehand, he was not displeased with himself and his career, and he enjoyed a good gossip, which might swiftly turn into a monologue where most sentences began with the word 'I'. He probably talked too openly when he had his glass of dry sherry each evening at the local pub or perhaps Special Branch had already put an informer on to him. For whatever reason, Superintendent Smith was now sufficiently concerned to apply for a warrant to 'turn over his drum' and in turn to interrogate me.

He was shortish and fat, with a fair complexion roughened by a countryman's exposure to the sun and the wind and the rain. He had small eyes and his gaze slipped and slid around the room, looking for hiding places, assessing the contents, summing up the occupant's status. I had a packet of cigarettes on my desk, to which he kept on helping himself throughout the interview. He was egregiously, almost insolently, polite, wielding the word 'sir' like a blackjack at the end of most sentences. Along with the obsequious tone, there was a phoney air of comradeship, verging on conspiracy. 'You an' me, sir – we're men of the world, sir. We've seen most things in our time. We could be mates, except you're the officer class I can see, sir, and I'm an other rank.'

He began by formally asking me to hand over the spare typescript. I said it was not in the office and asked him, as a matter of interest, what would happen if I refused to let it go.

'Oh, that wouldn't be clever, sir. My word, no. You see, I'd have to get a warrant and bring in some of my men to search this office of yours. I have to tell you, sir, these young fellas you get in the Force today – they're a clumsy bunch an' no mistake. They'd have to go through all your files – an' I expect you've got some real important ones here, sir, your best authors an' all that. Could be they'd knock over a bottle of ink, right over those important files. Don't worry, sir, I'd make 'em apologise to you – in person, like. But those files wouldn't look too good, no, sir.

'Another thing. Young coppers are so careless these days. They smoke like chimneys – oh thanks, sir, don't mind if I do – an' they don't always stub the fags out proper. Leave 'em burning all over the place. Lot of wood round here, sir, I can see. Make a real little blaze, that would!'

I reached for a cigarette from the rapidly diminishing packet and took my time lighting it. He was playing with me; he knew this game inside out from long practice – as he proved from his next remarks.

'You were in the forces, I reckon, sir. You look a military gent, if I may say so. You remember that old saying, sir, "You can't beat the army." Lots of squaddies tried but where did they end up? In the glasshouse, that's where. It's the same with us, sir. Now I know your firm's got a daybook and a private ledger. It couldn't run without 'em. Under the terms of the warrant, I could impound 'em both. And, like I say, sir, these fellas who work for me can be damn careless. Not the training we went through. Could be – I'm only saying "could be" – those vital files got mislaid or lost forever. Scotland Yard's like a bloody rabbit warren – excuse my language, sir. Things go missing and never turn up again. Of course, you'd get a written apology from a very senior officer – maybe even a Deputy Assistant Commissioner – but it'd be difficult to run your business and hang on to those important clients without the essential files.'

I said, 'Okay, I get the point. You're saying – if I try to play rough, you can play a hell of a sight rougher. Right?'

'You said it, sir, not me.' His tone grew harder. 'It wouldn't have to stop there, either. That nice old Riley of yours, sir. You park it in the road outside your house in Hampstead, don't you? One morning, you might go out to drive off and find the local police had towed it away. The same thing could happen another time. And another time.'

'But there are no parking restrictions in my part of Hampstead.'

'You're right, sir, there aren't. But there's such a thing as obstructing the Queen's highway. Badly parked cars, no lights on at night – they can be a real menace. Like I said before, you can't beat the system. I'm telling you all this for your own good, sir. You made the point just now. We can always play rougher. And anyone gets into our bad books, it's a hell of a time before he gets out again. You follow me, sir?'

I nodded, not trusting myself to voice my feelings.

He continued crisply. 'The colonel told me there's a spare copy with an American publisher. That was naughty of you, sir. With all this pending, you didn't ought to have sent it abroad like that. I'm giving you exactly one week to get it back. At eleven o'clock this day week, I'll expect you at Scotland Yard with that typescript and a signed warranty that no other copies exist. Don't miss that date, sir – otherwise, things could be very awkward for you.' He took one last cigarette from the packet, lit it, stood up and lumbered out of the room.

It was an abject defeat. I had absolutely no doubt that, had I stood up for the 'publish and be damned' principle, he would have carried out his casual threats. And if I had tried to raise the matter with some higher authority, it was only my word against his; even if pinned down, he could always claim to have been trying to be helpful in telling me how clumsy young policemen could be. My only private consolation, a small one, was that he had jumped to the wrong conclusion over the whereabouts of the spare script which, of course, had never left London.

At the handover, there was one other consolation. I was ushered into a ground floor room at Scotland Yard, facing the Embankment and the Thames just beyond. The sun, still quite low in the sky, blazed furiously through the uncurtained window. The room contained a trestle table with nothing on it, two chairs on one side with their backs to the window and one chair on the other side of the table. I was left on my own in the empty room for nearly fifteen minutes – the usual softening-up trick. Then the penny dropped. I took one of the two chairs and moved it round the table to make a pair for the solitary chair. Then I firmly sat down in the remaining one. Through the sun's fierce rays, my head and shoulders cast a deep dark shadow across the wooden table.

At length, Superintendent Smith and a thin bald man who never spoke a word entered the room. I stayed seated. They hesitated, scraped their feet but finally had to occupy the two chairs opposite me. Their faces were caught in a kind of searchlight through the sunshine bouncing off the glittering river, their eyes began to stream as they tried vainly to focus on the dark mass that was my head and shoulders, silhouetted against the translucent windows. I had managed to reverse the childish trick.

Mr Smith did not suffer the discomfort for long. He flicked through the carbon copy of *The London Cage*, to make sure the pages were complete and glanced through my covering letter which stated that there were no other copies in existence. He had to shield his eyes from the sun's questing rays with one stubby hand. Then he stood up to indicate the meeting was at an end. There were no handshakes.

Evans Brothers were magnanimous enough to let Colonel Scotland keep the two-thirds of the advance already paid. Seven or eight years later, under the new Labour government and with further help from Tony Greenwood, who had been elevated to the peerage, a slightly revised version of the book was published with fair success but not to compare with the sales it would have achieved when the vogue for war books was in full swing. Nevertheless, Colonel Scotland, then a very old man who was to die shortly, did not have to suffer posthumous vindication.

Just now and then, the wheel comes full circle. Superintendent Smith, on retirement at the age of sixty, a few years after this episode, decided to write his memoirs. The *Sunday Pictorial* offered him £50,000 – half a million pounds in today's terms – for serial rights. The government, at the instigation of MI5, banned him from revealing his secrets. The deal collapsed.

9

THE MOON AND THE EMPTY HORSES

Every agent has one: the client who rings up several times a week for a cosy chat, either because he needs reassurance – there really is life out there, beyond the desk and the accusingly blank sheet of paper – or, if he is newly published, to celebrate that fact with his guide and friend or, if he is an old hand, to make sure that the bloody agent, who rips off his hard-won earnings, is actually at his desk and not drinking champagne under the gaze of the cherubs at the Ritz. Most of the calls arrive unerringly at the wrong time. Either the agent is genuinely in a long and important meeting or, running late, he is dashing out of the office for a lunch date with a publisher to whom he hopes to sell a book or two, or at half-past six, when with the aid of the office bottle he is letting the rigours of the day wash over him before staggering home.

In 1970, Roderick Mann was the showbusiness correspondent of the *Sunday Express*, which then had a three million circulation and a solid appeal to middle-class, middle-aged readers. The debonair Roddy had many friends among the Hollywood stars and his weekly column was read with relish. He had recently written a witty novel entitled *Foreign Body*, a satirical smack at Harley Street, which I had sold to Cassell's in London and their parent company, Macmillan, in New York.

Although he had written another humorous novel many years earlier, he still felt, I think, the newness of book writing and all the arcane practices of the book trade. Thus he was liable, in the nicest possible way, to spend ten or fifteen minutes at a time on the telephone, asking direct questions, followed by supplementaries. On the day in question, I had several urgent letters to dictate and a large contract to check carefully before it went by hand to an author who was passing through London.

So when my secretary, Veronica, entered my room and said that Mr Mann was on the phone, I asked her to say I was tied up but would call him back. That was at about ten-fifteen. An hour later, he telephoned again. The message was the same – but with the added assurance I would get back to him the moment I was clear. At about twenty to one, yet another phone call. I was on the point of dashing out to lunch, in any case, and I asked Veronica to say I had already left.

At around three o'clock, he called for the fourth time. Veronica, looking mutinous, swept into my room. 'You've just got to speak to the poor man,' she declared. 'Lying on your behalf, I've run out of excuses. It's time you did your own dirty work!'

Abashed, I said, 'Put him through.'

Roddy's voice said in my ear, 'Are you doing anything at six o'clock tonight?'

Oh Lord, I thought. Does he want to corner me over a drink or two and ask more insipid questions? Aloud, I began to say, 'Well, er . . .'

Before I could think of an excuse, he cut in, 'I've been trying to get hold of you all day.'

'I know. I'm so sorry. It's been one of those days.'

'The point is,' he went on, 'David Niven's at the Connaught. He's flying to the States tomorrow afternoon, so a drink tonight's his only free time. You see, he's writing a book and I've told him about you. He wants to meet you.'

'Bless you, Roddy,' I said. 'You're a friend. That's fine – I'd love to meet him.'

'I'll see you there. Six-ish. He always has the same suite on the second floor.'

In the intervening years, I have often lit a metaphorical candle in thanks to Veronica as well. Had she not turned rightly mutinous, I would not have taken Roddy Mann's fourth call. He would almost certainly have given up in disgust and David Niven would very easily have found another agent. The only small consolation over 'the big one that got away' in such circumstances is that the agent who is left with nothing on the end of his line almost never discovers what he has missed.

David Niven had been having a not-so-quiet drink of champagne with his friend John Mortimer when I arrived. He was taller, broader in the shoulder and looked physically stronger than his screen image. And, like so many actors, he had the endearing knack of appearing to concentrate totally on his immediate audience. That facility, coupled with those deliberate gestures, shuffling the knot of his tie, running a forefinger between his collar and his neck, presented him in his favourite guise – the man who was always either put upon or put down. No one has ever matched him as the teller of funny stories but the punchline almost invariably showed him as the butt. His childhood had been a sad one, thanks to his uncaring stepfather, and at Stowe he courted popularity by being a professional silly idiot, the form prankster who was bound to be caught out. Joining the regular army, he served as a junior officer in the Highland Light Infantry in the early 1930s. But his career did not prosper – there was apparently an affair with the wife of a naval officer – and he was given the choice of resigning his commission, which he took, or being cashiered.

Some while later, when we knew each other well, I was able to tell him the outcome of a story he told in *The Moon's a Balloon*. I had heard it from Lieutenant-Colonel H.L. Percival, DSO, a contemporary of his in the HLI, who early in the Battle of Alamein was transferred as CO of Second Battalion The Buffs because our previous colonel had been blown up in a bren carrier. Hugh Percival had attended the regimental farewell dinner for David Niven, who in his book tells how his own CO, who hated his guts, spoke of his imminent ruin and then asked him gloatingly what he intended to do when he was back in Civvy Street.

Niven responded to the challenge. He stood up and said he was going straight to Hollywood. In a few years, they would see his name up in lights. The whole mess, majors, captains and subalterns, roared with laughter: typical of young Niv, full of jokes right up to the last.

The aftermath, which I told him, was thus. Not many years later, when the HLI battalion had finished its posting in Malta and was back in the United Kingdom, that same CO and the battalion adjutant were walking across Leicester Square to the Army and Navy Club after seeing a show in the West End. The colonel, no doubt musing on the world of entertainment, paused and said, 'I wonder whatever happened to young Niven?'

The adjutant nudged his arm and pointed silently towards the front of the vast Empire Theatre. There, spelled out in the brightest of bright electric light bulbs above the title were the names 'ERROL FLYNN' and 'DAVID NIVEN', and underneath them *THE DAWN PATROL*.

On that first occasion, with much collar-easing and tie-adjusting, he agreed to hand over the first 20,000 words of the 'ghastly little book' friends like Roddy had persuaded him to try. My heart sank a little when he said it was handwritten but I need not have worried. His bold copperplate was easily readable and I devoured the sample at home that night. On the telephone next morning before his departure for Heathrow, I assured him of my genuine pleasure over both the pathos and the wit – in the latter case, particularly that wonderful scene when the 'boy David' dogs the footsteps of the prostitute and hampers her business. He kept on asking if I was just being polite and I kept on protesting that I fully meant what I said. At length, he accepted my praise and appointed me his agent.

In spite of his acting commitments, the book developed steadily and, from my besotted viewpoint, was getting better and better as it went along. David had charmed a secretary at the Connaught Hotel to make typed copies from his handwritten version in her spare time. There were, however, a few non-literary problems. Almost twenty years earlier, he had written a novel entitled *Round the Rugged Rocks*, which had been published by Cresset Press, later absorbed into the Bodley Head. It was a highly autobiographical novel; indeed it covered the same territory and the same episodes as the almost finished *The Moon's a Balloon*. Through ignorance, David tended to pooh-pooh the matter. After all, *Rocks* had been out of print all this time and was long forgotten. Why drag it up again? When I discovered that publication rights had never reverted to him, I felt there could be a double problem. There might be grounds for an action for plagiarism from the publishers. In addition, the Cresset Press contract almost certainly contained a clause granting them the option on his next full-length work. David had lost his file copy years before and if he were at this late date suddenly to ask for a new copy from the Bodley Head, suspicions would at once arise.

It would be equally suspicious if, as his agent, I were to write on his behalf and ask for the publishing rights in *Round the Rugged Rocks* to revert to him. Why all this sudden – and professional – interest in a forgotten piece of fiction? In the end, I concocted a deliberately naive letter for David to sign; he was thinking of drawing up a new will and had been advised to get his affairs in order first. One loose end was the publishing agreement for that ancient book of his. He would never allow such a juvenile piece of work ever to be reprinted and it had been out of print for many years. So would the Bodley Head be kind enough to drop him a brief note, letting him have his publishing rights back? (There was no mention, of course, of the new book that was almost finished.)

Like the gentlemanly firm they usually were, the Bodley Head agreed to his request. I had hardly taken a deep breath of relief when another problem presented itself. Although as tough as rawhide when terms were to be discussed, David had one thing in common with that girl in *Annie Get Your Gun*. He couldn't say no. Over the years, various publishers, including his old friend and fellow member of White's, Jamie Hamilton, had written to say they would be delighted to publish his memoirs. The reply was invariable: each publisher was assured that, if he ever got down to the task, that publisher would head the list of candidates. Now the promises were about to be called in. There was not a little acerbic correspondence and telephoned cries of 'Foul!' and in the end I had to invoke the first come, first served formula, which favoured Hamish Hamilton.

Many years later, Niven showed me two letters from his friend, Jamie, that shrewd publisher. The first, written some long time before *The Moon's a Balloon* had been started, expressed the keen wish to publish any book the actor might care to write, with the proviso – 'but please, whatever you do, never write a book about Hollywood.' After *The Moon*'s enormous success, Jamie wrote to him again to say how gratified he was. He added, 'But please, never, never write *another* book about Hollywood.' Niven's next was, of course, *Bring on the Empty Horses*, which enjoyed almost as big a success as *The Moon*. That year, he thought of having a Christmas card printed which would reproduce Jamie Hamilton's first proviso on the front, with the worldwide sales figures of *The Moon* on the reverse and Jamie's second proviso on the inside page with the *Empty Horses*' sales results on the back page. Hamilton, as chairman for life of his publishing house, which he had sold to Roy Thomson in 1965, was then approaching eighty and his sense of humour had not expanded with age. Charitable friends prevailed on David to think again.

So the firm of Hamish Hamilton won the British and Commonwealth volume rights in *The Moon's a Balloon* for an advance of £7,500 – in today's terms, worth about £55,000. It was quite a brave offer, particularly as there was no paperback support at that stage. Up to that time, twenty years ago, no film actor or actress had gone into print with a personal story aimed at the general reader. There had indeed been heavily illustrated biographies in paperback, expanded from fan-magazine articles or studio handouts, but no first-person, in-depth memoirs. David Niven was to start a fashion that continues to this day.

To recoup at least part of their sizeable advance, the publishers needed to sell paperback rights long before their own hardcover publication. Roger Machell, the most senior director after Jamie Hamilton himself, took on the responsibility, conscientiously pursuing all the reprint houses with early proof copies. But nobody came to bid. Clarence Paget of Pan Books telephoned me and patronisingly suggested that the first third or so of the book was quite interesting – Niven's childhood, schooldays and unfortunate military experiences – but that the last two-thirds, dealing with Hollywood, was 'terribly boring'. If the author would agree to tearing the book in two, Pan would publish the first part on its own and pay an advance of £500. I told Clarence to get lost. Machell was in full agreement when I reported the incident.

A week or so later, he called me. There was one offer on the table; it was from Coronet Books, the paperback subsidiary of Hodder & Stoughton, and the terms were an advance of £500 against a flat 7½ per cent of the published price on home sales and 7½ per cent of the price received on exported copies.

I said, 'Oh, for Heaven's sake, Roger. David'll never accept a miserable five hundred quid – half of which goes to you, anyway! Can't you push 'em up to a thousand? Four figures begin to look a shade more respectable.'

Within twenty-four hours, Roger Machell called me again. Philip Evans, the editorial director of Coronet, would increase the advance to £750 – but that was that. If we wanted a penny more or a ½ per cent increase in the royalty rates, would we please go and look elsewhere? Roger answered my unspoken question by adding he was convinced Phil Evans was not bluffing. The paperback grapevine, as he and I well knew, was strong and sinuous. You could be sure Phil knew his was the only bid in town. After a lot of arguing – he was inclined to toss the Coronet offer away as beneath his dignity – I managed to persuade David to accept it on the grounds that an advance was only an advance; if the paperback edition did well enough, as, swallowing hard, I was certain it would, the royalty income would continue to flow in.

The story had a happy ending. Eighteen months to two years later, when the Hamish Hamilton edition had sold well over 100,000 copies and the Coronet paperback was approaching a two-million copy sale – it was eventually to sell in excess of three million – Phil Evans rang me one afternoon. He was, he said, feeling terribly embarrassed over *The Moon's a Balloon*. The advance was now laughably academic, thank goodness, but here was one of the biggest selling paperback books of all time with a flat 7½ per cent royalty, the kind of rate an absolute beginner might expect. Did I think my client would accept if the rate was increased – *retrospectively* – to 10 per cent?

Phil and I were (and still are) good friends. I have to admit that the first thought crossing my mind was an unworthy one. He must still be enjoying the afterglow of an excellent lunch. Who ever heard of a publisher, who was legally entitled to pay a modest royalty to an author, of his own free will offering to raise that royalty by one-third and then go further by backdating the increase to the first copy sold? But, as he went on talking, my long-held belief in the truth of Lord Byron's comment about Barabbas' being a publisher began to crumble. Phil was sincere in his offer, which had the backing of the Hodder & Stoughton main board.

David Niven was very touched when I told him the news. He was inured to the Hollywood system where, in Samuel Goldwyn's phrase, an oral agreement wasn't worth the paper it was printed on and lawyers gnawed their way through contracts like a pack of rats in the sewers. Apart from the extra money, which would work out at over £150,000, it was the dramatic generosity of the gesture that appealed to the actor in him. Up to that point, every time he flew into Heathrow from his summer home in Cap d'Antibes or his winter home in Château d'Oeix, Switzerland, he would scrutinise the bookshelves and get me to castigate Hamish Hamilton or Coronet if copies of their respective editions were not on sale. From then on, Coronet was exempted from blame.

A year or two afterwards, Phil Evans had a terrible car accident when driving in the pouring rain in Gower Street. For sixteen weeks he lay in a coma at University College Hospital, while his many friends in relays sat around his bed and talked to his unresponding form. He eventually regained consciousness and through his indomitable will gradually taught himself to function again, although for many months after being discharged from hospital he was largely confined to his home in Fulham. On his visits to London, David Niven tended to pack in an appointment 'every hour on the hour' but he always found time to hire a chauffeur-driven car to take him to Fulham to spend the afternoon with Phil. He kept the visits private and I only found out about them from a chance remark dropped by Phil himself.

But I must retrace my steps and deal with another débâcle associated with *The Moon's a Balloon* – the American rights. With the British hardcover and paperback rights stowed away, although Hamish Hamilton's initial publication was still months ahead and with a £10,000 offer for first serial rights from the *People* – the so-called 'quality' Sunday papers no doubt still thought that actors should be whipped from parish to parish – I was looking for fresh worlds to conquer. A battle-plan was drawn up and approved by the author. I would airmail one copy of the bulky typescript, which ran to about 500 pages, to New York where our reciprocating agency, Paul R. Reynolds & Son, could have a further seven copies xeroxed. I had already drawn up an agreed list of seven New York houses and one Bostonian. When the copies were ready, I would fly over to New York and hand-deliver them to my chosen targets. To promote a sense of urgency, I was going to tell each one that I intended to remain in their city for a further ten days and would then board an aircraft home. The auction would be automatically closed.

In the eighteen months or so since I had first met him, David Niven's warmth and wit had proved appealing. And I was genuinely taken with the book itself. He had managed to get the rhythms and vocabulary of his speaking voice into his writing; the wry self-knocking of his anecdotes was also a refreshing change from the 'I am the greatest' air which one then associated with the stars of the Hollywood system. In fact, I had come to like Niven and his book very much, which may well have tinted my views of its potential success a more rosy colour. Ideally – and in my long experience it is only an ideal – an agent's feelings towards his clients and their output should be neutral and objective. Geese may each have a beak and feathers and two wings and two webbed feet – but they are not swans. Anyway, I had airily suggested to David that in order to keep the poor or the not wildly enthusiastic away from the door, we should establish a 'floor price'. No bids below a certain figure would be entertained. The figure was to be $35,000, then worth nearly £30,000.

My first target was an obvious one: Michael Korda. Not only was he editor-in-chief at Simon & Schuster with its aggressive sales force and imaginative promotional schemes but he was also the nephew of Sir Alexander Korda of London Films, in more than one of whose productions Niven had appeared. So I had arranged to see Michael as my first appointment on my first working day. Lugging the heavy script with me, I entered his office on the umpteenth floor of their then offices, almost opposite St Patrick's Cathedral on Fifth Avenue. I knew that, as a further bonus, Michael Korda had been educated in England, sounded English and understood the self-deprecatory sense of humour far better than most Americans. The omens were good. The fact he was wearing jodhpurs and had a weird collection of headgear, including a Foreign Legion képi, a bowler hat, a British policeman's helmet and a cowboy's hat on various shelves on a side wall of his office, only gave him an added feeling of British eccentricity.

I set the thick rectangular package down on his otherwise unadorned desk and launched into my sales patter. This was one of the most extraordinary books to come my way. Apart from the world-wide appeal of the author's name, the book itself was full of great stories, featuring other such famous names as Errol Flynn, Sam Goldwyn, Marion Davies, Clark Gable, Ronald Colman – indeed, almost all of that galaxy of stars that had lighted up Hollywood for the past forty years. It was – slight pause for an imaginary roll on the drums – David Niven's autobiography.

Michael Korda, short, slight, bespectacled, slowly raised his eyebrows. 'Niven is an old, ham, British actor,' he pronounced.

'Oh come on, Michael, he's a big star.'

'He's never played better than second lead. Hasn't made a big movie in years.'

I decided to change tack. There was no percentage in discussing the many films David had made and his respective status in them. I said, 'He's been promised the lead on the

Johnnie Carson Show and the Merv Griffin Show and a spot
on the Today Show.'

The world-weary eyebrows slowly ascended again. 'They
all say that. It never happens.'

The only thing left was a personal appeal. 'Michael, will you
do something for me? Read the first thirty pages – that's all. If
you aren't hooked by the first thirty pages, okay, fair enough.
But my guess is, once there, you'll want to read on.'

Cinéastes will recall that dramatic scene in *The Informer*
where Victor Maclaglan has betrayed Sinn Fein for cash and
the British officer does not want to soil his hands by actually
touching the pieces of gold, the sovereigns. And so, with the
tip of his swagger cane, he pushes the heap of money across his
desk while Maclaglan twists his cap in his giant hands. Michael
Korda had no swagger cane – a pity, he should have switched
his hat-collecting fetish to types of walking stick – so, using the
back of his knuckles and his fingernails, he gently prodded the
bulky typescript towards my side of the table.

'I wouldn't read the first three pages,' he declared. 'Sheer
waste of time. I repeat – Niven is a ham, old, British actor. The
book may go down on your side but here it spells disaster.'

Although none of my other visits was quite as bleak, *The
Moon* did not rise high in the New York sky. Several houses
claimed that the asking price of $35,000 deterred them; they
did not want to insult me or my author by putting up a
modest bid. Undeterred by that aspect, Norton bid $10,000,
as did William Morrow. Atlantic Monthly Press, a small,
distinguished Boston house, whom I did not expect to bid
at all, surprised me with an offer of $15,000. At last, by weary
stages, the top bid emerged at $17,500 from Putnam's. The
wife of John Dodds, the senior Putnam editor concerned,
had been an actress of some note, whose career culminated
in her playing the role of the blonde foil in *I Love Lucy*. She
had known Niven slightly in Hollywood, thought his book a
winner and encouraged her husband to bid.

By then, I had dropped the *hauteur* of a $35,0000 'floor'.
The eight members of the auction had been hand-picked. If
none of them would offer even as much as two-thirds of the
asking price, the next eight down the scale were most unlikely

to bid up. Time was slipping away; I was due to fly back to London in another two days. If I could only persuade John Dodds to increase his offer to $25,000, the gap might just be acceptable to my client. He went up to $20,000 without too much bother and, after consulting the redoubtable owner of the firm, Walter Minton, crept as high as $22,500 – but that was it. Not a cent more. If I pressed any harder, the offer would only be withdrawn. I knew Dodds too well to even hope he might be bluffing.

I had arranged to telephone David Niven in Switzerland on my last night in New York. Feeling utterly miserable, I did so. There must have been an electric storm in the Alps because the line crackled and spluttered and went faint at times. Bellowing away, I gave him a rundown on the results of the auction, mentioning twice that the top bid was from Putnam's at $22,500.

I had expected him to get either angry or sarcastic but he was calm, almost benevolent, saying it was quite close to our agreed figure. There, I thought, grace under pressure – no wonder the man had been a member of No. 4 Commando in the war, and had done secret and daring tasks for General Montgomery during the Second Front. He went on to say that as a matter of principle we should reject the Putnam offer. Although close to our figure, it was still beneath it.

With several repetitions because of the dreadful line, I urged him to accept the offer. From a publishing aspect, New York was a booksy little village. It would be known all over that I had come to auction his memoirs. If I went away empty-handed, the general view would be that there was something wrong with the book. Hamish Hamilton were due to publish in the UK in a few months' time. It was imperative to sell the American rights before then. We would have lost impetus; Americans hated bringing out a book months after it had appeared in Britain because that would give the British publisher a clear run at the Continental open market. And so on. Somehow, my vehemence, coupled with the Wagnerian thunderstorms rolling round the Alps, won him over. He told me to go ahead and clinch with Putnam's.

As soon as I was back at my desk in London, I telephoned

John Dodds with the good news. And then, as I always did, I
sent an airmail letter confirming the details, with a blind copy
to David. Dodds was a man of honour but even someone in
that select category can fall under a Madison Avenue bus.

Two days later, I received a telephone call from my client.
This time, unfortunately, the line was crystal clear; his screams
of rage penetrated my skull. What the hell was I playing at? I
had distinctly said $32,500 on the phone from New York. He
was not going to accept a piddling offer like $22,500. How
could I have had the nerve even to put it to him? Get on to
Putnam's at once and tell 'em to go to hell and take their offer
with them.

'George, I clearly heard you say thirty-two thousand five
hundred dollars. Not just once but twice. Even then, I wanted
to turn it down but you persuaded me. Twenty-two thousand
five hundred – I wouldn't even have looked at it! You tell 'em
to stuff it. I don't accept their dreary little sum. That's all there
is to it.'

I said, 'Look, David, I'm terribly sorry. You obviously
misheard me with that terrible line. But I definitely said
twenty-two thousand five hundred. And after we'd discussed
the whole shooting match, you agreed I should accept. So I've
just gone ahead and done it.'

'Well, damn well undo it then.'

'But I've given my word – and yours.'

The silence lasted several seconds. Then he said, 'All right,
let it go ahead. But I'm telling you, George – another slip like
that on your part and you're out.'

I apologised again, although in retrospect I cannot see why
I should have done so. It was hardly my fault that atmospheric
conditions had caused him to mishear the figures. Even so, I
made him a sporting offer. If the ultimate earnings of *The
Moon* in the States fell short of $32,500, I would make up
the difference out of my own pocket. Allowing for agent's
commission, that meant my maximum loss could amount to
$9,000, at that time rather more than £7,000. I did not have
that kind of money lying around in my current account.

There was little cause for anxiety. On publication there,
Niven swept across the United States on a triumphant tour,

almost a royal progress. In spite of Michael Korda's gloomy prophecy, he *did* appear with top billing on the Johnnie Carson and the Merv Griffin Shows – and on the Today Show. The reviews were mainly cordial, apart from a vicious one in the *New York Times*; the reviewer wondered whether on gazing into his shaving mirror each morning Niven ever saw anything. Putnam's sold nearly 200,000 copies of their hardcover edition and sold the paperback rights for over $350,000. Korda's sister firm, Pocket Books, bid up to that figure – but were outbid. If he had had the perception to read the first thirty pages of the typescript, Simon & Schuster and Pocket Books could have had the chance of sharing all the rights for one-tenth of that sum. (Michael was perhaps a shade less dogmatic in his pronouncements at our subsequent meetings.) All in all, David Niven made about three-quarters of a million dollars from the American rights. The present-day sterling equivalent would be close on £3 million.

This is the moment perhaps to explain his views on taxation. When the war broke out in September 1939, his Hollywood career was building nicely. The climate was good, he had made many friends locally and America would remain at peace for more than another two years. He gave it all up and hastened back to Britain to enlist in the army. He could have kept his head down and enjoyed the sunshine and the prospect of good acting parts in safety for the next five or six years, as James Mason and a few other Britons did. For his sacrifice, he was greeted not with a cheer but with an Inland Revenue demand for unpaid taxes amounting to £30,000 – nearly £1 million in today's terms. Even when his friend, Winston Churchill – whose tax planning when he came to write his own memoirs was far more effective – tried to intervene, the Inland Revenue was adamant. David Niven's patriotism left him penniless, trying to exist on army pay for the next five years. He took a solemn vow with himself, he told me, that if he survived the war, never again would he contribute to the British exchequer.

And he kept that vow. He spent the first few years after the war resident in Hollywood and subject to United States taxation, far less than the 83 per cent prevailing in his homeland. Then he established permanent residence in the Swiss canton of Vaud and set up a Swiss corporation to which he assigned his services as an actor and later the copyrights in his books. As a keen skier and swimmer, he divided his time between his chalet at Château d'Oeix, where he spent rather more than the six winter months in order to maintain Swiss residence, and his villa in the south of France at Cap Ferrat. Under UK tax laws, if a British subject owns no property in the United Kingdom and spends one complete year out of the country, he or she is not liable to local tax, provided that the country of permanent residence has a tax-exemption arrangement with the UK – as France and Switzerland have. Indeed, as time goes by, the individual may spend up to a total of 182 days each year on visits to this country without incurring any tax penalty. When I first met him in 1970, David Niven was in that happy position.

After his death, several of his obituarists wondered why, as an actor of some distinction with a fine war record, he had never received any form of decoration or honour. Rumour has it that any member of the 'great and the good' class has to pay his annual dues – his taxes – before becoming eligible. Rex Harrison, with homes first in Portofino and later in New York, had to become an octogenarian and find himself a British address before getting his knighthood. If the rumour is true, it has a certain logic; why should eminent people who do not directly support their country receive honours and awards from it? The only irony is that the fount of all such titles and decorations should herself have been a non-taxpayer for most of her life.

Unlike many of his subsequent imitators, David's two volumes of memoirs strictly avoided all 'kiss and tell' aspects. This was due, no doubt, partly to breeding and partly to that old-fashioned notion that what went on between the sheets was a private matter between the two persons concerned. His modesty in print was all the more remarkable because, during his pre-war bachelor days and in that period between marriages after his first wife Primula died in a tragic party accident, he was held to be a pre-eminent swordsman in the fencing salons of sex. Roger Moore, himself a witty raconteur almost in the same class, used to tell an anecdote illustrating that reputation.

As near neighbours, Prince Rainier and David Niven had become warm friends but fell out over some minor tiff, which developed into weeks of silence on both sides. Each of them was missing the other's company but was too proud to make the first overture. At last, a message came from the royal palace in Monaco, suggesting they should bury the hatchet and dine together at a favourite *bistro* in the Old Port at Cannes. David accepted.

He took a few preliminary drinks to ease his nervousness and was well away when he greeted his princely friend. They had another bottle or two of champagne to celebrate the reunion and both were fairly maudlin as the evening progressed.

David said, 'Rainier, ol' buddy, I envy you from the bottom of my heart. You're an absolute monarch. You say, "Off with his head" and – bingo! – it's off. That's power all right.'

'Not nowadays,' Rainier answered. 'that might have been so in olden days but not now. *You're* the one I envy. All those women in Hollywood. Flinging themselves at you. Tell me, David, of all the hundreds you must have had, which one made the biggest impression on you?'

'S'easy,' David said, his head floating but with a suspicion of alertness tethering it. 'The best little hoover in the whole of Hollywood was Grace . . . Gracie Fields!'

There are two phases in the successful publication of a book. They are the writing and the selling. As Jeffrey Archer put it it to me in an interview, 'I could see that few authors were professional about publicity. Agents were professional, publishing houses were professional, authors imagined that when they handed the book in, that was it. I believe you are exactly half way when you have handed the book in. Any author who does not realise that is either a snob or a fool – he can take his choice.'

On that basis, David Niven was a real professional. Jamie Hamilton decided to throw a party in the week before publication of *The Moon's a Balloon* for members of his own staff, reviewers and some of the senior buyers from W.H. Smith, John Menzies, Hatchards and others. He hired a private room at the Savoy. My office was only a short walk away and Niven, who had various points to discuss, called there first. On the way, he asked if I knew the various book buyers who would be there. I said I probably knew some of them but, anyway, you could always tell book buyers at a publishing party. They congregated in a corner and talked gossip non-stop.

He said, 'Look, I'll spend a few minutes being civil to Jamie and his boys and girls. If you wouldn't mind hanging about? Then I'll mosey over and you can point out the buyers. Okay?'

It worked out exactly as he planned. He was his witty and debonair self, thanking Jamie graciously for all he had done, cracking a joke with Roger Machell, flirting outrageously with the lady copy-editor and generally being the life and soul of the party for five minutes or so. Then, saying he really ought to circulate – 'among my fans, ha-ha' – he sidled over to me. I was able to point out the book buyers, who really had grouped themselves in a corner, and David sauntered over, doing his adjustment-of-the tie exercise and introducing himself. For the next twenty minutes and more, there were roars of laughter coming from that corner as he poured out jokes and anecdotes and flattery. I heard him say, 'Yours must be a wonderful job – I do envy you. All that power. Able to make or break a book. And I guess you have to be terribly shrewd to know in advance what will take off and what will flop. Fabulous.' You could see them swelling with pride. Roger Machell told me the following week that the buyers present at the party had more than doubled their orders in the next few days.

Again, when he arrived in New York to promote the American edition, Walter Minton and the other senior executives of Putnam's greeted him when he stepped out of the elevator at 200 Madison Avenue. Before they could take him off to the boardroom for drinks, he asked if they could give him a few minutes. They must have thought he wanted to use the lavatory, but he asked the receptionist where the workers hung out and was shown to the post room. Expertly, he chatted up the staff, discovered their first names and learned items of their personal lives before he rejoined the boardroom celebrations. From then on, every time he called at the office, he would pop his head round the door of the post room and say, 'Hi, Sadie, all okay? Hope your mother's lumbago is improving' and similar things to the other inmates.

There were, I am sure, genuinely decent motives behind his behaviour. He had been an outcast long enough in his youth to know the effect of a friendly remark or gesture from someone senior – not least a famous film star. And in any event he was predisposed to liking the human race. But there was also a streak of self-advantage in his act, as was later proved. John Dodds, his editor, told me months afterwards that at five o'clock, closing time at Putnam's, on a wet weekday, there was an urgent message from the 'Good Morning, America' Show, one of the two biggest breakfast-time television shows in the United States. If a copy of *The Moon's a Balloon* could be rushed to them at once for the editor to 'gut' overnight, David Niven would be interviewed in the lead spot the following morning. Every single occupant of the post room, along with some junior secretaries Niven had chatted up, volunteered to take the book to the studio, Dodds said.

In England, the best and most famous launch-pad for his three published books was the Michael Parkinson Show, one of the most popular programmes of its day. Playing his role of the down-to-earth, no-nonsense, Yorkshire tyke, Parkinson was the perfect foil for the sophisticated, man-about-town air which was Niven's public persona. Even the gruff baritone of the one blended well with the upper-class tenor of the other. And Parkinson was clever enough – and humble enough – when Niven was in full flow with his anecdotes to give him his head and merely feed him another opportunity if the flow momentarily slackened. The show was televised live late on a Saturday evening. On the first occasion, at the launching of *Moon*, BBC2 was due to close at midnight but Niven was still going strong after a full hour and whoever was in charge of the programme had the wit not to pull the plug. The millions of viewers watched and listened, enchanted, until close on one in

the morning. On the Tuesday and Wednesday of the following
week, repeat orders from the bookshops poured into the Great
Russell Street offices of Hamish Hamilton.

In spite of the extraordinary writing success he plunged
into, David Niven did not rush to exploit the new medium.
Another four years passed before the sequel, *Bring on the
Empty Horses*, was published and then another six before
the novel *Go Slowly, Come Back Quickly* appeared. And it
was not for want of pushing on my part. His film career had
declined once he could no longer play dashing young heroes
and, although he had scored some individual successes in
Separate Tables and the first of the *Pink Panther* films, during
the 1970s, the final decade of his acting career, he appeared in
many bad to indifferent films. It was not as though the acting
side brought in the bulk of his income. Each of his books
probably earned him at least four or five times as much as
any one film he made in the same period.

The answer was – clubbability. As that *New York Times*
reviewer shrewdly suspected, David Niven needed to reflect
off other people. Writing is notoriously the lonely art. The
empty room, the desk, the chair, the blank sheet of paper –
no one else can help the writer at that moment of truth. Even
if he dictates the words into a machine, he ends up talking to
himself. For the first time round, it was a novelty for Niven
and he had the added incentive of writing about a place and
a time he loved. Thereafter, it became a chore. At the end of
it all was the carrot of success, bestseller lists, TV interviews,
crowded signing parties and to be the focus of attention but
for him it became increasingly difficult to write in the summer
when the sun was sparkling off the Mediterranean or in winter
when the snow was crisp and powdery on the *pistes*.

Making a movie was so different. You were never left
alone with your thoughts. At the worst, there were always
technicians around to share a joke and hear a new anecdote.
After over forty years of making dozens of films, there were
almost certain to be actors and actresses in the cast with whom
you had worked before. Relaxing over drinks in the evening,
there was all that catching up to do – who was sleeping with
whom, was X's marriage really on the rocks, was it true

that . . .? David Niven had by then become a well-loved uncle figure in the movie world. Ever since pre-war Hollywood in the 1930s, his good manners, genuine modesty and sporting ability had made him popular and towards the end of his career, he had out-soared the shadow of envy and calumny. Patrick McNee – John Steed of *The Avengers* – whose wit and breeding resembled Niven's, once told me how on location in India when making *The Sea-Wolf*, virtually Niven's last film, the much older man had befriended him and had gone out of his way to make him feel at home.

David used to vie with his friend William Buckley, the American writer, over which of them could come up with the most inappropriate and meaningless title. The *Moon's a Balloon* is a quotation from an e.e.cummings poem. The title of the sequel derived from an instruction by Michael Curtiz, the Hungarian-born film director who made *The Charge of The Light Brigade*. He wanted to indicate the carnage of the battle by showing a line of riderless horses crossing the skyline. His command of English was flawed and he shouted, 'Bring on the empty horses!' The last published book, a novel, drew its title from a remark made by a West Indian nanny who had grown to love the Niven family during their stay on the island. As they waved goodbye on their departure, she called out, 'Go slowly, come back quickly.' There was to have been a fourth book, a suspense novel, but the author only lived to complete less than a quarter of it in draft. In earlier years, I had often jokingly quoted him that old publishing trade saying, 'Books that don't get finished don't get published.' Had I then realised how true that was to prove in his case, I would have urged him even more to keep his head down over the writing desk.

The last American contract I negotiated for him was very different from the first. He had fallen out with Putnam's, his original publishers on that side, on the grounds that they had settled a 'nuisance suit' without first consulting him. There is a charming and rather pathetic little scene in *Bring on the Empty Horses* in which a high-class brothel is run upstairs in a private house. The madame's little daughter sits, playing with her dolls, at the foot of the stairs and the famous film stars descending, in both senses of the verb, often pause to ruffle her hair or join in the game with the toys. Some weeks after the book's appearance Putnam's received a letter from a lawyer acting on behalf of a woman who purported to be the daughter, now grown up, claiming damages on the grounds that she was identifiable and thus had been brought into 'ridicule and contempt'.

The legal action had little or no merit. The book does not mention the name of the madame or the address of her house. There could have been – and perhaps were – a dozen different establishments of that kind spread around Beverly Hills, each with its small girl playing with her dolls. But Putnam's took a pragmatic view. By the time they had consulted their own expensive New York lawyers, had sworn affidavits and perhaps hired private detectives to investigate the claimant 3,000 miles away and then the expense of fighting the case in Los Angeles, it would be far cheaper to settle out of court. Which they did – for $5,000. The first David heard of it was when his next royalty statement contained a debit of $2,500, half the cost of settlement. It was a legitimate charge under the contract, except that the publisher should not have acted unilaterally.

David was furious. He had always held that nuisance suits were a particularly unpleasant form of blackmail. Moreover, he had a ferocious New York lawyer named Lee Steiner. As he said to me, 'If only Lee had had the chance of handling the case. He'd have had the other side screaming for mercy and even paying some money themselves – just to be shot of him!' But all he could do to register his dissatisfaction with Putnam's behaviour was to leave them: a strong enough rebuff.

So for what was to be his final American contract, although we could not then have realised it, I had to deal with Sam Vaughan, a genial vice-president of Doubleday. David and I had worked out a small ploy beforehand. I told Sam that I was looking for a two-book contract with a $1 million advance, to be pooled between the two. Sam, as a proper publisher should, tried hard to persuade me to accept a lesser sum but I stuck and stuck to the magic seven figures until at least we seemed to have reached an agreement.

High up over Park Avenue, Sam, a big man, stretched an

arm across his desk. 'Okay,' he said, 'a million bucks. It's a deal. Shake?'

'No,' I said, 'it's not a deal.' He looked at me thunderstruck. I went on, 'I want one million and five bucks. That's the deal.'

'But why the extra five?'

'So that whenever one of his chums asks him what he got, he can always say, "More than a million dollars." Okay?'

'Hell,' said Sam, 'let's not be pikers. Let's make it a million and fifty.'

The first book under the Doubleday contract was to be *Go Slowly, Come Back Quickly*. As usual, the British edition was published a month earlier by Hamish Hamilton, so that the author could complete the local publicity launch before flying to the States and repeating the performance there. Also as usual, the highlight of the British promotion was to be his appearance on the Michael Parkinson programme on the Saturday night before publication. The Parkinson interviews for the first two books had each been exceptional, crackling with prime Niven anecdotes, cleverly set off by the host's questions. The very big audience no doubt expected the third to be best of all.

But it was not to be. David seemed strangely ill at ease. As I watched the screen, I could tell that this was not the professional diffidence, the oft-rehearsed act of the supremely confident man pretending to be shy. He stammered, there were half-finished sentences and long pauses; twice, he missed the punchline in an anecdote. He also appeared to be in some physical discomfort. He was sweating and his shirt collar really did seem too tight. Had I not known that he, always the true pro, never drank anything stronger than lemonade in the hospitality suite before appearing on television, I would have reckoned he was the worse for drink.

He telephoned me at home on the Sunday evening. He said, 'Did you watch the show last night?' I said yes. 'It was pretty bloody awful, wasn't it?'

Again, I said yes. There was no point in prevaricating, being polite.

Then he told me a strange story. He got back to his suite

at the Connaught after eleven o'clock and poured himself a glass of champagne from the drinks cabinet. He felt rotten, both because he knew he had been a flop and because of great physical weariness. His strength seemed to be draining away and a feeling of lassitude taking its place. Just then, he noticed that an envelope had been pushed under his door. He picked it up, saw it was addressed to him and removed the letter. Then he opened the door and looked up and down the corridor. There was no one in sight.

The letter, he told me, read something like this:

Dear Mr Niven,

Forgive a stranger's intrusion but I watched you on television tonight. You were clearly not your usual happy self, if I may say. My husband and I are guests at the hotel, and I was a trained nurse before marriage. It seemed to me from your performance that you might have suffered a minor heart attack. Several of the symptoms were present. In any case, I do strongly recommend you to have a thorough medical check-up at the earliest opportunity.

Yours sincerely,

After he had read the letter over to me, he gave a bit of a giggle – the Niven trademark – and said it was a nice sort of letter to get when down in the dumps. I said I was sure she meant well but could not imagine there was anything wrong with his heart. And I meant the remark. He was a spry and athletic seventy-one-year-old, who watched his diet carefully and who kept himself in trim by vigorous swimming in the summer and cross-country skiing in the winter.

David had already decided to follow the stranger's advice. He attended the Mayo Clinic on arriving in New York for the second leg of the publicity tour. There he was diagnosed as being in the early stages of motor neurone disease, which at the time, 1981, was almost completely unknown to laymen – and to most doctors as well. Apparently, it attacks the nerve-ends at the extremities of the body and gradually works towards the centre. There is no recognised cure.

Generous-hearted Sam Vaughan, who by now had developed a warm friendship with David, wanted him to cancel the coast-to-coast American tour but he was equally firm to keep his promises. Finally, there was a compromise and the tour concentrated on a few main centres which included Chicago, San Francisco and Los Angeles, apart from the starting-line in New York. David had plenty of rest-periods between public appearances. Even so, the stress of the arena, added to the secret knowledge that he was in the early grip of an incurable disease, took its toll. When I saw him again, soon after his return, I was struck by the realisation that his body, which had never carried surplus weight, seemed much leaner and his face more lined.

He had less than two years to live. The growing irony was that, as the disease attacked his vocal chords, his voice, that precious instrument which by an inflection or a modulation could raise an anecdote to a small work of art, was gradually rendered into a succession of dalek-like sounds. But his sense of humour was never defeated. He once said to me on the telephone, while it was still just possible to make out individual words from the croaks and gargling sounds, 'Peter-Ushtinov-shays-I-shound-juss-like-a-drunken-Russian-general-and-he-ough'a-know!' Cocooned by good friendship and the protection of his wife Hjordis, he slowly withered away until death mercifully released him in June 1983.

He was a brave man.

10

HOME FROM THE SEA

After winning the 1500 metres gold medal in the Rome Olympics, Herb Elliott, the Australian runner who was never beaten in an important race, came to study at Cambridge. We met through a mutual friend, Jack Pollard, an Australian journalist, and Herb invited me to handle the book he intended to write. One of his most fervent admirers was Chris Brasher, himself an Olympic gold medallist, having won the steeplechase in the 1956 Games, and who was now, four or so years later, sports editor of the *Observer*. Chris and I met quite frequently through our connecting interests and soon became business friends.

He had had much to do with setting up the first Transatlantic Single-Handed Race, sponsored by the *Observer*, in 1960. The race was the result of a half-crown wager among members of the Royal Western Yacht Club at Plymouth and four contestants set out from the home port. The winner was an unfancied old man, aged sixty, named Francis Chichester. The following year, also with *Observer* backing, he sailed the course again single-handed and reduced his record by a substantial margin. A few months later, Chris Brasher told me that Chichester had never used a literary agent but in his view badly needed one. He had mentioned my name: would

I come along for an early evening drink at St James's Place to meet him – and his formidable wife, Sheila?

She had had the nous during the war to buy Number 9 St James's Place cheaply; it was one of a terrace of tall, narrow Georgian houses on the north side of the cul-de-sac, a few doors away from the rambling building then inhabited by the firm of William Collins. The Chichesters ran a small map-publishing business on the ground floor. Upstairs was the drawing room, a kind of *salon* that occupied the whole breadth of the house. And it was there that Chris introduced me to my host and hostess.

Francis was on the short side but sinewy and with a pair of muscular, capable-looking hands. He was grey-haired, balding and wore steel-rimmed glasses; he had a quizzical gaze and there was a mischievous pucker among the lines down his rather hollow cheeks. Sheila was big – an ample, bosomy woman with fine blue eyes and a slightly querulous note in her very upper-class voice. I sat on a plump sofa and sipped dry sherry as we chatted.

I already knew something of his sailing exploits and Chris Brasher had briefed me on the almost miraculous recovery from lung cancer which he had made just a few years earlier. Then a heavy smoker and something of a worrier, Francis had been diagnosed as having a malignant tumour in one lung; a leading specialist had warned that even an urgent operation to remove the lung might be too late to save his life for any real length of time. Sheila, a devout believer in the power of faith-healing, persuaded him to forgo surgery. She took him to the south of France where rest, prayer and what we now call organic food restored him to at least part-health. As he grew stronger and because of the supposedly beneficial effects of salt breezes, he was encouraged to take up sailing. Within those few years, Francis had become strong enough and expert enough to sail *Gipsy Moth* single-handed across the Atlantic 'the wrong way' – east to west – and win the *Observer* Trophy. He owed his life to Sheila – and was not allowed to forget it for long.

What I had not realised before meeting him was his immense skill and experience in navigation. He was indeed perhaps the greatest navigator of the twentieth century below the jet stream. He had been one of that small band of pioneers – Bert Hinkley, Amy Johnson, Jim Mollison, Sir Alan Cobham, Colonel Lindbergh – who had flown old, rickety, single-engined aircraft thousands of miles over then uncharted and dangerous territory. He himself had flown from England to Sydney, Australia, on to New Zealand and then northwards, island-hopping, on his way to Japan until a near-fatal crash halted him. In those far-off days there were no ground-to-air beacons, no navigational aids, no satellites beaming bearings, no handy air-traffic controllers. The pilot, nursing his plane and doing his own navigation, had only the compass and the sextant to rely on. A small island 200 or 300 miles away would be the merest speck on the map. If the compass bearing was out by even half a degree, it would be possible to fly right past the island without knowing whether it lay to port or starboard.

If simplicity is part of genius, Francis Chichester might well have qualified. He thought and thought, and finally hit on the answer. If you take the correct bearing and then deliberately lay off five degrees to port, you know that when you have flown the proper distance, the island must lie to the right, in other words, to starboard. So at once you have halved the possibility of error.

It was a pleasant, ice-breaking meeting. No commitments had been made when Chris and I left; as I came to learn on many a future occasion, Francis was a man of swift and decisive action when alone at sea but a complete ditherer on land. Sheila was the domestic decision-maker and fortunately she decided to ask me to handle his writing affairs. We had a further meeting, when I quickly realised they had a real problem to sort out.

Allen & Unwin had paid him an advance of £200 with modest royalties for his book about the single-handed race, *Alone Across the Atlantic*. For his next book describing the record-breaking attempt the following year, they had again paid him an advance of £200 on account of modest royalties. He was now considering an interim autobiography, covering his whole career to date, including the pre-war flying, his war service, his illness and extraordinary recovery, and his sailing feats. Allen & Unwin, nothing if not consistent, were offering him £200 advance and modest royalties.

I explained to the Chichesters that the publishing firm had been run for many years by that bearded Methodist, Sir Stanley Unwin, who had written a standard work entitled *The Truth About Publishing*.* His 'truth' was simple, if somewhat one-sided: authors are awful people. They never deliver a book on time and even when it finally arrives, it is either too short or, more likely, far too long, badly typed, full of crossings-out. Authors are always trying to borrow money or write libellous passages or upset the smooth running of the publishing house in any way they can. Publishers, on the other hand, are good folk. They are sober, industrious, painstaking, honest – well, most of them – and, above all, reliable. What a pity and a paradox that they should have to rely on those unreliable authors to earn their daily bread. As Walter Harrap once said to me, wagging his head, 'You know, George, ours would be a wonderful job if it weren't for authors!'

The following morning, I telephoned Philip Unwin, who had taken over the firm from his uncle, and explained that Francis Chichester had invited me to act for him. From Unwin's tone, I sensed that agents were confined to an even lower circle of hell than that of authors. However, he did condescend to repeat the firm's offer for the memoirs – a £200 advance, payable half on delivery and half on publication, against a starting royalty of ten per cent. I told him the book was worth more. *Alone Across the Atlantic* had already earned out its advance and was in credit by several hundred pounds. He refused to raise the offer. I tried again. He still refused. Rashly, I was beginning to lose my temper. I said, 'I'll make you a bet . . .'

He cut in, a shade primly, 'I am not a betting man.'

'All right, I'll put it another way. Let me make you an offer. If I can't get someone else to put up ten times as much – £2,000

---

* I had read the first edition. Later impressions were toned down to a degree.

– within one week from now, you can have the book at your price – £200. Okay?'

He agreed.

My hand was sweating as I put down the phone. £2,000 was a lot of money in the early 1960s, more than a year's salary for a middle-grade employee. Francis Chichester was becoming well known in sailing circles and he had received considerable publicity from the *Observer* stories but he was not as yet a famous public figure. At that time, even generous publishers expected to pay no more than two-thirds of potential sales in the shape of an advance. To earn back £3,000 in royalties, a book would need to sell up to 15,000 copies, which would put it well into the bestseller list. It seemed a daunting task. What if I failed and in a week's time had to go crawling back to the superior Mr Unwin to accept his offer of £200? What indeed would my new client say, having to settle for that indifferent amount *minus* £20 as agent's commission? Except that I would obviously have to resign on the spot and forfeit any chance of commission; and quite rightly, having succumbed to petulance at the wrong moment.

At that moment, my memory was tugged. Not long before, Hodder & Stoughton had appointed a general editor, a youngish man named Robin Denniston. He had learned the trade the hard way under the ruthless Calvinism of Billy Collins. (As George Hardinge, another of the brilliant young men who flew towards Billy's candle, once said to me ruefully, 'Billy drives you into a nervous breakdown but at least he pays your hospital expenses!')

Robin could almost have been a character out of a Graham Greene or John le Carré novel. Westminster and Oxford, a trained parachutist from his National Service days, the son of a Royal Navy officer who had served with real distinction in the Secret Intelligence Service during the Second World War, he had that vague, slightly shambling air that concealed a sharp and incisive mind. Untidy, with the knot of his tie screwed round almost under one ear and, more often than not, a spot of blood on his collar where he had nicked himself shaving, he did not resemble the prototype of the smart young executive. He kept a harmonium in his room at St Paul's House and played it at times of high emotion. He had a knack, a useful knack as it turned out, of telephoning agents at regular intervals to ask if they had a book available that might interest Hodder's. If the answer was 'No', he did not waste the agent's time in idle chatter but thanked him politely and rang off.

He had called me, as it happened, the previous day, so that I knew he was still looking for books. Moreover, having worked at Collins, a few doors away from the Chichesters, he probably knew something about the man. I got through to him, explained that I was offering the memoirs, as Allen & Unwin had made an indifferent offer, and said that the price was £2,000 advance, take it or leave it. He had the exclusive first refusal but I needed a really urgent decision. He promised to get back to me – fast.

I sat and wondered – but not for long. About forty minutes later, Robin rang back. We were in business. He had talked it over with 'the family', who were prepared to back his judgement. The deal was on.

At once, I telephoned Philip Unwin. Try as I might – and I did not try very hard – I could not keep a gloating tone out of my voice. 'I didn't need a week,' I said. 'I didn't need a day, I didn't need an hour, even. I've spoken to Hodder's, who are happy to match the £2,000. So that's it, I'm afraid.'

It was not perhaps surprising that, some years later, when Philip Unwin came to write the official history of George Allen & Unwin, he should observe that the company had a good and friendly relationship with Francis Chichester until he took to himself 'a rapacious agent'. Alas, as so often in life, one man's rapacity is another man's sagacity. *The Lonely Sea and the Sky*, Chichester's memoirs, sold over 70,000 copies in the hardcover editions and several hundred thousand copies in paperback. The American edition was a success and the book did well on the Continent in half a dozen or more translations. Francis must have earned close on £50,000 from all the various sources. *Post hoc* but definitely not *propter hoc*, his erstwhile publishers fared less well. 'Industry and all the virtues' saw them losing a niche but never finding a role in the new world of big publishers; they became Unwin Hyman in a takeover and were later swallowed up in the Murdochian trough of HarperCollins.

Not long before the book appeared, Francis let me in on a secret. The following year, 1965, he was planning to sail single-handed round the world, stopping once in Sydney, Australia, and then proceeding around Cape Horn and back to Plymouth. It would be the first such venture since Slocum and he was having a new *Gipsy Moth*, the fourth, specially designed and built for the voyage.

I was thrilled. I had not been involved in a big expedition since the conclusion of Fuchs's Antarctic crossing. This new one had the right 'sniff' to it. Although I realised it would be expensive to mount – the building of a new boat by a specialist designer would not come cheap and, besides, Francis would be losing the best part of a year (or more) away from his map business – privately, I thought raising the money through a sale of rights would be a walkover. Not for the last time, the rose-tinted spectacles turned out to be dark glasses. Denis Hamilton, editor of the *Sunday Times* and himself a keen sailor, was given the chance to publish and then syndicate regular progress reports, which Francis would beam back from the radio telephone he would carry on board. His reply was succinct – along the lines of 'We all admire Chichester for his sailing exploits but let us not forget he will celebrate his sixty-fifth birthday during the voyage. My readers will not be interested in the doings of an old-age pensioner all on his own for a year or so.'

Before even approaching Hamilton, I had of course checked out the *Observer*, which was in the process of organising the second quadrennial Transatlantic Race. Chris Brasher was enthusiastic but David Astor, the editor, and his management felt they had devoted enough space and indeed money to single-handed sailing in general, and Francis Chichester in particular. I next tried Hugh Cudlipp, the panjandrum of the Mirror Group, who actually owned a boat. His verdict was the same as Denis Hamilton's – but more pithily expressed. Things were not looking good.

Then a chink of light appeared. I had had some friendly deal-ings with Alastair Hetherington, the editor of the *Guardian*, who had backed one or two small expeditions I had handled. I mentioned the Chichester venture to him; he was not a sailor but preferred fell walking and climbing. Luckily, he consulted his industrial correspondent, John Anderson, an experienced seaman, who gave the thumbs up. The paper agreed to put up £500 to cover reports over the first leg of the journey, with the option to renew for the second leg from Sydney to Plymouth. It was not a fortune but at least it was a start in the right direction.

Denis Hamilton, who came from humble origins in the north of England, had recently appointed a young newspaperman from the smokestacks of the north-east to be his managing editor. His name was Harold Evans. He was pale-faced, with spiky dark hair and heavy, horn-rimmed glasses; this was long before the image-makers shaped the hair and inserted the cornflower-blue contact lenses for his numerous television appearances. Then he was an impressionable provincial with a belief in his ability as a squash player that was to be rudely shaken. Introduced to one another within days of his arrival by Brian Glanville, my novelist client and the *Sunday Times* chief football correspondent, Harry and I were regular squash opponents and soon became friends. He had been allotted £1,000, ostensibly to spend in dribs and drabs on minor projects. He had the nose for a good story and the panache to blow it all on Francis's voyage. Hodder & Stoughton chipped in with several thousand pounds to commission the resulting book and the International Wool Secretariat, which was developing a campaign to publicise its name and functions, put up a good sum to have its twisted skein symbol painted on the bows of *Gipsy Moth IV*. Australian sheep farmers were the biggest supporters of the IWS and the fact that Sydney was the stopover point had become an important consideration. Whitbread, whose chairman and head of the family firm, the Colonel, was a friend of Francis, was the final sponsor, not only giving a generous donation but also lending free of charge its publicity expertise. So, bit by bit, the kitty was filling up, although it never overflowed with spare cash.

By this time, I had come to know Francis pretty well and was convinced that, given a touch of luck or divine providence, he had the strength, the skill and the determination to make the circumnavigation. But looking back after more than a quarter of a century, I can appreciate why experienced newspaper editors should shake their heads in doubt. He would have his sixty-fifth birthday during the voyage; he had had an almost miraculous remission of the lung tumour a few years earlier, but who could tell what effect the strain of long hours on watch, the physical effort of continually raising and lowering the sails without help, and the psychological pressure of weeks and months of solitude, most often encompassed by a blank sea and a blank sky, might have on him? And how would it be possible to sustain the excitement of the pioneering voyage over that long period, when the passage of 500 nautical miles would take up barely an inch on the map?

For the book rights I would use the Farquharson standard form of publishing contract; for newspaper and ancillary rights, I would draft a detailed letter contract to be signed by the respective purchasers and countersigned by Francis; at least, that was the theory. Francis had a quizzical interest in how things worked, a faculty that was of great advantage on a lone voyage when it came to make-and-mend. He could take a complex piece of machinery such as a compass or a radio receiver to bits, think hard about how each functioned and where it fitted into the apparatus, track down the missing or broken screw or wire or plug, adapt something else to take its place and get the machine working again.

Partly out of inquisitiveness and partly, I eventually came to realise, out of a sense of impishness, he would adapt the same techniques to a clause in a book contract or a paragraph in a letter contract. The trouble was that words, unlike bits of machinery, could be made to fit into too many areas of a sentence or a paragraph. Francis would query a phrase in, say, the clause on territorial rights. What exactly was the 'open market'? What was so 'open' about it? Why should an American edition be allowed into it after a certain lapse of time? I would find myself explaining for the fifth or sixth time that (a) his previous agreement with Hodder's and even those with Allen & Unwin contained exactly the same clause and they had worked effectively to date; (b) that the open

market was an advantage to a successful author as it meant that
both his English-language publishers, British and American,
would be competing in that territory and should therefore
sell more copies in aggregate than if one or the other had the
market exclusively. He would at length accept the point and
lie back, basking like a lizard on the rock until shooting out
his tongue again to capture the impatient fly. Then there could
be another long inquisition, this time perhaps on why book
publishers gave only six complimentary copies to the poor
author without whom . . . There were times when I could
cheerfully have crept into Camper & Nicholson's boatyard
after dark and bored a large hole in the stern of the almost
completed *Gipsy Moth IV*.

Apart from Robin Denniston, who with the family's full
backing had invested a substantial advance on behalf of
Hodder & Stoughton for British book rights, two further
remarkable men, both journalists, were associated with the
venture. One was Murray Sayle, the other John Anderson.
Murray, a large, beaky-nosed Australian, had joined his
fellow countryman, Bruce Page, as a reporter for the *People*
when under Sam Campbell's inspired editorship it was vying
raucously with the *News of the World* at the lower end
of the market. Hitherto, the *Sunday Times* had been a
preserve mainly for middle-class, ex-public-school, Oxford
or Cambridge journalists. Harold Evans was beginning to put
together a nucleus of provincials and 'outsiders' like himself,
the new hard men of the newspaper world, and he chose Bruce
Page to run his 'Insight' team. Murray Sayle followed along.

He had a quick wit, a ready tongue and what seemed an
infinite capacity to absorb alcohol. On the afternoon a few
hours before Francis's triumphant return to Plymouth Sound,
Murray, whose task it was to carry out that first immensely
important interview, had been imbibing an inordinate amount
of champagne along with others of us at Lady Astor's house
on the Hoe which Sheila Chichester had taken over for
the occasion. Sharp-eyed viewers of the BBC television
programme must have seen him teetering on the quayside
as he argued vehemently about Vietnam and only just getting
aboard the harbourmaster's launch with a despairing leap as

it went to greet the returning hero. And yet the published interview was brilliantly effective. There was a geniality to the man that only the most curmudgeonly could resist. There was also a touch of real courage. When *Gipsy Moth IV* was nearing Cape Horn on the second leg of the voyage, Murray went down to the tip of South America and hired a madcap local pilot with a single-engined aircraft who flew him in a storm out to sea to meet the yacht. It was blowing a gale, and the plane was tossing and lurching around a cloud-driven sky but, leaning out as the plane swooped down, he secured that famous photograph (a *Life* front cover) of the battered boat with one small sail aloft as the giant waves creamed above it.

Less colourful but equally skilled in his craft was John Anderson. As founder's kin, he had been educated at Winchester College; he had a sponge-like capacity for absorbing facts, and the ability to write fast and well on a wide area of subjects. One of his special skills was to take someone else's written draft or transcribed dictation and edit it into readable English but still preserving – indeed improving on – the other person's characteristics and individual flavour. He did an invaluable job on both Francis Chichester's major books and was later to play an even more important role for an even more quirky and difficult man, Lord George-Brown.

The crowd that saw Francis off from Plymouth was a small one, consisting mainly of people directly concerned with the project. As always, whenever a national newspaper secures rights in a story that has been or is about to be, the opposition ostentatiously ignores it. Only when the story has become a national event will the other papers cover it. Francis had been in a crabby mood during the run-up to his departure, since Alec Rose, a Portsmouth greengrocer who was a keen amateur sailor, had suddenly popped up and challenged him to a single-handed race around the world. The circumnavigation had been Francis's own idea; I strongly suspected that the interloper was trying to cash in on the publicity. In any case, he would not be ready to sail for some months. If Francis accepted the challenge, as he was much tempted to do, he would have to hang about for many weeks when his nerves were already on edge. Besides, the challenge was laughable. On the one hand, an experienced long-distance sailor, an acknowledged expert navigator with a yacht specially designed for non-stop fast cruising; on the other, a weekend sailor, who messed about with boats when he was not weighing up the sprouts.

'Francis,' I said, 'it's as if I were to challenge Cassius Clay to fifteen rounds in the ring. I wouldn't last eleven seconds – but think of all the publicity I'd get. Publicity at *his* expense. It's the reflected glory angle. Same with you and this man Rose. Merely going up against you would get him into the news, because everyone knows you're the best. Ignore him. You made your announcement way back. If he wants to have a go, let him make his own publicity.'

Alec Rose did, of course, potter round the world in fairly easy stages and was given a knighthood by Harold Wilson, whose scattering of largesse during his various premierships included in its erratic aim a raincoat manufacturer who went to gaol, a property dealer who blew his brains out soon after being knighted, a crooked lord who ran a glass-bottling firm, and the Beatles. Rose's attempt was backed by the Mirror Group and towards the end of his long-drawn-out voyage, a celebration lunch was given at which his wife was the guest of honour. Hugh Cudlipp gave the main speech and kept referring to the hero of the hour as 'this humble greengrocer'. He noticed that Mrs Rose was showing increasing signs of unease, indeed anger, and asked *sotto voce* if something was troubling her.

'My husband is not a greengrocer,' she declared. 'He is a high-class fruiterer.'

In the 1960s, the *Guardian* London office was in the same Grays Inn Road building that housed the *Sunday Times*, a great convenience when it came to sharing the regular progress reports beamed by radio telephone to the GPO special unit on the North Circular Road in the Brent district of London. And each week the interest and the enthusiasm grew. Britain was going through a bad patch; inflation had begun to creep in, Churchill died, the unions were flexing their biceps, there seemed to be more ash than glow in Wilson's glib 'white heat of technology'. And yet here was this old-age pensioner battling against the elements all on his own, using only the winds to propel him southwards down the wide sweep of the Atlantic Ocean and then, once round the Cape of Good Hope, eastwards into the Roaring Forties. It was classic, it was heroic, it made many readers feel that the old bulldog spirit was still there.

Even at the launching, Sheila Chichester's sharp eye detected something strange in the way *Gipsy Moth IV* took to the water. There appeared to be a problem with the keel – or so she thought. Apparently, it did not show up in the sea trials prior to the voyage itself. But, once he was well out at sea, Francis realised that the design of the keel meant that he could not leave the yacht to follow her own devices for hours on end under the self-steering apparatus but had to steer her manually for much of the time. Hence, he had to reduce his rest periods, so necessary for a man of his years. It was an emaciated and weakened Francis Chichester who had to be helped ashore in Sydney Harbour at the end of the first triumphant leg. Sheila had already flown in to greet him and over the next six weeks or so she nursed him back to full strength and vigour. Simultaneously, the yacht was hauled out of the water and the keel rebalanced.

In the opening pages of *Gipsy Moth Circles the World*, he had some bitter, almost vindictive, words to say about the shortcomings of the original design. John Anderson, Robin Denniston and I did our best to persuade him to omit the passages. After all, in its first guise the boat had got him half-way round the world and that kind of criticism, occurring so early in the book, struck a petty, jarring note. But he was adamant. Part of him wanted the truth to be told, however hurtful it might be to someone else. And yet another part of him, I suspected, wanted the world to know all the handicaps he had had to overcome in his truly global success. If that were so, it emerged from a deep pride within him, not a superficial vanity.

The *Sunday Times* had shrewdly 'booked' Francis for the duration of the whole voyage, whereas the *Guardian*, then far less affluent than it now is, had paid for the first leg to Sydney with an option to renew for the second half. *The Times*, one of the many daily papers that had rejected the opportunity before Francis set off, now offered him through its Sydney correspondent £1,000 for the daily-paper rights over the rest of the voyage, thus cunningly bypassing me. The first I heard of the offer was in a telephone call from Sheila. For at least some days after his arrival, Francis's weakened state meant that he had to stay in bed under sedation for much of the time. Thus, there was almost no chance to talk things over with him. Sheila, I knew, urged him to accept the bigger offer – after all, there was twice as much money involved. Even when he was in full health and vigour, he was more often than not swayed by her dominant personality; he never forgot – nor was he allowed to – that he owed the prolonging of his life to her faith and courage. In his weakened state, he was a pushover.

My own feeling, which I tried to put across by cable and telephone but with no success at all, was that one should keep faith with those who had shown faith at a time when the gamble was greatest. Now that the story was front-page news and a leading item in television bulletins, chequebook journalism was on to a sure thing. The story could only get bigger and better the nearer he came to his Plymouth home port. With more and more book rights being sold and syndication payments from the newspapers building up, the Chichesters were already certain to make a large sum of money – and deservedly. Why, therefore, discard one of your early backers who helped to make it possible for the sake of £450 net? That was the gist of the argument I kept sending to Sydney but to no avail. The *Guardian* lost out, although John Anderson, who had already struck up a friendship with Francis, based on his own love for seamanship, was magnanimous enough to stay on as his initial editor.

And so the scene was set for the triumphant homecoming on a warm summer evening. Plymouth Hoe made a natural proscenium and a large crowd had gathered on its slopes – although nothing like the quarter of a million which most newspapers reported. There were perhaps a tenth of that number. But we had stood there patiently as dusk infiltrated the cliffs on either side of the sound and crept across the quiet waters. *Gipsy Moth IV* had ghosted in, grey in the twilight with the grey mainsail furled to the mast. The plan was that Lord Montague of Beaulieu, a family friend who owned an open white Rolls Royce, would meet Francis at the Royal Western Yacht Club's building by the water's edge and drive him through the crowded streets of Plymouth to the Guildhall for a press conference. As already mentioned, Murray Sayle, along with Sheila and Giles, the Chichesters' son, had gone aboard that afternoon for the first vital interview.

I have usually tried to follow the Duke of Edinburgh's wise advice, 'Take every opportunity.' Having already drunk several pints, it seemed, of champagne since lunchtime and knowing that the press conference might run for an hour or more, I made straight for the men's lavatories on arrival at the Guildhall. I happened to glance across at the next stall and there was this shortish man with steel-rimmed spectacles and grey hair escaping from under his baseball cap. His face, his neck and the backs of his hands were burned an ochre-y brown.

'Welcome home, Francis,' I said. 'Well done.'

'Thanks, George. How much did you get for that *Life* photo?'

'Which one do you mean? There were quite a few.'

'The front-cover one,' he said. 'You know – the one with *Gipsy Moth* passing the Horn.'

'Oh, that one. £500, I think it was.'

'Not enough,' he said. 'You should have got more.'

Francis and Sheila remained for several days at the Astor house on the Hoe while he regained his land legs and, indeed, the strength that had been sapped through the long homeward stretch of the voyage. He was now Sir Francis and the plan was that he and Sheila were to sail *Gipsy Moth* in easy stages along the south coast and up into the Thames Estuary. They would heave to at Greenwich and then go ashore for the formal knighting by the Queen. Then the yacht would proceed upstream to Tower Pier for a City of London civic welcome and a Lord Mayor's lunch at the Guildhall. It was to be a splendid finale to a great exploit by an old man.

The day before *Gipsy Moth* was to leave Plymouth *en*

route for London, I had a panic-stricken phone call from a senior official at the International Wool Secretariat's office just behind Pall Mall. The word had come through that Sheila Chichester had ordered the IWS insignia on either side of the bows to be painted out. Apparently, she did not want any nasty commercial advertising to lower the tone when the yacht tied up at Greenwich. This was, of course, the culmination of all the Wool Secretariat's dreams and the reason why they had gambled substantial sums of money on the outcome of the voyage. The arrival in the estuary, the slow passage up to Greenwich, the knighting itself and then the final leg to Tower Pier with ships' sirens hooting in tribute would all be covered by television and several million viewers would see that the IWS was the main outside patron.

I was completely in sympathy with my 'wool' friend. There was a letter contract, signed by Francis, which stated that in consideration of a certain payment *Gipsy Moth IV* would at all times throughout the voyage and for so many weeks thereafter display the IWS symbol prominently on both sides of her bows. I managed to get hold of Sheila on the phone to discover that she had already arranged with a local chandler for a painter to delete the signs first thing next morning. I tried to explain that the step would be a direct breach of the contract and could have grave consequences – but she was adamant. In her view, it would be a grave insult to Her Majesty if *Gipsy Moth* turned up, 'looking like an advertising hoarding, George!' I argued for a while but, as I knew from experience, when she worked herself into that mood, she was impervious to reason. One might as well try diverting an avalanche as talking her (as she had just become) ladyship into the path of common sense.

A desperate moment needed a desperate remedy. I arranged a double bluff with the 'wool' man and then telephoned Plymouth again – this time, insisting on speaking to Francis. I told him the wool people were hopping mad (true). I said they had consulted their lawyers (untrue), a rough, tough City firm, who were about to draw up an injunction (untrue). If Sheila went ahead next day with having the insignia painted out, the yacht would be impounded. She would never leave Plymouth until the injunction had been heard and any resulting lawsuit settled, which might take two or three years. So, instead of tying up alongside *Cutty Sark*, another heroine of the oceans, and walking up a jetty to greet Her Majesty, he and Sheila would have to take a train up to Paddington and presumably a taxi for the onward journey. I concluded by saying it seemed a bit of a shame.

The bluff worked. By the time the word came through to the chandler, his painter had, I believe, already blotted out the insignia on one side but he managed a workmanlike replacement, accurate enough to deceive the eyes of those millions of television viewers during the investiture. And that was the main thing.

I can remember only one other instance when I deliberately misled a client by twisting the facts, indeed lying, for what I felt to be his or her ultimate benefit or what I strongly held to be the honourable course. The IWS never would have issued an injunction against Francis and Sheila, even though they had a virtually foolproof case. The resulting publicity might have hurt the Chichesters but it would have been extremely damaging to the initiators: a large organisation up against the individual, the old hero attacked in his hour of triumph – what a field day the popular newspapers could have had. But Sheila who, strangely enough, had had a successful career in publicity and with her steamroller tactics had helped greatly to promote her husband's career, should never have embarked on such a high-handed and unfair action.

That controversy had been kept private but a very public one was to occur soon afterwards. When *Gipsy Moth* reached Greenwich, as I have already mentioned, Francis and Sheila were to disembark and walk up a wooden jetty to a spot where Her Majesty would greet them. After a brief chat, Francis was to kneel on a specially prepared footstool and the Queen would dub him Knight. It was to be a short and simple ceremony, but carried out under the full gaze of the television cameras, both BBC and commercial, and in front of thousands of spectators, crammed behind ropes and barriers.

Sheila rightly saw herself as a working member of the crew during the leisurely sail along the south coast and naturally wore trousers as part of her working kit. Again, with the keen wind that so often blows along the stretches of the Thames Estuary, a strong gust might cause some embarrassment if she changed into a skirt for the royal ceremony. Thus far, the approach was blameless. The problem was that in physique Sheila was the noblest Roman matron of them all, with wide hips and ample buttocks to match. With magenta-coloured silk trousers stretched tight across the lower half of that generous frame, her progress up that narrow wooden jetty was the focus for all eyes and lenses, stealing the limelight from the hero of the hour and eclipsing the Queen's sedate costume. It was fortunate, perhaps, that she did not have to stoop down to the footstool for a double accolade.

The popular press next day grabbed at the episode. Should women wear trousers? Had Her Majesty been insulted? Would this new-fangled fashion sweep through Ascot and other social venues? Even the more serious newspapers ran articles on the symbolism of trouser-wearing and the changing roles of the sexes.

After the ceremony, *Gipsy Moth IV* continued her triumphant progress up the Thames under power, with anchored ships and barges giving peals of applause on their hooters and Tower Bridge raised as, swanlike, she glided under the ironwork and anchored at Tower Pier. Then to the Guildhall and speeches and applause and toasts, until at last a Lord Mayoral limousine drove Francis and Sheila back home to St James's Place. The City of Westminster, not to be outdone by its neighbour to the east, had arranged for brightly coloured pennants to crisscross the narrow street at roof level as a final welcome back to the local hero. He and Sheila had invited me to join them at home after the Guildhall ceremony. It was very quiet, almost hushed, after the feasting and the fuss, as the three of us sat there in the drawing room and made small talk in a sense of total anticlimax.

John Anderson told me quite early in 1966 about a young man he had encouraged through publishing a few articles by him in the *Guardian*. His name was Robin Knox-Johnston. With the help of a brother and experienced dhow-builders in Bombay, he had constructed a boat named *Suhaili* and was sailing her via Cape Town back to the United Kingdom. John told me that his protégé under a modest exterior was a tough and ambitious fellow. Then almost twenty-seven years old, he had passed all his merchant-seaman officer's exams and had much experience of the oceans. He was also a junior officer in the Royal Naval Volunteer Reserve. John had written to tell him about me and Knox-Johnston in reply suggested a meeeting on his return. *Suhaili* was due to tie up at Tower Pier in two or three weeks; on the appointed day John and I walked along the wooden jetty and down on to the landing stage to greet the two-man crew.

Their mother and father and other members of the family were there for the welcome home, and so there was no chance for more than a handshake and a few words of congratulation. Even in that brief encounter, I liked what I saw; we arranged for him to call at my office a week later for a detailed discussion. We talked about a book describing the building of *Suhaili* and the voyage home but I had to tell him that in my view the prospects of success were limited. It might be too technical for the general reader and he himself was not yet well known enough in sailing circles to warrant wide sales there. We met again over the weeks and, gradually, it emerged that he had a much more exciting project in mind. It was to carry out the first *non-stop* circumnavigation of the world.

That, if it succeeded, would be the most tremendous feat. Francis had pointed the way but even a determined and resourceful man like him had been forced to spend some weeks in Sydney, recuperating in health while the keel of his boat was rebalanced, as a half-way halt. *Gipsy Moth IV* could have sailed no further without that precious break. Robin had proved *Suhaili*'s endurance up to a point by sailing her without a pause from Cape Town to the United Kingdom but was she solid enough to survive the Roaring Forties and the Cape Horn gales in a voyage that might last the best part of a year? Her cruising speed was around four knots, which meant that, allowing for the doldrums on the outward and inward tracks, an average of 100 nautical miles a day would be her potential. From start to finish, the route would be close on 30,000 miles. So the voyage could take at least ten months.

What would be the psychological pressures of the enforced loneliness for that long period on a young, high-spirited man? Francis had survived without mental scarring but he was an old man with the vital juices damped down by the years – and something of a loner as well. Again, his period of solitude on each leg of the voyage had been less than a third of what Robin could expect to endure. Irrespective of his skills as a sailor and navigator – and I had no qualms about them – the all-important factors were the fortitude and guts he might display over a seemingly unending stretch of nautical crises, large and small, and the enveloping sense of utter loneliness. There was in fact a real air of modesty about this rangy young man with the curly brown hair and the curly beard. His family hailed from Northern Ireland and he had been born on St Patrick's Day; underneath the modest exterior one could sense the utter conviction of the Belfast Protestant, tempered – unlike so many of his compatriots – with a strong sense of humour. He had been born and raised in England and educated at Berkhamsted, where Graham Greene's father had once been headmaster. John Anderson, a subtle judge of humanity, was convinced of Robin's abilities and it did not take me long to agree.

(Before he set out from Falmouth, the *Sunday Mirror*, his sponsoring newspaper, had him thoroughly examined by a psychiatrist who pronounced him 'distressingly normal'. Within twenty-four hours of his return over ten months later, the same psychiatrist put him through the same tests to discover just what mental or emotional damage the months of solitude might have caused. The verdict was: 'even more distressingly normal'.)

During the next year and a half, he had to make up for the long holiday away from money-earning and he rejoined the merchant navy for a limited period. He also had to justify his RNVR commission by spending some while on active service with the Royal Navy. We kept in touch sporadically by letter and then in the winter of 1967 a dejected Robin Knox-Johnston called at my office. Not realising that an agent's duties extended beyond the selling of book rights, he had written to close on fifty companies to seek their support for his non-stop bid. The net result had been a few dozen tins of beer and a £5 voucher. It was with some relief that he agreed to leave me to look for funds.

John Anderson had already told me that the *Guardian* would not be able to back him and so I went at once to Chichester's major patron and my regular squash opponent, Harold Evans, now promoted to the editorship of the *Sunday Times*. He declined, as I rather suspected he might. His newspaper had not only published numerous progress reports and feature articles during the voyage of *Gipsy Moth IV* but it had also serialised a few months before my approach Francis's book on the subject. That struck me as a good enough reason for rejection and I switched at once to Mike Christiansen, editor of the *Sunday Mirror*, to whom I had sold several profitable – at least to the respective authors – serials in recent months.

Then Harry Evans called me back. At the instigation of Murray Sayle, he was thinking of running a lone-sailor, round-the-world, non-stop sailing race. The *Sunday Times* would pay each accepted entrant a modest fee and equip his boat with a radio telephone for transmitting progress reports. The prize for the winner would be a 'Golden Globe' and a further payment. Would Robin care to enter? I felt incensed – and told Harry so. It had always been held – and still, I hope, is – that when an editor is approached over a future project or an unpublished book and is offered publication rights, the matter is treated as strictly confidential. The editor does not use any information he may have acquired in that way in his newspaper, unless he buys the right to do so. I said to Harry that I felt he had breached the unwritten rule. He argued that he and his features team had been discussing over quite a lengthy period how best they might cash in on the great success they had achieved through backing Francis Chichester and that my approach on behalf of Knox-Johnston had merely triggered off the final scheme. The stand-off merely stiffened Robin's and my resolve 'to show 'em'.

Knowing that Kenneth Parker, Cassell's senior editor, was

an enthusiastic weekend sailor, I returned to the firm that had done so well for and from the first big expedition I ever handled, Fuchs' Antarctic crossing. They put up a solid advance for the British book rights, split between a third on signature of contract, a third on delivery and a third on publication. Then Mike Christiansen weighed in with a bold gesture – £5,000 for the newspaper rights. (That is equivalent to about £45,000 today.) It was a great gamble. However resolute and skilful the lone sailor may be, there is always a risk that a negligent steamer will run him down in the crowded approaches to the English Channel or a freak storm may smash his boat like matchwood or the constant battering of the wind and the waves may damage a mast beyond his capacity to repair it.

One event, right at the start of their relationship, almost brought it to a premature end. To get to know him better away from the formality of an office, Mike had invited Robin out to lunch; he thought it would be amusing to choose the venue of the *Hispaniola*, a large boat that had been converted into a restaurant and was now moored permanently along the wall beneath the Embankment. During the lunch, a police launch went past at some speed, its bow wave caused the *Hispaniola* to rock – and Robin fell off his chair into the gangway. Long afterwards, Mike confessed to me he could see in that moment his large wad of money sinking fathoms deep to the floor of the Atlantic. If a seasoned sailor could not keep his balance on the gentle Thames, how would he fare in a roaring gale around Cape Horn? But, much to his credit, Mike Christiansen persevered, even though his boss, Hugh Cudlipp, himself a sailor who had turned down Francis Chichester a few years earlier, would not even attend the party. (Cudlipp did turn up to the post-voyage celebration in the *Mirror* building but he was not his usual vociferous self.)

Ever since 1960, I had been visiting New York on business every spring and autumn, always staying at the decrepit but homely Royalton Hotel on West 44th Street. There may have been cockroaches – 'Croton bugs', we experts called them – in the bathrooms and weird contraptions that made the beds rock up and down if you put a quarter into the slot but the linen and towels were always clean, the staff never changed and George, the night porter, remembered all his regular visitors. Today, at treble or quadruple the old prices, the hotel is a designer-ridden horror with bland young men and women standing by the exit and mechanically repeating 'Have a nice day' at fifteen-second intervals.

In those early days, just around the corner on Sixth Avenue stood the Fawcett Building. The Fawcett brothers owned Gold Medal Books, then among the two or three biggest paperback companies in the United States, and a host of magazines, one of which was *True* Magazine. It had latterly been a right-wing publication, strongly endorsing the gun lobby, and specialising in articles on hunting and shooting. Charles Barnard, the new editor, wanted to steer it towards a more general approach. He was a widely experienced journalist and a good writer; before long we had struck up a warm friendship that still exists, quarter of a century later. He knew I had represented Chichester and when I told him about Robin's plan, he was immediately enthusiastic – to the concrete extent of putting up some very useful dollars for the American feature rights and arranging to fly over to London to meet my client. By this time, *Suhaili* was moored at St Katharine's Dock where Robin was working on her full time. One afternoon, when I went to inspect progress – it must then have been late April and he was due to set out from Falmouth in a little over a month – the first sight I saw on stepping aboard was the powerful editor of *True* Magazine, shirtsleeves rolled up and a smudge of paint on the side of one cheek, stretched out to scrape and then paint the planking beneath the bunk. He was a full member of the team and I felt like a bench reserve in my gent's City suit and polished shoes.

Robin, along with Kenneth Parker and two *Mirror* men, sailed *Suhaili* along the south coast to Falmouth, where the snooty harbour master, although a graduate of the same shipping line, British India, condemned him to a remote berth under the harbour wall. (That same harbour master the following year, dressed up in his resplendent official uniform, wanted to be the first to congratulate the returning hero under the gaze of television and press cameras – but he was not invited on board.) By now, the *Sunday Times* had announced its race and at least half a dozen competitors had entered, although Robin would be the first to start by a margin of some weeks. We had both taken the view that what Harry Evans and his newspaper did was their own affair. We had been the first to announce that Robin was going to attempt a non-stop circumnavigation and, as far as he was concerned, it had nothing to do with the *Sunday Times*. In other words, he never entered their competition and was not issued, as the official entrants were, with one of their radio telephones.

But that did not stop Harry sending a reporter to interview 'our boy'. It must have been 13 June, the day before his departure. Turmoil fell from the air; that awful feeling of 'Have I forgotten something vital?' enveloped all of us who were helping to load the stores. First aid? – yes; a pair of scissors to cut his nails and his beard, if need be? – yes; cigarettes at the rate of a pack a day? – well, maybe; something to light them with? – hell, where is the cigarette lighter and the fuel? And so on. The calculations were hampered by the exquisite feeling of hangover that penetrated most of us. The team was staying at a friendly small hotel and pub in an alleyway just off the harbour: the Captain's Cabin served pints of smooth West Country ale.

Some of us must have had sore eyes, for the reporter was indeed a sight. Clad in a dove-grey suit with a Leander-type pink tie to match the pink ribbon around the panama hat that rode lightly on his crisp curls, he pranced delicately between the bollards, the coils of rope and the remaining stores cluttering the harbour wall. He demanded an interview there and then with Robin, who looked at him for a searching moment and then turned his red-rimmed eyes on me.

'That little prick's from the *Sunday Times*, isn't he?' I nodded. 'I think I'll throw him in the harbour.'

Robin was – and is – immensely strong. He could have tossed the journalist over the side with one hand. By now, Ken Parker, sniffing trouble ahead, climbed ashore from *Suhaili* and came up to us. We drew Robin out of earshot, agreed that the preening visitor deserved a good spanking – but now was not the right moment. No one in the team wanted to do the

Sunday Times a useful turn but on the other hand there was no point in needlessly upsetting them. Give the 'little prick' a brief interview – and be done with it. Robin contented himself by saying that, if he were ever to win their Golden Globe, he would fling it in the harbour instead, and, humour restored, agreed to be interviewed.

The following morning, 14 June 1968, he slipped his mooring and quietly headed out towards the open sea, accompanied by a *Sunday Mirror* launch for last-minute photographs and messages. There were only a few family and friends to wave him farewell from that remote corner of Falmouth harbour.

As the weeks went by and *Suhaili* trudged ever further south towards the Cape of Good Hope and then still more southwards and eastwards into the Roaring Forties, other swifter contestants set out to claim the reward, until there were ten of them pursuing Robin. But, one by one, they fell away. John Ridgway had to put in to a South African port when his boat was damaged in a gale. The same fate befell his one-time rowing partner, Chay Blyth. Some lasted the long push to Australia – but that was the limit. And still Robin plugged serenely on. Moitessier, the great French lone sailor, was closing in fast and seemed likely to overtake *Suhaili* in the Cape Horn area but then the Frenchman decided to keep sailing eastwards, across the southern Atlantic, past South Africa and on till he came to the Pacific islands.

And then there was Donald Crowhurst. He was apparently the kind of man to be seen propping up the bar at a rather flashy county club, dressed in a slightly too tight double-breasted blazer with crested gilt buttons, a Guards-type striped tie and a froth of white handkerchief protruding from his left sleeve. He had, it seems, boasted of his prowess as a single-handed sailor in the pubs and clubs around Portsmouth, and had been interviewed on local radio to a point where the *Sunday Times* called his bluff, equipped him with a radio telephone, paid him some money and pressed him to perform. After some weeks at sea, he began to put up prodigious daily mileages and, in spite of his late start, looked like catching up with the leaders in the early spring of 1969.

Francis Chichester had been appointed judge of the *Sunday*

Times race. It was his task to interpret the all-too-ambiguous rules that had been drafted in a hurry and to ensure, as far as possible, that no competitor cheated by putting ashore, taking on fresh stores or equipment or receiving assistance from an outside source. He telephoned me and asked if I knew anything about Donald Crowhurst. I said he had the reputation of being a blowhard and had apparently broken down in tears on the night before his departure, but that was only gossip I had picked up from the *Sunday Times* Grays Inn Road office.

'What's the point, Francis? Why do you ask?'

He lowered his voice like a conspirator. 'Just a weird hunch,' he said. 'I'm beginning to think – *maybe* – the fellow's a phoney.'

'Good God! But he's doing so well.'

'Exactly, George. Too damned well. At least, that's how it's starting to look.'

He went on to blind me with science. Many weeks before, when he was well into the southern Atlantic, Crowhurst had gone off the air and had maintained radio silence. Now he had started transmitting again; he was well past Cape Horn and indeed, according to his latest position, not far short of the Equator on the return leg. Francis had calculated the maximum daily knottage of Crowhurst's boat, with special reference to the distances claimed since he had begun to report again. Even with favourable winds throughout, it all looked a little too good. And Francis knew from personal experience that the prevailing winds in the southern ocean and the South Atlantic would not have been consistently favourable. Either Crowhurst, the weekend sailor, was beating all the professionals at their own game – and by an extraordinary margin – or he was cheating. Next day, I went round to Francis's office, and was shown the maps and charts on which he had plotted Crowhurst's progress. Even to my untutored eye, the trail of dots with dates against them looked mighty strange.

When he asked my advice, I said that he should report his suspicions under the seal of confidentiality to the *Sunday Times*. After all, I said, he had a great reputation to protect. Were Crowhurst to win the Golden Globe and later on it emerged that he had grossly cheated and that Sir Francis Chichester, the judge, had been suspicious from an early stage and had done nothing about it, Crowhurst would not be the only figure in the dock.

Months later, the facts emerged. Donald Crowhurst had sailed across the Equator and had then turned to starboard and put in at a remote fishing port on the east coast of South America. His plan was to stay hidden ashore, until the honest competitors had completed two-thirds of their voyages and were steering northwards from the South Atlantic. He would then embark and race back ahead of them. When he did so, R/T messages told him of the growing suspicions against him. He was already on a short psychological fuse and the thought of returning to Portsmouth not in a cloud of glory but to face an inquisition proved to be the detonator. He jumped off his boat, which was found drifting weeks later.

One tragic repercussion was that a Royal Navy officer, who had taken leave to compete in the race and who would have come in a comfortable second to Robin, fearing that Crowhurst was overtaking him, pushed his catamaran too hard. One of the hulls was damaged and he had to limp into the Canaries and end his great effort.

And still Robin kept plugging on. Soon after rounding the Horn, he 'went off the air'. Apparently, a fault developed in his radio telephone. He could pick up radio messages and weather forecasts from the Falkland Islands but could not transmit messages. (I write 'apparently', because I had learned some time before that he was not just a bluff, hearty sea-dog but was as competitive as they come, though he always kept within the rules. I have never pressed this point with him and it may well be that the apparatus for transmissions did develop a fault. At least, we can say that his radio silence kept his few rivals guessing – not least Crowhurst, who then seemed to present the biggest danger.)

A month went by, then two months and three months. Even those in his dry-land team, who knew that Robin was as tough as the teak that went into constructing *Suhaili*, began to have faint tremors of worry. But he must have fiddled with that radio apparatus to good effect. One Sunday evening in springtime, I was sitting at home reading a typescript, when the telephone rang. A voice announced that the Portishead radio station was calling. Would I accept a ship-to-shore call from the mid-Atlantic? I said yes – and there was Robin sounding as though he had just got back from a pleasant weekend's sailing. Everything was going fine, although he had run out of cigarettes. He was south-west of the Canaries and should be in sight of Falmouth before the end of the month. He had tried to call his family but they must have been at evensong. Woud I please tell them the news and send his love?

It was a moment to savour. He was safe – and that was the great thing. And he had more than repaid the confidence and support of his friends and sponsors. What made me enjoy my celebratory large scotch all the more was the smirking thought that the ten 'hares' who had actually entered the *Sunday Times* race had gone hopping and puffing and skipping out of the newspaper's columns, whereas the 'tortoise' had kept quiet and gone plodding on to be the solitary finisher.

Even then, the *Sunday Times* managed to get one last sting in the tail. There is an island a mile or two off Falmouth Harbour. Having spent over 311 days at sea on his own, Robin took the most direct route back, leaving the island on his starboard side. But in its nautical wisdom, the newspaper decreed that the finishing line was on the other side of the island, which involved his having to tack against the current and the winds and spending another hour or so at sea.

Falmouth was then a small seaside town and port with narrow streets and quaint alleyways. On 22 April 1969, it was swarming with people waiting to greet the hero. The *Sunday Mirror* had hung banners across the streets. Along the harbour wall, there was hardly room to move. The buzz and excitement grew as the small yacht came closer, and at last anchored a few hundred yards offshore. The harbour master, who had been less than helpful the year before, dressed in a uniform that would have made a Swiss admiral jealous, rushed to and fro in his launch.

As Robin had not spoken face to face with human beings for many months, he was to be broken in gradually. His two younger brothers, Chris and Ian, and I were to go on board

Suhaili with a bottle of champagne, and chat for a quarter of an hour before he came ashore and held a press conference. The stench and squalor of the cabin needed a Dante to describe. A pair of rugger stockings were so stiff with dirt that they almost stood up by themselves. Robin had been awake and on his feet non-stop for thirty-six hours, to avoid being run down by one of the many ships crowding the approaches to the Channel.

After the opening congratulations and the first nose-tingling draught of champagne, Robin took me aside. He had been thinking, he said. He wanted to double my firm's commission – from 10 to 20 per cent – as a measure of his gratitude for the help given.

After another swig, I said, 'Bob, this champagne's getting warm. Let's finish it and go ashore. We'll have one hell of a party tonight, then you have a good night's sleep – and we'll forget you ever mentioned it. But next to having you back in one piece, it's the nicest thing that's happened today.'

I could not help contrasting his homecoming with the one three years earlier.

Robin and his supporters had made a vow before his departure that on the night of his return he would sit down to the largest and juiciest steak in the whole of Falmouth, washed down with at least a bottle of fine red wine. The press conference over, we all trooped into the hotel dining room and the giant steak, sizzling gently with a plateful of chips, was placed before him. He smiled with delighted anticipation. For over 300 days, he had lived on a kind of permanent Irish stew, which he replenished regularly with tinned beef and vegetables. All that time, he had been dreaming of this moment, he said. He managed two mouthfuls of the steak and a few sips of the wine, and then had to admit defeat. Sheer fatigue, the excitement of the hour, the enveloping warmth of the reception and, above all, the physical contraction of his appetite through all those months at sea had done for him.

During recent weeks I had been interested in Francis' reaction to Robin's approaching success. He had reacted strongly – overreacted, in my opinion – when Alec Rose made his futile challenge and he had been nettled when

Harold Wilson arranged a knighthood for Rose. As Sheila put it in her upper-class minor key of a voice, 'A knighthood for that greengrocer, George – it's unthinkable! What *are* we coming to? Why, he called in at ports where I didn't know they had ports.' And now here was this young, handsome mariner who was about to create a world record and, perhaps, cast a deep shadow over his own. I privately suspected that Francis would be antagonistic.

I did him a grave disservice. He was genuinely pleased and when they met for the first time – Francis was staying at a luxury hotel a few miles out of Falmouth – they at once got on well. Robin already had a great respect for what Francis had achieved and for his supreme navigational skills, and Francis admired the young man's endurance, his courage and, perhaps above all, his modesty. As the appointed judge, he was to hand over the Golden Globe to Robin at a special dinner, organised by the *Sunday Times*, the following evening.

But there was to be one last twist of the knife. As it was a *Sunday Times* knife, it inevitably proved to be blunt. There had been a report that Robin's voyage had not been non-stop. *Suhaili* had been caught on a sandbank off the coast of the South Island, New Zealand, as the tide was running out. Robin had taken the opportunity of going over the side and careening her hull. When the tide came in again, she floated off the temporary obstacle and sailed on eastwards. It had either been a deliberate and skilled manoeuvre, or an accident: no doubt Robin would argue with a straight face that he had misjudged the tide and the presence of a sandbank. The question was – did the brief stopover contravene the race rules?

That afternoon, a few hours before the dinner, Francis called his committee of experts together to determine the problem. There was himself as race judge. Then there was Charles Barnard from *True* Magazine, who had flown over specially to greet his protégé and who just happened to be at the hotel. As a teenager, Charles had done some sailing with his family around Cape Cod but was somewhat rusty. The third and last expert was myself. Apart from wartime troopships, my experiences on water were largely limited to a few brisk rows on the Regent's Park lake with my sons. Besides, I had to disqualify myself because, as Robin's agent, I had a direct interest in the outcome of our meeting. At which point, Charles disqualified himself as the American magazine publisher.

Francis said, 'Right, boys, having got that out of the way, let's get down to sorting out these damned rules.'

Which we did, to the ultimate benefit of the only finisher, the newspaper and its lucky Golden Globe, which did not end up at the bottom of Falmouth Harbour, as threatened.*

Francis continued to keep himself in fine physical trim. He went in for yoga and spent hours standing on his head. Most weekends, he would fast, living on copious draughts of water and thinking to expel poisons out of his system that way. With his questing and experimental mind, he was alert to any innovations that might ease the physical effort required by a sailor. I recall setting up a lunch for him to meet Chris Bonington, who had recently become a client. Francis had heard about the technical mountaineering device called a 'jumar', a ratchet on the rope, employed by a climber on vertical rock without footholds. He was wondering whether it might be adapted for ascending a mainmast – and the lunch table was soon covered in pages of sketches as the two experts in their fields bounced ideas to and fro like ping-pong balls.

Over the next year or two, he spent much of his time sailing off the Hamble and occasionally taking a leisurely trip across the Atlantic where Sheila and Giles, or one of them, would act as crew. When he told me that he was being pressed to enter the 1972 single-handed race, I did my best to dissuade him, even though some rich inducements were on offer. I had a nasty feeling it would be like the case of the famous boxer who has one fight too many or of the racing driver who stays on the circuits when his vision and the speed of his reactions are that much worse than when he was at his prime. Francis

* As I recall, we introduced a new rule stating that competitors must not attach their boats to any form of 'artificial or man-made obstacles'.

had nothing to prove, as I told him. There was no one in the race who could come close to matching his achievements.

But when his mind was set, nothing was going to deflect him. He entered – and I drove down to Plymouth the day before the start to wish him Godspeed. We met in his suite at the Holiday Inn, the hotel he had officially declared open two or three years before. Behind it was an old pub, newly rechristened The Gipsy Moth. This was indeed Chichester country. We had not met in person for six or eight weeks, as it happened, and privately I was both surprised and saddened to see how thin he had grown. He had always been a spry, wiry type with no spare flesh but now there appeared to be an inch or two all round between his shirt collar and his neck. Those square wrists and muscular hands seemed to have shrunk. That afternoon, he took me down to the harbour to go aboard *Gipsy Moth*. She was moored well away from the harbour wall. The tide was out and there was a drop of perhaps fifteen feet from the top of the wall to the surface of the water. We were to be rowed out to the yacht but first had to climb down some slippery, seaweedy, iron rungs let into the harbour wall.

In the usual way, there would have been some barbed remarks about landlubbers unable to cope and how the youngster – I was fifty-five – couldn't keep up with the veteran. But not this time. Francis's progress down the ladder and into the rowing boat beneath was even more shaky and uncrisp than my own, and when he finally sat down heavily in the boat, I could see his chest heaving for breath. This man, I felt, isn't fit to sail a boat on the Norfolk Broads, let alone the broad Atlantic with its gales and storms. I had a hunch that Sheila felt as I did but was going to give him the chance of one last grand sailing gesture. And I couldn't go charging in at the judges and demand that he be medically examined and then disqualified on the grounds of ill health.

I watched the start of the race next morning from the grandstand of the Hoe and saw *Gipsy Moth*, hugging the cliffside, disappear to the west and crossed my thumbs before driving back to London. Perhaps I had misjudged the situation, not for the first time, and Francis would use his years of experience to preserve his energy. But a few days

out, he was run into at night by a French trawler without
lights. The mainmast was broken and *Gipsy Moth* drifted as
a helpless hulk until Francis could be taken off and the yacht
towed back into Plymouth. Even then, another French boat,
full of nosy tourists, came in too close and interfered with the
rescue operation.

Visiting him in Plymouth Hospital a few days later, I could
see that he was even physically weaker than he had been at our
meeting earlier. But his spirit was as combative as ever. He was
highly indignant over a report that hinted that the collision
with the French trawler had been his fault and insisted on
drafting, with myself as scribe, a letter to *The Times*, hotly
denying the calumny.

My wife and I were due to take a motoring holiday, touring
Scotland, in 1972 and we left London on the morning of 26
August. We were half-way up the M1 and were thinking of
stopping for lunch when a message inside my head told me
urgently to switch on the car radio, which I kept permanently
tuned to what was then the Third Programme. The announcer
had just begun to read the news. The first words I heard were,
'We regret to announce the death of Sir Francis Chichester.' In
my heart, I had never expected him to leave Plymouth Hospital
on his feet but, even so, the news of his final voyage caused
a pang.

11

EXILES

Michael Joseph was a man of wit, charm and distinction. To
prove him the possessor of such qualities, one only has to refer
to his remark, 'Authors are easy to get on with if you are fond
of children'; or part of his speech at the Foyle's Jubilee Dinner
in 1954. 'Publishing is merely a matter of saying Yes and No at
the right time'; or his cabled reply to the angry novelist who
demanded an immediate decision on his script, as he had other
irons in the fire: 'SUGGEST YOU EXTRACT IRONS AND
INSERT MANUSCRIPT'.

When I was a young and raw agent, Michael, who had been
himself a leading agent with Curtis Brown before the war and
who was now looked on as one of the outstanding publishing
talents, went out of his way to seek my advice on a book
about ponies. He knew I was agent for Pat Smythe, then the
most famous horsewoman in Europe, perhaps the world. My
knowledge of ponies was nil, as Michael would have realised,
and I was not a total fool; it never hurts to flatter a tyro,
who one day might have a good book going begging. But
the warmth with which he pursued his enquiries quite won
me over.

He had been married to Hermione Gingold, the actress, but,
some years after that marriage ended in divorce, he wed Anthea

Hodson, the daughter of Lord Justice Hodson. She had been his secretary and knew at least the rudiments of publishing, but was still a learner when in 1958 at the age of sixty Michael died. Beneath his benign exterior and ready wit, he must have been a worrier; he suffered from stomach ulcers. Apparently, an inflamed ulcer gave him more than usually severe pains, he pooh-poohed treatment, the ulcer burst, peritonitis set in and in those early days for antibiotics it was too late to save him.

Perhaps he had had a premonition, for not long before his death he sold the firm to *Illustrated London News*, which in turn at the end of 1961 was taken over by Roy Thomson, then on the rampage in the media world. The three most senior directors at Michael Joseph Ltd, all of them professional publishers, felt that they were being bought and sold like cattle; they walked out, with the objective of taking over Jonathan Cape through the financial backing of Sir Allen Lane. (If I may advertise my own wares, any reader interested in finding out what happened next in the fifty-yard journey from Bloomsbury Street to 30 Bedford Square should read Chapter V of my book, *Scribblers for Bread*.) Peter Hebdon, one of the trio, soon rejoined Michael Joseph but the firm was still left in a perilous position. It lacked a senior editor and a commanding presence such as Michael himself had provided. Many people in the trade thought it might soon go under. Anthea, choking back the tears, told me on the telephone that she had rung Spencer Curtis Brown for support and he had said brusquely that his agency had no time for losers. Innes Rose and I assured her of our complete backing.

At that time, Farquharson's had for several years represented British rights for a small New York agency run almost single-handedly by Robert P. Mills. Some men and women become agents because they think it an easy path to riches, others because they like the secret power of treating with authors at their most vulnerable. Bob Mills was an agent because he loved good writing and wanted to do all he could to enhance it. He had an eclectic client list; the potentially most exciting name on it in the early 1960s was that of James Baldwin.

We tend to forget that almost a century after the American

Civil War the great gulf between black and white had still not been bridged. I remember driving a hire-car from Washington south across the Mason-Dixon Line, through Virginia, the Carolinas, Georgia and Alabama, noticing the segregated buses, the 'Whites Only' cafés and bars, black families in the backwoods living in a rusty old sedan jacked up on bricks, the general air of torpor and hopelessness in the shanty towns of the South. In 1960, driving through the squalor of Harlem on my way back from across the George Washington Bridge, I braked too abruptly before a pedestrian crossing. An old black woman, lugging a heavy bag on the crossing, stopped and spat at the car. A gobful of hate slithered across the windscreen. James Baldwin was the angry voice of the dispossessed. Two other Negro writers, also as it happened Farquharson clients, Richard Wright and in his satirical way Chester Himes, had preceded him but Jimmy's was the voice and the force of the new day.

He wrote like an avenging angel but his prose style was the only ordered thing about him. Short and slight with brittle thin wrists and small, seemingly boneless hands, he had bulging hyperthyroid eyes and broad rubbery lips. He had a melodious voice and a frequent laugh, a cross between a cackle and a giggle. He was an overt homosexual years before Wolfenden opened the closet doors an inch or two and if he had come to London via France would probably have had a sailor from Marseilles in tow. He never had any money. The advances on his books were big and growing bigger with each new work but he could never stay long in one place, he spent lavishly on his travels and on his friends and the hangers-on who claimed to be friends. I came to realise that his frequent visits to our (then) Red Lion Square office were not prompted so much by affection and respect as the knowledge that he could always borrow £50 or £100 at short notice. (£50 in 1960 would be about £600 today.)

Above all, he was brave. He was staying in a Swiss *pension* on one occasion. A band of German tourists were also guests and when they came into the dining room for breakfast, one of them, a big, burly young man, would walk past Jimmy's table, run the palm of his hand across the frizzy head and say, 'Good morning, nigger.' After the second time, Jimmy jumped up and challenged his tormentor to a fist fight. He weighed about nine stone and his opponent would have been almost twice as heavy and a head taller. Baldwin got thrashed – but that was the end of the tormenting.

His regular British publisher was Michael Joseph. Bob Mills had told me that a big novel, *Another Country*, was on the stocks. Bob, who was as laid back as he was shrewd, reckoned that, properly launched, it could be Jimmy's breakthrough novel, ending up at the top of the bestseller list. He knew, as I did, that Michael Joseph would buy a Baldwin novel sight unseen but he asked me to hold off. 'It's virtually finished,' he said. 'Just needs a final runthrough, minor editing. New York'll soon start humming about it – that's the time to strike. Okay?' I agreed. It would be crazy to sell it short.

A week or two later, Jimmy called at Red Lion Square. As ever, he needed a loan; the petty cash box was virtually empty and I had to send one of our staff to cash a cheque at our bank. The author and I chatted while this was going on. He told me he had been to Spain as a judge for the Prix Formentor. He had spent much time with George Weidenfeld, apparently another judge, and even now was staying at the London flat of Weidenfeld's senior editor. They badly wanted to publish his new novel.

If ideas could be fed into the national electricity grid, George Weidenfeld would light up London. He could look through one's client list and come up with a dozen ideas, some of them quite tolerable, for books through which he might 'borrow' the author from his regular publisher. Some of his thoughts were pretty fanciful. For example, if I had told him that my clients included Enid Blyton, John le Carré and Morris West, he might well have suggested a novel about a boy spy with Blyton writing the opening third, le Carré covering the boy's training at the Circus and West the finale where the young hero has to spy on the Pope.

He loved to cosy up to big names and powerful people. Always on the move between New York, London and Tel Aviv – he was an avowed and sincere Zionist – he was mercurial, intelligent and a great acquirer of authors. But many agents came to suspect that he was more interested in the pursuit than its aftermath; like the farmer who spent all his time hunting down the hares but who somehow failed to remember that the main object of the exercise was to sell the skins and cook the meat. George Weidenfeld never appeared to be equally caught up with the more mundane side of publishing – like chatting up the head buyers, cherishing the reps, getting invoices out on time. Many well-known people appeared on his list but few genuine bestsellers, whereas the firm of Michael Joseph had proved again and again that it could sell books better than most and as well as any rival. Michael's launching list in 1936 had included *How Green Was My Valley*. Twenty-five years later, H.E. Bates, Paul Gallico and C.S. Forester were just a few of the major novelists whose London 'home' was a narrow Georgian terrace house in Bloomsbury Street.

Jimmy Baldwin, I well knew, always listened to the last voice that spoke. Here he was, having spent a week subjected to the magnetic Weidenfeld personality and even now under the proximity and pressure of staying at a senior editor's flat; he was already attracted by the idea of a new publisher. I have always held that, unless a publisher behaves badly or negligently towards his author, the agent should be a marriage broker, not a divorce lawyer. Michael Joseph had done a good job for Jimmy thus far and in my opinion would sell far more copies of *Another Country* than Weidenfeld & Nicolson could. But what to do? It was getting on for 11.30 in the morning, far too early to call Bob Mills in New York for advice.

Denis Hamilton, when editor of the *Sunday Times*, was notorious for his occasional indecisiveness. Once he said to me with a sigh, indicating his cluttered desk, 'The buck stops here.'

'Yes,' I replied. 'And for a hell of a time, too.'

He gave me a wounded look.

This time, I had to move the buck – fast.

First, I insisted that Jimmy must have lunch with me that very day. There was an hour to kill but I put him in a spare room with a telephone so that he could call up various friends in London. In those days the calls went through the office switchboard and I quietly tipped off our operator to put any calls he might make to Weidenfeld & Nicolson at the back of the queue. When I went into the room once to make sure he had settled down happily, I found him joking on the phone with an old friend, Ava Gardner (O lucky man!). My secretary booked my usual table at The Ivy for one o'clock. Then I set to work.

I knew that Peter Hebdon lunched frequently at The Ivy, which was a furlong from his office, and that Anthea also used it, though not so often. I rang Peter, explained the situation and said that, if they wanted to keep Baldwin, he and Anthea had better drop whatever other lunch engagements they might have and book a separate table at The Ivy without fail. Peter, that great seller of books and jovial companion, saw the point at once. I took a deep breath and pressed on. It is normally the agent's job to prepare a new contract but with Baldwin chatting away in the next room, I could not risk his discovering my plan. So I wanted Peter Hebdon to have a new contract prepared in his office, including the same terms as in the previous one except that the advance was to be doubled. I had already explained that according to Bob Mills, whom Peter knew and respected, *Another Country* was going to be an exceptional novel.

It was a lot to ask. Peter was a bluff, tough Yorkshireman but he knew me well enough to accept that I was in for the long run, not the quick kill, whereby the agent tries and too often succeeds in making the publisher overbid and end up with a big, unearned balance that eventually has to be written off. Great fun for the agent and his pocketful of commission but too often disastrous for the publisher and dissatisfying to the conscientious author. I did not have to stress that the deal must attract Baldwin with a tempting sum of money due on signature of contract. Peter Hebdon had a quick word with Anthea, who picked up the spare telephone in his room and we had a brief three-cornered chat. They agreed.

So Jimmy and I took a cab to The Ivy. We had a couple of drinks before lunch, a bottle of wine with the meal and a brandy or two with our coffee. It was that

nice world-without-end hour when all the rough corners
are magically smoothed off. I happened to look across
the room, then turned to Jimmy and said, 'Talk about
coincidence! There's Anthea and Peter Hebdon over there.
Small world. I think they've finished – let's get 'em over for
another cognac.'

I waved and they joined our table. Jimmy knew Peter quite
well and the four of us had a pleasant, if inconsequential, chat.
Then I told Jimmy he ought to go back with them to their
office. It was his lucky day, I said. We had fixed a new
contract on vastly better terms and there would be some cash
in his pocket as soon as he signed his name on the last page. I
had to rush back to my own office for an appointment but if
he had any problems, he only had to pick up the phone and
call me. So off he went, shepherded by his two publishers,
one on each side. He did indeed ring me half an hour later
but not with a query over the contract. Having now signed
up with Michael Joseph, he wondered what he should say to
his host, the Weidenfeld & Nicolson editor, when the latter
returned from work that evening, fully expecting him to sign
up with them.

'That's easy, Jimmy,' I said. 'I half thought of that and
arranged for Peter to pay you £200 in notes out of the advance
on signature. Did he?'

'Oh, sure.'

'Well then, grab a cab, go round to the flat, pack your bags
and check in to a hotel for the night. You've got an hour or
two – but don't hang about. Okay?'

It was a long time ago, over thirty years. To borrow
Marlowe's mighty lines:

. . . but that was in another country;
And besides, the wench is dead.

In this context, 'the wench' would be Anthea Joseph, who
died young of cancer. Peter Hebdon, who always drove
himself hard, died from a heart attack on the last leg of
a round-the-world business flight. Jimmy Baldwin died at
the end of 1987, a shell of the man he once was. As the

temporary survivor of the quartet, I look back with sadness at their premature passing but with genuine pleasure over the episode itself. In a world that even then was turning towards the 'me first', 'never had it so good', snouts-in-the-trough outlook, where lawyers would make fortunes because no one could be trusted to keep an oral promise, it was a shining example of trust. James Baldwin trusted me enough to sign at my bidding a document I had not read; I trusted Peter Hebdon and Anthea Joseph to draw up a contract for his signature that would not cheat him. And they trusted my word, based on that of Bob Mills, the prime agent, that *Another Country* was going to be an exceptional novel.

As indeed it proved to be on publication. The book was widely praised, it shot to the top of the bestseller lists in New York and London, and stayed there for weeks, and a year later Corgi had a comparable success with the paperback edition. It brought its author riches and additional fame. And yet it was the acme of a mercurial career. Already, Baldwin was viewed with suspicion by the more intransigent American blacks like Malcolm X and the Black Panthers. When that crafty politician, President Kennedy, tried to defuse the racial tension by calling James Baldwin to the White House as an advisor, many of his people felt he had sold out. He never advocated the bullet and the bomb as the panacea for the black man and woman's burden. With Jimmy, it was always *The Fire Next Time*, never now. That was part of his generous spirit, his magnanimity, but it lost him admirers among his own people during the divisive decade that spanned the Vietnam War.

His final years were mainly spent in France, at the 'Matisserie' of St-Paul-de-Vence; a cushioned exile but a sad decline. He had broken off from his sage mentor, Bob Mills, and had taken on a black woman agent who worked out of Paris. His writing was now sporadic and no longer memorable, a reworking of an age that had been overtaken by new and different variations on the old problems.

Seven years after that episode, Harold Evans, editor of the *Sunday Times*, telephoned me. He had heard from a reliable source that Kim Philby, the traitor-spy who had fled (or been allowed to flee?) from Beirut to Moscow, was writing his memoirs. Why didn't I pop over to Moscow, meet Philby and become his literary agent? His son John happened to be living in Gayton Road, Hampstead, a hundred yards or so from my home. He was in regular touch with his father and could fix up things for me. All that he, Harry, required from the tip-off was first crack at the British serial rights in the memoirs.

To say that I was confused when I put the telephone down would be a serious understatement. Through the good offices of my client, Brian Glanville, then the *Sunday Times* chief football correspondent, I had met Harry in the first few days of his arrival in London from the northern provinces. I had to a minor extent shown him the ropes; we played squash once or twice every week, had done some useful business together and had long become friends. Even so, he had just made a strangely quixotic gesture. Why introduce an agent at all to the scene? A middle man would only push up the prices on his client's behalf. Harry himself would only be interested in the newspaper serial rights but of course he knew that two worthy publishing houses, Hamish Hamilton and Michael Joseph, were part of the Thomson empire, along with his own paper. It would be the simplest and most profitable move to make a comprehensive bid for all the 'printed word' rights in Philby's book.

Then the rouble dropped. Even if it cost more, keeping the traitor at arm's length would be a diplomatic move if the authorities or public opinion came down on the newspaper. Having an auctioneer in the ring might sanitise the bidders by concentrating the censure against the man who called for the bids. I never discussed the point with Harry Evans but, assuming these suspicions were correct, I did not then blame him nor have I since. In his shoes, I too would have wanted to interpose a barrier between myself and a sordid traitor.

Before I had thought things through, John Philby called on me. A shy, almost passively quiet young man with fair hair combed down in a fringe across his forehead, he only seemed to come alive when discussing photography. I gathered he wanted to become a professional. I admired him for his courage in maintaining his rather unusual surname but wondered privately whether his father's misdeeds and public shame had helped to bring on his great reticence.

After supper that evening, I went for a long walk on Hampstead Heath. Part of me was attracted to the prospect of visiting Moscow, then still a remote and guarded city. (I assumed that the KGB must have approved the writing of the memoirs and thus the way would be made easy for my visit.) Another part of me was fascinated by the opportunity of meeting the enigmatic Philby in the flesh. I had met Churchill several times during the war, and Roosevelt and Stalin at the Tehran Conference. Stalin had given an overwhelming impression of cold evil but what brand might permeate Philby? And, of course, it would be a very profitable coup to handle his book.

Somewhere between Parliament Hill and Kenwood, I decided it was not for me. Whatever the favourable factors from my point of view, the man was despicable, a quiet assassin who had betrayed British secret agents to his Russian masters, and who had lied and intrigued his way from Spain to Washington DC, as far as Whitehall, taking in and undermining the Establishment wherever his slimy path wound. Why provide a man like that with a forum and a megaphone? I would ring Harry Evans on the morrow and say politely, 'Thanks – but no thanks'.

Before I could do so, his editor-in-chief, Denis Hamilton, called me. He was furious. He said, 'I never thought it of you, George, but you've become a real shit!'

'What are you getting at?'

'You and Kim Philby.'

'But . . .'

He cut across my answer. 'You know George Brown is going to denounce you in the House this afternoon? As a traitor to this country.'

'I doubt that, Denis. Very much.'

'What makes you think he won't?'

'George is a client of mine.'

That was no bluff. Through the industrial correspondent

of the *Guardian*, John Anderson, Sir Francis Chichester's friend, I had been introduced to the Foreign Secretary, that extraordinary man-child. Lacking most formal education, he possessed a razor-sharp intellect and could skim through an eight-page closely typed brief in two minutes, extracting the 'juice' from the Foreign Office's measured 'On the one hand, this . . . On the other hand, that'. And yet after one gin and tonic too many, his petulant tantrums would outdo the yells of a spoiled three-year-old. But he was a big man for all that, and he had long grown disenchanted with Harold Wilson's posturings and pettifogging intrigues. There would soon be a bust-up. Sensing it, George Brown was quietly beginning work on his memoirs, *In My Way*, assisted by John Anderson. Ironically, within eighteen months of Denis Hamilton's tirade, I would be selling serial rights to his newspaper for £35,000 (worth almost £300,000 today).

But unlike *I Pagliacci*, the comedy had one more act to run. There was no denunciation by the Foreign Secretary in the House of Commons that afternoon but there was a polite summons to the Foreign and Commonwealth Office to meet the Permanent Under-Secretary of State, Sir Denis (now Lord) Greenhill. I proceeded up the marble stairs behind a tail-coated flunkey, taken along various corridors and brought face to face with Sir Denis, a man in his mid-fifties with smooth hair and a smooth face. I cannot say that he further resembled Lord Castlereagh and there were no bloodhounds in evidence. He waved me to an antique chair on one side of the open fireplace and then sat down on the other side. Another flunkey brought in a teapot, milk, and two cups and saucers on a mahogany tray. The cups and saucers were of the finest china, seemingly as fragile and light as eggshells.

Sir Denis told me what I already knew: that Philby was an out-and-out villain, who for many years had betrayed his country's secrets and sent many brave men to certain torture and death. HMG could not stop him from writing his memoirs, which were bound to consist of disinformation, but they did want to prevent the book from having credibility. If it were represented in Britain by a well-known literary agency with a high reputation – 'such as yours', he added – that would automatically make it much more credible. I had been in the infantry in the war, he said, and fought at Alamein; he hoped I would be enough of a patriot to forgo the Philby book.

I told him I could not understand what all the fuss was about. A good many hours ago, I had decided to have nothing to do with Philby and was on the point of passing my decision to Harold Evans when first Hamilton, and now he, had jumped to the wrong conclusion. The stable door was indeed bolted. But the horse had been firmly inside all the time.

He thanked me, we finished our tea and then, like a good host, he saw me to the head of the marble stairs where we shook hands. Throughout the visit, a strange sensation had been creeping through me, a kind of *Last Year at Marienbad* dream-feeling. I seemed to have been in this place before, experiencing the same kind of encounter. And then I realised. As Ernest Bevin, a previous dweller in these marble halls, had said of George Lansbury's speeches, 'Clitch! Clitch!' This was the ultimate cliché, dragged in by every third-rate espionage film or TV drama: when the head of the service debriefs the operational agent returned from enemy territory.

Sir Denis put a friendly hand on my shoulder and asked in a quiet voice, 'Did you drive here in your blue Alvis?'

I smiled and shook my head before moving off but I thought Oh no, now you've spoiled it. That cheap little trick, employed many years before by Superintendant Smith of the Special Branch, you can't fool us, we know all about you, Big Brother is watching. I could well understand a brutal copper flexing his invisible power to impress a possible suspect but I did not expect the Permanent Under-Secretary to show off like that. Two phone calls, one to New Scotland Yard and one in reply, would swiftly establish the make and colour of my car. It was as much as to say, 'Okay, you've behaved as we wanted you to this time round but don't forget the long arm of the FCO if you're ever tempted to stray again.'

As far as I was concerned, he then was and would remain a green hill far away.

12

PULLING RANK IN THE HIMALAYAS

In September 1975, I clambered aboard a Pilatus Porter high-wing monoplane at Kathmandu Airport. The City suit had been swapped for breeches, scarlet stockings and trekking boots; I was toting a heavy rucksack, replete with down jacket and trousers, sleeping bag, long-johns and all the paraphernalia needed for a walk up to the thin, cold air of the Himalayas. Backed by Barclays Bank as its main sponsors, a British team led by Chris Bonington had put four members on to the summit of Everest via the hitherto unclimbed south-west face. It had been a magnificent feat of mountaineering and Alan Tritton, the bank director most closely concerned with the venture, his American wife Diana and I were to trek up towards the Everest Base Camp and congratulate the team in person.

I was then fifty-eight and it was thirty years since I had last roughed it in the army. It was also four years since I had stopped playing squash. How the residue of all those business lunches and the lungs sooted up by many decades of steady smoking would cope with the new physical demands was a problem about to be faced. I was not alone as a beginner on the Everest trail. Diana Tritton, a tall Californian, had airily announced back in London that she had never walked more than four miles in her life. We were not sure whether she meant four miles at any one time or four miles *in toto*. In the event, she glided like a land-based swan up and down the steepest gradients without a sign of distress.

Kathmandu is on a high plateau, some 6,000 feet above sea level, with the mountain range about twenty miles to the north. The plan was to fly to Lukla, an airstrip scratched out of the lower range at 8,000 feet, where we would meet our Sherpa guides and helpers carrying tents and cooking equipment. From there it was shanks' pony through the pine forests along the Dudh Khosi river, across the swaying Hillary bridge, and then plodding higher and higher to Namche Bazar, Khumjung, where Ed Hillary had built a school and a hospital for the local sherpas, on to Thyangboche Monastery and then the last few miles to Base Camp at 17,000 feet. My feelings of doubt were not lightened by the first sight of the Lukla airstrip, when the Swiss pilot skilfully dived through the cotton-wool wisps of cloud to make his approach. The runway, which ended in a steep wall of rock, had a vertical slope on its eastern side and an equally vertical drop to the west. To add the exclamation mark, if one were needed, several crashed aircraft, which had been dragged off the runway, littered the sides of the strip. But the landing was smooth, we humped our rucksacks and other gear off the plane, joined up with the Sherpas and then began one of the most momentous two weeks of my life.

It was back to nature with a vengeance. The truism has to be stated: there were no telephones, no postal service, no cables – none of those essential adjuncts to aid the self-esteem of the modern businessman. Everything to be used on the journey had to be carried, food, tents, camping gear. We Western adults were embarrassed, ashamed even, to see Sherpa girls of twelve or thirteen, always smiling, putting a couple of rucksacks into a wicker basket and then hoisting it on to their backs by means of a leather strap which they placed across their foreheads. Barefoot on the rough track, they leaned forward as they walked, to take the weight on their heads and necks. I did at least carry my smaller pack for overnight use but knew that I would collapse in a heap after a few yards if I had tried to transport the bigger one. You quickly become attuned to nature, waking with the light, trekking for two or three hours each morning, taking a light lunch and a rest in the heat of the day; then another couple of hours' trek, covering perhaps ten miles in the day. The Sherpa leader would find a convenient camping spot, his helpers would erect the tents, the cookboy would get his fire going and cook yakburgers on a kind of barbecue and anyone who wanted to stay up chatting after supper would need to put on a down jacket as at those heights the temperature dropped like a stone after dark. Then to bed on the ground with only a groundsheet or a plastic strip between the sleeping bag and the hard ground. And sleep was never sweeter.

The lung-creasing, leg-muscle contortions involved in the trek – like an ant climbing up and down the teeth of a giant saw inclined upwards at an angle of forty-five degrees – and the narrowness of the track meant that we walked at our own pace in a single file that stretched several hundred yards from front to rear. That was another real luxury for me. After years of continual talking – to authors and publishers in person or on the telephone or muttering inanely into a tape recorder – it was a balm to trudge along in silence, gazing at the glittering peaks on either side, close enough, it seemed, in the clear, thin air, to reach out and touch; walking delicately along a track with a drop of several thousand feet a pace to the right and watching a lammergeyer with dark wings like two perplexed eyebrows finding a thermal current in the void some hundreds of feet beneath me and soaring effortlessly as far again above; following the Sherpa cook up a steep incline and round the corner when he stopped abruptly, went down on his knees and said in a devout tone, 'Sagarmatha! Sagarmatha!' He had caught the first glimpse of Mount Everest, a holy shrine to the Nepalese, and now I could see it, framed in a notch of closer mountains, massive and dreadful as it loomed against the afternoon sky with its eternal plume of cloud astride the summit. There was the never-ending tinkling of the prayer wheels, tugged by the winds across the Thyangboche Monastery plateau or the hands of the faithful; the wizened Buddhist abbot whose piety and benevolence were matched only by his commercial instincts for raising funds for the training of more monks – these are images my memory could never reject.

The reunion with Chris's climbing team and the BBC television crew who had accompanied them on the mountain was celebrated with Sherpa beer, that sludgy, sour concoction made from fermented yak's milk. (At least, that was the recipe I was given; I would hate to think of other possibilities.) The celebrations were muted because Mick Burke, an old climbing comrade of Chris and the others, many of whom had been with him on the successful first ascent of Annapurna five years before, had gone missing high up on the mountain. Mick, an expert cameraman as well as a fine climber, had been in charge of the high-level film work. Dougal Haston and Doug Scott had been the first pair to reach the summit, followed by Pete Boardman, the youngest ever to get to the top, and Sherpa Pertemba. Mick had last been seen above Camp Six when the weather turned bad and a blizzard set in. He had great drive and determination; the feeling among the team was that he almost certainly made the summit but perished on the way down.

Our trek ended back at Syangboche airstrip at an altitude of around 11,000 feet. The surroundings were dramatic. At the end of the airstrip was a deep gorge, beyond which the proud snowbound triangle of the holy Mount Amadablam, one of the highest peaks in the range, soared into the dazzling sky. On a spur north-east of the strip and about 1,000 feet above it stood the Japanese Hotel with its plate-glass windows looking out at Everest. The party was now reduced to the Trittons and myself, Chris Bonington, Doug Scott and members of his family who had trekked out to meet him. The rest of the team and the BBC crew had gone ahead back to Kathmandu, civilisation and the first long hot bath for three months. It was a Saturday. There was to be a large press conference at the British Embassy in Kathmandu late that afternoon, followed by an embassy party for the team and local diplomats.

Storms and bad cloud conditions meant that only one Pilatus Porter would be able to fly out from Kathmandu. The aircraft's capacity was five unladen adults or, with all the climbing gear to be loaded, three adults at most. Chris had to be one of them as the leader and Doug Scott another, as the 'summiteer'. Alan and Diana Tritton did not want to be separated and, as someone with experience of press conferences might be useful, I was selected for the last seat. The plane arrived, piloted by the cigar-smoking Emil Wick, a Swiss aviator of exceptional skill in mountain flying. We shoved our gear on board and were about to say a temporary farewell to the others, who would be flying out next day.

For several days past, we had crossed paths – literally – with the Indian ambassador to Nepal, his wife and their two young sons, who were having a gentle trek on the lower ranges. He seemed a pleasant enough man but she was *formidable*. Sounds carried in the thin air and her hectoring tones could be heard around distant corners long before their entourage came into sight. They had arrived at the landing strip not long before the plane touched down.

Her husband looked abashed but now she came storming in and confronted Emil Wick. 'My husband is the Indian ambassador,' she declaimed. 'On his behalf, I am commandeering this aircraft! We have to return urgently to Kathmandu.'

Emil gently pointed out that 'these gentlemen' had already booked it. She gave us a scornful look. It has to be said that 'these gentlemen' looked like a trio of real rogues, not least Doug Scott who, with his straggly hair and beard and wire-framed spectacles, appeared the eternal hippy. I had several days' stubble on my face and had not combed my hair; Chris too was unkempt. She repeated her claim in an even more strident tone.

Emil's normally placid face had a worried look. He drew us on one side. India had great clout in landlocked Nepal; if it were ever to close the land and air routes, as had happened in a diplomatic *détente* a few years earlier, Nepal would be commercially throttled. Emil and his co-pilots drew their flying licences from the Nepalese government. If he refused the Indian ambassador, and this – er – woman were to get her husband to lodge a formal complaint, there could be big trouble. He hated suggesting it but would Chris . . .?

Emil Wick had been a good friend for a long time – not only to Chris's and other British Himalayan expeditions but to all nationalities. In an emergency, his and the other pilots' skill and experience in touching down on rugged airstrips in adverse conditions could mean the difference between life and death for an injured climber. Chris and Doug smiled, and shrugged. We began to offload our gear from the Pilatus Porter.

There was a triumphant smile on the face of the ambassador's wife, as she stood ready to board the aircraft. Her husband had the good grace to look away. As the last rucksack was lifted off, Doug turned to her and in a mild voice asked if she would mind telling us what business called her party back to Kathmandu so urgently.

'Not at all,' she replied. 'There is to be a special party at the British Embassy tonight. His Excellency and I have been invited to meet the leader of the British Everest expedition and the climbers who reached the top!'

'That should be interesting,' said Doug.

The 'hijacking' of our seats had its own aftermath. A week later, I flew back to London via Delhi in advance of the main body to help prepare their reception. In 1975 – and perhaps still today – the British Airways flight to London left Delhi at one o'clock in the morning and the Air India flight at two o'clock. Wandering around a deserted reception area – the restaurants had long closed for the night and there were no bars – I bumped into Dermot Purgavie, the *Daily Mail* journalist who had reported the Everest ascent, and told him the story of the ambassador's wife. He wrote it up on his return for his paper, which gave it a big splash. London correspondents of Indian newspapers picked it up and reported back. The ambassador, it seems, was given an official reprimand by the Indian government and his career prospects were greatly reduced.

But there was still to be one last great moment back in the mountain range itself. On the next day, the weather was fine, and Emil Wick was able to fly twice from Kathmandu to Syangboche airstrip and back. The Trittons and Doug Scott with his family occupied the first flight, which left Chris Bonington and me as the last survivors. Lift-off was in itelf quite eventful. The strip ended on a cliff edge with a deep gorge immediately ahead and the great white wall of Amadablam a

short distance – or so it appeared – beyond. The plane would
only get airborne towards the end of the strip, so that the pilot
then had to climb and wheel sharply either to his starboard
in the general direction of Kathmandu or to his port in the
direction of Mount Everest. Chris wanted to take some aerial
photographs of the face of Everest and Emil Wick was only
too willing to oblige.

Traversing the eternal snows and the icefields and the rocks
protruding like dark, splintered bones in a light aircraft that
almost bounced in the updrafts verges on the indescribable –
and I will try to avoid the temptation of Clovis. More was to
come. The Pilatus Porter is a high-wing monoplane, which
made it impossible for Chris to get vertical tracking shots
of the mountain. He shouted his predicament to Emil Wick
over the roar of the engine, and the pilot grinned and stuck
up his thumb. On the next run, he pulled the aircraft over so
that it was virtually flying on its side with the starboard wing
upright in the thin air. Chris, wedging his feet against a seat
to give himself purchase, had a clear view for filming. I had
a unique ringside seat – or, rather, stance. From Base Camp
to summit, Everest rises from 17,000 feet to just over 29,000.
We must have been flying at around 24,000 feet and just a few
hundred feet away from the surface of the mountain, so that
in one long look I was able to take in the great menacing bulk
which narrowed both in perspective and in shape until the very
summit was cloaked in the perpetual plume of cloud.

The flight back to Kathmandu was almost an anticlimax.

Dougal Haston was the climber's climber. Lithe as a cat, he was
always either exerting his great physical strength and endurance or, like a cat, relaxing totally. The BBC TV film of the
1975 Everest expedition shows him draped at his ease against
a rock, Jacques Fath black sombrero tipped down on his nose,
every muscle relaxed. But his climbing feats belied the pose.
His winter ascent of the North Face of the Eiger, his sharing
the first ever ascent of Mount Annapurna with Don Whillans,
his pioneering climbs on severe routes in his native Scotland,
made him the friend and idol of mountaineers everywhere.

His admirers were not exclusively masculine. He was tall with curly fair hair and deep-set blue eyes. Although he was shy and monosyllabic among strangers, almost dour in his attitude, he must have exuded a sexual attraction. Barclays Bank threw a large 'welcome back' party for the Everest Expedition at their main banking hall in Lombard Street. The press and television were invited. Dougal and I were having a quiet chat when I was swept aside by a pack of female journalists, who clutched at the poor fellow with their scarlet fingernails and seemed about to give a fair imitation of the Maenads at work. By 1975, he had taken over the running of a mountaineering school in Leysin, Switzerland.

Dougal was not just – in fact, not at all – a hard man of the hills. In his youth, he had occasionally drunk too much and got involved in fist fights and in his early thirties when I knew him, he still smoked an occasional joint. But now it was more likely to be a glass or two of vintage wine than a flotilla of beer pints that loosened his taciturn tongue. As I came to know him better and perhaps began to enjoy his confidence, he would now and then show me with some shyness an article or a short story he had written. He was, after all, a Scottish graduate; the prose style was crisp and vivid, the inner meaning often symbolically strange. I was impressed and encouraged him to keep on writing. He began work on a novel with a climbing background.

Many writers, indeed some of the more experienced ones, suggest to their agents that they should submit the work-in-progress in instalments. I was always against the practice – with one exception. If the writer was genuinely at a crossroads in the plot and needed some professional advice on which road to take, there could be grounds for submitting the existing script. But it is impossible to judge the impact of the full novel on the strength of the first 10,000 words and all the agent can say at the best is, 'Well done, so far. Keep up the good work.' The trouble is that if you read the first 10,000 words and make comments and then the next 10,000 words and make comments – and so on – you cannot see the wood for the trees, and the storyline soon becomes overly familiar. I used to remind my clients that the word 'novel' means 'new'. The agent should come to the finished work as fresh as the publisher will and the reading public will in their turn.

I did not have to press my theory on Dougal. He wanted to hug the plot and the characters to himself. We kept in touch, usually by telephone, as he was not much of a letter-writer, and I contented myself with his fairly sketchy progress reports. But then, one Friday afternoon, the call came through from Leysin that he had finished. He said he would post the complete typescript to me over the weekend. I was well pleased.

Over that weekend, I thought a good deal about him and his novel. The anticipation was great; I could only hope that the sustained effort he had put into it would not prove a waste of his time. On the Monday, the news broke. Dougal Haston had been tragically killed in an avalanche while skiing by himself on the slopes.

The following morning, the parcel arrived. I tore off the outer wrapping. Inside was an amusing little note from Dougal, asking me, please, to ring him with my views when I had read the novel, not delay the verdict by writing a letter.

I cancelled everything else and began to read. The main character was a man who ran a Swiss climbing school. He was an expert skier and in the afternoons when the hot sun had loosened the deep snow high on the slopes, he would deliberately ski into likely avalanching areas and use his hair-trigger reactions and speed techniques to dart away again when the first rumbles led to a massive fall. Dougal, indolent as a purring cat, almost seemed to be slumped in the armchair across from my desk, as I read on.

13

IN PURSUIT OF RUDOLF HESS

In the late 1960s I met an Australian journalist, then with the *Daily Mail*, named Desmond Zwar. He was working on a book with the American colonel who had been in charge of the accused at the Nuremberg Trials, more than twenty years earlier. A client of mine, Dame Laura Knight, had been an official war artist at the trials and Zwar wanted to include some of her drawings among the illustrations for the book. I was struck by his professionalism and his nose for a good story, and recommended Dame Laura to accept.

Some months later, he approached me again. He had made friends, he said, with a Colonel Eugene Bird of the US Army. Gene Bird, who had been a junior officer at Nuremberg, was now the American commandant at Spandau Jail in the leafy suburbs of West Berlin. At one stage, Spandau had housed all those senior German war criminals who had not been hanged or, like Goering, escaped the gallows through suicide. But one by one, they had been released – all except Rudolf Hess. Each month in turn, the United States, the USSR, Great Britain and France were responsible for providing 100 or more sentries and guards under the command of a senior officer. All to make sure that one aged, decrepit and supposedly insane Nazi did not break forth and overturn both the democratic process and the West German 'economic miracle'.

The so-called official reason for his prolonged detention was that any change required the approval of all four powers. The three Western ones would be only too glad to see the back of Hess and be shot of the vast expense of his solitary confinement but the Russians resisted, because the monthly meetings when the guarding changed hands gave them an extra link to the West. It was a feeble reason, because numerous links through diplomatic channels and the United Nations already existed. Far more likely, to my mind, was the suspicion that Hess 'knew where the bodies were buried'. By May 1941, when he flew on his solo mission to Scotland, the war was already going badly for Britain; Greece had been lost, Crete was doomed and in the Western Desert Rommel's advance the month before had cut off Tobruk and reached the Egyptian frontier. There was a strong and growing mood among senior politicians like Lord Halifax for an arranged peace. There had even been surreptitious meetings in Sweden between unofficial envoys on both sides. Had Hess underestimated Churchill's grasp on power and hoped to bring off a dramatic peace coup? In any event, he could be aware of the names of the pacific quislings and the extent to which they were prepared to roll over and raise their paws in the air. Far better, therefore, to keep the genie in the bottle with the cork jammed tight.

Desmond Zwar had already spent a good many hours in West Berlin with Colonel Bird and was now accepted as a friend. Bird, he told me, spoke fluent German, having stayed on after the war and married the daughter of a prosperous local paint manufacturer. The British commandant could not be bothered to learn German, the French commandant believed that his native tongue was the single essential for civilised discourse and the Russian would never speak to an ex-enemy. So Gene Bird was the only one to call on Rudolf Hess in his cell and hold lengthy conversations with him. He had gained the old man's confidence and, although it was strictly forbidden for all ranks from commandant downwards to take any item into or remove any item from the jail, he had smuggled in a small camera and taken shots of Hess in his cell gazing at his

Luftwaffe uniform or pointing to a wall map or smiling to camera. As professionals in our separate spheres, Zwar and I knew these unique still pictures were valuable.

I encouraged him to collaborate on a book with Bird, who came over to London for several meetings. He was dark-haired, plump-faced, with a soft Southern accent – a strange mixture of shrewdness and gullibility. I felt it proper to point out to them both that the US military authorities in West Germany might not take kindly to a fairly senior officer spilling the beans in such a delicate area. Gene Bird pooh-poohed my caution. His bosses, he said, wanted nothing more than to wind up the Hess farce and return Spandau to civilian use. Indeed, he added, he had been given several large cartons of official documents relating to the jail with instructions to destroy them. He had, however, lodged them in his garage for the time being. One of them, a big, brown exercise book, appeared to be Rudolf Hess's diary.

Desmond Zwar worked with zeal and skill. By late 1969, he had finished the typescript of *The Loneliest Man in the World*, which covered Hess's early days, his Great War experiences, his first encounter with Hitler, his whole-hearted adoption of the Nazi creed, his rise to deputy-Führer, the flight to Scotland, imprisonment in Britain, Nuremberg, being found unfit to plead and incarceration without limit. It was a strong and oddly moving story, enhanced by transcriptions of dialogue which Gene Bird had secretly recorded inside the jail. Hess, no doubt, had been and still was a fervent disciple of the worst Nazi beliefs but he was now well into his seventies, a prisoner for almost thirty years. Many people of my generation, while fully accepting that the Nazi hierarchy was the embodiment of evil, had felt uneasy over the Nuremberg Trials. They smelled strongly of retrospective justice. The German war crimes were not, legally speaking, crimes at all, since there were no specific laws in existence at the time for them to break. '*Vae victis*', as the Goth chieftain shouted. 'Woe to the conquered!'

There would be no great problem in finding a British publisher. The trick would be to choose the one who was most likely to obtain a wide spread of reviews. Zwar and Bird had, between them, no wide readership and so their

book would need to be well noticed. I therefore selected
Tom Rosenthal, who was running Secker & Warburg with
considerable panache. As a Jew in charge of a distinguished
firm founded by another Jew and developed by a third, he
would also be a useful counter to any unfounded charges that
The Loneliest Man in the World was anti-Semitic in making
public Hess's plight.

It was a short walk from my office in Red Lion Square
to Tom's in Carlisle Street, off Soho Square. On the way,
I rehearsed my tactics for the coming encounter. He was a
tough and experienced negotiator, so my plan was to ask for
a bigger advance than he would probably want to pay and
expect to be knocked down several points – a fairly obvious
manoeuvre. But where to set the opening offer? Privately, I
was prepared to accept £5,000, equivalent to about £40,000
in today's terms. So I decided as I walked to ask for £7,500,
expect him to underbid deliberately with a £2,500 response
and after some genteel haggling meet him in the middle – in
other words, at my expected £5,000. The thing to do, I knew,
was to get one's blow in first, mark out the firing range with
the opening shot.

But the tactic failed. Tom, a suave host, offered me a pre-
lunch drink and showed me his latest toy, a large tape recorder
with a mystifying spread of buttons, dials and flashing lights.
He then said that, as this was to be a discussion concerning the
publishing rights in an important book, he would like to have
my permission to record our oral cut and thrust. I nodded my
agreement. Clearing his throat and squaring his shoulders, he
switched on the machine and made a speech to his audience
of one. It went rather like this.

'George, I am not going to beat about the bush. We
all know that agents love to haggle – it makes them feel
they're doing their job properly. But I have neither the
time nor the inclination for that rigmarole. I have done
my sums thoroughly over the prospects of *The Loneliest
Man in the World* and I am going to make you an offer for
British Commonwealth volume rights including Canada. It
will be just the one offer, take it or leave it. Not – let
me stress – an opening for bargaining. I am only inviting

you to say yes or say no on behalf of your clients. Is that perfectly clear?'

'Yes, Tom,' I said.

'Right. Here it is. I offer you £10,000. What do you say?'

'Tom,' I said, 'you're a hard man. I realise when I'm beaten, when there's no point in trying to argue. Okay. I accept the £10,000.'

I must add in parenthesis that the widespread reviews achieved by Secker & Warburg and their diligent sales of the hard-cover edition, together with a canny sale of paperback rights, eventually cleared off the advance and indeed provided a reasonable surplus for the authors. United States rights were promptly snapped up by Tom Guinzburg of Viking Press, who insisted on changing the emotive title to *Prisoner # 7*, which he felt was more appropriate for American readers. When the time came, they failed to back his judgement to any noticeable degree.

The third leg of the tripod would be the sale of serial rights. Here, there was an obvious target – the *Sunday Express*. Founded at the end of the Great War by Max Aitken, later Lord Beaverbrook, that dreadful little man who turned irresponsibility into the eighth deadly sin, the newspaper under the guidance of holier-than-thou Scots like John Gordon had built a solid middle-class, middle-aged readership in the next fifty years. John Junor, another Scot who had seen active war service in the RNVR, became editor in 1954 and remained at his post for the rest of his working career up to 1986. Under his brusque but canny editorship, the paper had four main attractions for its readership – a knowledgeable gossip column, often privately fed by the proprietor, Beaverbrook, a witty showbiz column written by Roderick Mann, my client, a sound City column and serials of dramatic episodes in the Second World War.

The 'military serial' had been launched by Denis Hamilton, then editor of the *Sunday Times*, in 1956 with Field-Marshal Montgomery's memoirs. A decade and a half later, the Sunday papers had run through the important generals, admirals and air marshals; they had covered exceptional wartime events like the Battle of Britain, the sinking of the *Scharnhorst*, the

D-Day landings, Arnhem, Alamein and so on. Most of its rivals had long decided that the war was over but the *Sunday Express* was still soldiering on in 1970. There was a lingering controversy over Hess's flight to Britain and his continuing incarceration but the official version would probably never be released. Here was the next best thing, a unique eyewitness account of the man's present life with photographs that were obviously recent.

John Junor and I had been friendly sparring partners for several years. We lunched regularly at Boulestin; he had the disconcerting habit, if it was his turn to be guest, of urging me to order the house wine and not indulge in an expensive vintage. I never worked out whether this was a subtle way of asserting Scottish providence or of implying that I – or, rather, my firm – could not really afford the extra cost. Whatever, he was always a worthwhile companion; if opinionated, at least his opinions merited close attention.

As I expected, he jumped at the prospect of the Hess serial. But the asking price – £15,000 – made his brick-red face go redder. It was a very big amount, well over £100,000 in today's terms. I was not prepared to come down in price, as I reckoned that, if it came to the pinch, one or other of the less worthy Sunday papers would jump at the chance of sensationalising the story. And John's upbringing in the manse no doubt taught him that you don't put more than the going rate into the offertory plate. There was, in the modern jargon, a stand-off. Then an idea hit me. The staff of Sunday papers work late into the Saturday night and have the next two days off, returning to work on the Tuesday morning. John and I could easily fly to West Berlin on a Sunday and meet Gene Bird in his home surroundings. He could show us the town – the Berlin Wall, Checkpoint Charlie, the Olympic Stadium, culminating in a visit to the outside of Spandau Jail. It would give John the chance to assess Bird's honesty and his status, as well as the opportunity to see aspects of a strange city that only a local expert could provide.

And so one sunny Sunday afternoon, John Junor and I set off from Heathrow and, an hour or two later, touched down at Tempelhof in the heart of West Berlin. As the aircraft came in to land, the roofs of houses and the tops of parkland trees rushed past the windows. It was as though a small airport were to be built in Hyde Park, parallel with the Serpentine. We were met by the *Sunday Express* stringer, who drove us to the smart new hotel in what had been the heart of the old city.

That evening, we visited East Berlin. Like most Britons, when the dividing wall had been built, I imagined that travel between the halves of the city could only be funnelled through Checkpoint Charlie. But the subway continued to run. You boarded an underground train in the West and two stops later you had arrived in the East – under the hard stare of the Vopo, the *Volkspolizei*, in their grey-green greatcoats and black-peaked caps. Before you could emerge into the fresh air, you had to fill in various forms and 'change' five deutschmarks into the valueless (at least, in West Berlin) ostmarks. Being congenitally bad at form-filling and largely ignorant of the German language, I filled in all the wrong columns and caused delays for John and our stringer friend while contemptuous officials debated unintelligibly over whether to send me to the salt mines or let me go free. The latter course fortunately prevailed.

In the sickly yellow light of the streetlamps, the East was dreary in the extreme. Although it was not yet eight o'clock, there was almost no sign of life in the streets. The barracks-like buildings on either side might have been under strict blackout, for hardly a glimmer of light showed through the curtains. The three of us tramped across a bridge, our footsteps echoing loudly in the silent night. We were aiming for an 'interesting restaurant' John's local man had heard of; a soup kitchen in a slaughterhouse was more likely, I privately reckoned. At last, we came to the place. A heavy curtain stretched across the entrance. Tugging it aside, we entered.

A sumptuous sight greeted us. It might have been the original Quaglino's, not the present *chi-chi* version. The *maître d'*, white tie and starched shirtfront gleaming, greeted us with a smile. A glass of champagne, perhaps, before we took our table? Yes, he had Krug, Moët & Chandon, Perrier-Jouet, Laurent Perrier, the 'Widow' and indeed any other brand or vintage we cared to name. And when we sat down to dinner, the tablecloth and the napkins were of thick damask, white as newly fallen snow, the cutlery was silver, the wine list revealed twenty or thirty good burgundies and even more clarets. The food itself and the cuisine would have more than passed muster at the Connaught Grill. And nearly every table was occupied with jolly Germans enjoying their gourmandising to the full. Were they refugees from West Berlin, I wondered, rich businessmen and their wives or mistresses, enjoying the advantage of the strong deutschmark, or were they functionaries of the East German state, enjoying the fruits of political power? Whatever the answer, there was an almost palpable air of enjoyment in the richly decorated restaurant.

Our hotel in a smart shopping area of West Berlin was one of those replicas to be found in every major city in the world, evoking that stock response, 'If this is Thursday, it must be Frankfurt or Brussels or Houston, Texas, or wherever.' A notice in German, French and English on the wall of each identical room stated that continental breakfast was served in the basement swimming-pool area. I called for John in his room along the corridor and we descended silently in the lift. Neither of us was inclined to be bright and lively first thing in the morning.

As we sat at a small table on the pool side and ordered croissants and coffee, we noticed the place was nearly empty – except for three or four young men who were uncannily similar, tall with long blond hair, sunburned, well muscled, with wide shoulders and narrow hips. Each wore a silken cut-away jockstrap affair as a swimming costume. We took them to be instructors, awaiting the first pupils of the day, or perhaps lifeguards, but none of them actually entered the water. Squaring their shoulders, breathing in until knotted ridges of abdominal muscles stood out on their concave bellies, they sauntered up and down the side of the pool, preening themselves like matadors before the *corrida*.

I went on with my breakfast until a noise that was a cross between a snort and a groan came from my companion. Glancing up, I saw two of the young men in a close embrace, kissing each other passionately on the lips. A third tall young man sat, legs apart, at a table near us. His shorter companion was sitting on his knees; they were engaged in what might be bowdlerised as 'handling the situation'. Such scenes were not, I am sure, typical of the 'Caledonia stern and wild' in which my companion had been raised, nor indeed of the gentler mid-Kent rural scenes of my youth. Our breakfast appetite ruined, eyes averted, we retreated.

But the day improved quickly when Gene Bird called for us in his large black Mercedes and whirled us to the tourist sights; to Checkpoint Charlie, where there was a sinister gap along the eastern side of the Berlin Wall and guards with fieldglasses and sub-machine guns eyed each visitor who peered across; to the Olympic Stadium, which had been deliberately left to rot, with weeds growing up through the broken concrete and the houses in the neighbouring suburb that had been pounded into rubble by the Russian artillery twenty-five years earlier still as they were when the smoke and dust lifted; to the outside of Spandau Jail, that red-brick monstrosity with its screen of trees, clasping one old man inside its high walls; to a typical *Bierkeller* with its earthenware *Steins*, frothing beer and wooden shields with the arms of the old German principalities on the dark-stained walls; finally, for tea at Gene's comfortable house in an affluent neighbourhood.

He had not told us that his wife had been stricken with a form of muscular sclerosis, which confined her to a wheelchair. She radiated a kind of serene warmth that touched us both profoundly. I think it was her grace and courage, and the sustaining love between her and Gene as much as, perhaps more than, the other vivid impressions of our brief visit to Berlin, that made the tough, powerful editor of what was then the biggest selling 'respectable' newspaper tell me as we boarded the plane home from Tempelhof that we were in business.

There was to be a third act to the drama – and indeed a fourth. Since the early days of ITN, I had become friendly with Don Horobin and David Nicholas, two important members of the headquarters staff; by the time *The Loneliest Man in the World* was approaching publication, Nicholas, later to be knighted for his services to television, had been appointed head of ITN. At that time, a six o'clock bulletin as well as 'News at Ten' went out on the air. I knew that David and Don, once the earlier bulletin was under way, would have a free half hour or so for a drink and a chat. I also knew the structure of each half-hour programme; the first fifteen minutes before the commercial break covered the dramatic, often tragic, world news: to balance the output, they liked to have an upbeat, even 'inspirational,' three-minute item early in the second half. I had sold them TV rights to the Annapurna expedition, led by Chris Bonington, and the John Fairfax/Sylvia Cook world record for rowing across the Pacific Ocean. Another memorable feat by John Fairfax which was captured by the underwater television camera – diving overboard off Bimini in the Caribbean and killing a twelve-foot shark with his bare hands and a hunting knife – was considered too gory for family audiences. One could see the point. When Fairfax grasped the shark's dorsal fin with his left hand and sliced its belly open with the knife in his other hand, the beast's entrails rose in the blue sunlit water in a red misty trail and floated upwards in a bloody splurge.

Colonel Bird had already smuggled his 8mm movie camera into Spandau and managed to shoot a few minutes of black-and-white film – Hess walking alone in the garden, pausing to bend and sniff at a flower, turning and walking towards the camera, stopping and giving a broad grin with his face a foot or so away from the lens. The shots were ordinary enough and amateurish – but they were unique. Although ITN had a very modest budget for buying in outside film material, David Nicholas agreed to pay £5,000 for unlimited usage. He and Don Horobin had an even more ambitious idea. They had recently acquired some Japanese Super 8mm miniature cameras which had much higher definition than earlier types and which could shoot in colour. I had told them that Bird was about to visit his family in Alabama and would be returning on PanAm via London and Frankfurt. Why not get him to stop off for a few days and do a crash course with one of ITN's best cameramen? When his next turn came to be in charge of the jail, he could reshoot his Hess film with far greater professionalism.

There was another side to be exploited – tape-recording.

Three questions that had bedevilled military historians ever since the end of the war were: (1) When Rudolf Hess flew to Scotland in May 1941, was he aware that Hitler intended to invade Russia the following month? (2) If so, did he pass the word on to the British authorities? (3) And if he did, did Churchill warn Stalin, who failed to heed him? (The far-reaching consequences of Enigma still remained a closely guarded secret, known only to the higher reaches of Bletchley and a few senior leaders, nearly twenty-five years ago.) It would be a world scoop if Bird could record Hess admitting that he had known about the imminent invasion before he took off and had tried to warn his British hosts.

Gene Bird, with the enthusiasms of a schoolboy, was delighted to accept. He was in an anomalous situation. Semi-retired from the US Army, he spent three out of every four months attending to his father-in-law's prosperous paint business. Yet he was still on active duty for each fourth month and was kept on the strength, subject to military law throughout the year. Whatever one's private view of the nonsense in keeping an ancient, decrepit man locked up when he had spent thirty years in prison and was no longer a menace, if he ever had been, Bird was being invited to break the rules and regulations to which his country subscribed. Both Desmond Zwar and I pointed this out to him as forcefully as we could. We had previously, before the book was undertaken, made sure he realised the possible risks he would run when it was published. But Bird, who was both streetwise and somewhat naive, took everything in his stride.

He stopped off in London for the long weekend's crash course in camera work. I had supper with him on the second evening, when he announced ruefully that his large suitcase containing fresh shirts, a second suit *and* a typescript of the book had been wrongly flown on to Frankfurt. To him, it was just a nuisance, one of those slip-ups that happen with stupid baggage clerks. To me, it was far more sinister. Although we had sworn him to silence, I knew that he was so thrilled with the prospect of authorship that he must have spread the word far and wide – as, no doubt, he had mentioned the crash course to all who would listen. He should have kept the typescript locked up in his family safe, not packed with the clean shirts and underwear for customs officials to finger.

Unfortunately, the suspicions were well founded. The camera lessons completed, Gene Bird flew back to West Germany – to be greeted by security officers from the US forces. They had already noted the contents of his not-so-missing suitcase and apparently they interrogated him for several hours, having examined and then confiscated the brand-new Japanese lightweight movie camera in his briefcase. (ITN eventually wrote it off to the exigences of overseas risks.) A few days later, I received an official letter from the United States Army Headquarters, West Germany, ordering me to send them my copy of the typescript without delay.

My reply asked them to enlighten my ignorance by telling me the precise date when Great Britain had become the 51st state of the USA. It must surely be so, because I could not imagine that the armed forces of one sovereign state would give an order to a citizen of another sovereign state and expect that order to be carried out. Perhaps they would kindly send me a copy of the (I presumed recent) treaty in which Great Britain had surrendered its independence. My schoolboy sarcasm had some modest effect because, shortly afterwards, Gene Bird was on the phone, pleading with me to carry out the instruction. He was to retire summarily from his Spandau appointment and indeed from his part-time service with the US Army but, if we played ball, no further action would be taken.

I had to ask him – did he want to withdraw the book from all forms of publication? Surprisingly, the answer was no. Now that he was retiring from active service, the US government would have no further control over his actions. As I then pointed out to him, their letter to me had been sloppily worded. Instead of demanding the return of all copies, notes and relevant documents, and a signed and witnessed statement that their demands had been complied with – as the Special Branch had done in the case of Colonel Scotland many years before – they had merely sought the return of the top copy. All I had to do was first make several photocopies of the text and then despatch the original. Would he agree to my doing so? He did.

The Loneliest Man in the World was serialised in the *Sunday Express* and published immediately afterwards with considerable success by Secker & Warburg in Britain and by the Viking Press in the USA. ITN made up for the loss of their unused camera by transmitting Bird's original black-and-white footage of Hess whenever a suitable opportunity arose. All concerned, except Rudolf Hess himself, did quite well out of the venture.

I mentioned earlier that Colonel Bird was asked by his superiors to get rid of some boxes of old documents relating to Spandau and that he decided to store them in his garage. Among them he had discovered a large notebook with many handwritten entries – and he recognised Hess's writing. When the heat came on, he gave it to Desmond Zwar, his collaborator, for safe keeping. When Zwar decided to return permanently to Australia with his family, he thought that the notebook, now known as *Hess's Diary*, should be kept centrally for possible future publication, rather than accompany him to Cairns in somewhat remote Queensland. He entrusted it to me. Before he left for good, we consulted an international lawyer with specific knowledge of German federal law on the question of copyright. The 'opinion' was reassuring. As a convicted war criminal who had written the material since his conviction and who seemed unlikely to be released in the foreseeable future, Rudolf Hess had no rights in the matter and no claim to copyright. Nor in the event of his death while still in Spandau would his family have a tenable claim. Apparently, the case of von Speer, who had served a modest sentence in Spandau and on his release had written a successful autobiography, was not germane – on some subtle legal grounds that I failed to grasp.

As already mentioned, my knowledge of German is not even rudimentary. The inked handwriting was firm and legible; a colleague of mine, Vanessa Holt, who handled Farquharson's foreign transactions and who was fluent in German, was able to read it and give me her views. Apart from isolated jottings, the bulk of the text consisted of an address to the German people, which Hess had written in the early years of his captivity. When the Allies withdrew from West Germany, he expected to be appointed Führer of the Fourth Reich and this was the draft of his acceptance speech. He promised to lead his country to a glorious future, prosperous and powerful with a renewed fighting machine. The faults of the past had been due entirely to the insidious and malignant influence of the Jews, and his priority would be to eradicate any remaining Jewish remnants. And so on. These were the ramblings of a demented and evil old man.

But as I looked further into the notebook, I could see that he was only mad nor'-nor'-west. There was, for example, a neat, hand-drawn diagram of taps and piping with notes to show how the water flow into the shower attached to his cell could be improved. A brief essay, followed by two columns of dates, equated his old friend Hitler with Napoleon and demonstrated the uncanny similarity of stages in their respective careers, exactly 130 years apart. Napoleon crowned himself emperor; 130 years later, Hitler came to power. In 1810, Napoleon was the master of Europe; in 1940, so was Hitler. In 1812, the Retreat from Moscow took place; at the end of 1942, the Siege of Stalingrad was doomed, as was the Nazi invasion of the USSR. And the 1815 finale of one tyrant was matched by the 1945 finale of the other. It struck me then that a man whose mental powers must have been debilitated to some extent by years of imprisonment but who could work out for himself logical puzzles such as plumbing improvements and historical analogies could not be wholly mad. He must have fooled the psychiatrists at Nuremberg and prosecuting counsel such as David Maxwell Fyffe.

For some years, the notebook languished on a bookshelf in my office. Then, in the early 1980s, I had lunch one day with Eric Jacobs, a distinguished journalist who then had an important position on the *Sunday Times*. Towards the end of a good lunch, he swore me to secrecy and then told me, almost in a whisper, that two days later, on the Saturday, *The Times* would run a big 'splash' as a trailer and then next day its sister paper would lead with the first riveting instalment of – the Hitler Diaries.

I burst out laughing.

It was a disconcerting, if spontaneous, gesture. When he

taxed me with my rude disbelief, I said, 'Look, Eric, let's forget the Mussolini Diaries a few years back. You remember – two little old ladies in northern Italy wrote 'em. But, for God's sake, Hitler . . . his valet wrote a book, his quack wrote a book, Trevor-Roper wrote a book about the last days, dozens of people have written books or published diaries. Has any one of them mentioned Hitler *and* a diary? Goering never mentioned it, Goebbels never mentioned it.

'Hell, a diary doesn't just happen. You said there are several hundred pages. They must have taken hours to write up, day after day. They cover the war years, you say? Hitler fought a war on two fronts for four years. He was a very hands-on kind of leader. When on earth did he find time to keep the diary going? And why did no one see him doing it? Do you find time to write a detailed diary? I don't.'

He argued that the paper and ink had been scientifically tested and that Lord Dacre, lately Regius Professor of Modern History at Oxford, the quondam Hugh Trevor-Roper, had for a substantial fee scrutinised parts of the text. All I could say in reply was that, of course, a forger selling a fake would first make sure to use paper and ink of the right period. As far as a Cambridge man like myself was concerned, Oxford was the Latin Quarter of Cowley; we were unlikely to be swayed by the evidence of its professors.

'Common sense is the key,' I said dogmatically. It *had* been a good lunch. 'Hitler was a talker. He loved making speeches and listening to his own voice. If – *if* – he decided to keep a diary, he would have saved time and enjoyed himself more with a silent audience by dictating it. He had quite a few confidential aides; one or other of them must have known shorthand. The diary could then be privately typed up next day while the Führer went on with his war. By that reckoning, I'd believe it more if you'd told me the *ST* had bought a bunch of typed pages, not a literal manuscript.'

Hamlet put it well. 'The Times are out of joint.' But let us pass quickly from the blushes of those who were sucked in by the enthusiasm of the German magazine which first acquired the rights to the fake diaries. In the aftermath, I decided that the Hess diary, which at least was genuine, even if it was hardly a diary, might now be a topical item. I was not going to allow it out of the building, when photocopies could be made and circulated, so over a period of a few weeks representatives from the *Observer*, the *Guardian*, the *Sunday Express*, the *Daily Mail* and other newspapers came by appointment to sit in a spare office and study the large notebook. In the upshot, the general verdict was that the material might make an interesting psychiatric study or provide a useful source for historians but was far too bitty and anti-Semitic for newspaper publication.

There the matter might have rested, had not a German lawyer representing Wolf Rudiger Hess, Rudolf's son, got in touch. Shortly afterwards, Wolf Hess himself came to see me. Square-built and broad-shouldered, he had the same dark eyebrows and searching look as his father. He was apparently a successful and well-respected engineer in West Germany. He felt keenly that the notebook belonged to his family and should therefore be handed over to him as his father's direct descendant. I felt sympathetic towards the request. The notebook was serving no useful purpose gathering dust on my bookshelves, nor could it now gain any advantage for Gene Bird and Desmond Zwar. So, having received their written permission, I arranged to hand it to Wolf Hess on his next visit, along with a release document for his signature. The conditions for releasing it to him were that it must be kept safely and be made readily available to serious historical students and researchers.

More years were to pass before Rudolf Hess's mysterious death in 1987, still incarcerated inside Spandau. This modern Prisoner of Chillon spent half his long life behind bars. Was it just a case of 'Woe to the conquered – from the vindictive' or was there a more sinister motive impelling the conquerors' actions? Instead of falling for forgeries, perhaps Sunday newspapers could focus their investigative powers on finding an answer.

14

'YOU'VE GOT TO MAKE ME LOOK GOOD!'

Around 1980, Jeremy Hornsby, an industrial correspondent and an author of good standing, had a problem. I had acted for him on various occasions and so he arranged to discuss the matter with me. It was this.

Through his journalism, he had come to know Joe Gormley pretty well and Gormley, it seemed, respected his articles – to the extent that he had invited Hornsby to collaborate with him on his memoirs; in effect, to ghost them. The problem was that, several years earlier, Joe Gormley had signed a contract for their publication with Cassell's and had been paid an advance on signature. Then second thoughts had come creeping in. He had been elected to the National Executive Committee of the National Union of Mineworkers in 1957 and had worked his way up through politicking and force of character until becoming president in 1971. He would be due to remain in office until his sixty-fifth birthday in July 1982. But long before the end of the 1970s, he was finding himself surrounded by ultra-left-wing colleagues such as Laurence Daly, the General Secretary, the ambitious Arthur Scargill and Mick M'Gahey, the communist. Gormley, though intensely loyal to his union, was a pragmatist. 'Oh, that mine enemy would write a book!' He was all too well aware that publication during his presidency would make him and his book sitting targets.

So he had prevaricated with Cassell's. The firm itself had quite recently undergone several bewildering chops and changes as a result of its purchase by Macmillan Inc. of New York. Editors and other senior staff had come and gone, decisions – even, I was told, as petty as which brand of lavatory paper should be used in the washrooms – could not be taken on the spot but must be referred back to New York, and the wind of confusion seemed to blow erratically around the north-west corner of Red Lion Square. But the lowering of efficiency had not cloaked the fact that Joe Gormley owed them either a book or the money back. Hornsby wondered if, with Gormley's blessing, I could step in, sort out the mess with Cassell's and then handle the yet-to-be-written book. I agreed to try my luck.

Fortunately, the reshuffling of the senior staff had left one or two old friends still in place. Through the long delays, they had largely lost confidence and interest in the Gormley memoirs and when I mentioned that the earliest possible date for publication was more than two years off, one could sense the unspoken 'Let's get shot of this boring business, provided he pays us back.' It was only fair that he should – but Cassell's were even more reasonable in their approach by not claiming interest on what would now be a loan and agreeing further that repayment need only take place when a new publisher put up an advance. (It was still in parts 'an occupation for gentlemen', even fifteen years ago.)

My first meeting with Joe Gormley took place on a sunny morning at the (then) NUM headquarters in Euston Road. It was an imposing building, a fit residence for the centre of what was still one of the biggest and most powerful unions in the land, a symbol of the muscular working man. The president's room on the first floor was equally imposing, with a huge desk straddling one wall and a long U-shaped table for executive meetings occupying most of the remaining space. Against the far wall from the desk was a large refrigerator.

But Gormley himself was not dwarfed by his impressive room. I had read that in his youth he had done most jobs in his local colliery, including a long spell working underground. Of medium height, he had the thick neck and slightly sloping shoulders that signify great upper body strength. His handshake was firm and rasping. A newspaper profile had referred to him as 'a battered cherub', a description he liked so much that he used it for the title of his memoirs. It was apt. He had thick grey hair, dark, elliptical and rather shaggy eyebrows and a much-lived-in face. There was a strange air of knowing innocence about him. But one could see, almost from first glance, that the man was nobody's fool. To dance on the point of a needle when most of your comrades were trying to ram it into your foot required the quickest of wits.

He asked me if I would like a drink and, imagining that at eleven o'clock in the morning he meant either coffee or tea, I nodded. Then, in his shirt sleeves, he walked over to the refrigerator, took out two cans of beer and tossed one to me. There were no glasses in sight, so I followed suit when he pulled off the ring top and sat sipping the beer straight out of the can. Looking back on the episode, I reckon it was a test on his part to discover if I was one of those cissies who couldn't lower a drink unless it was in a glass.

We chatted for a while and then his driver walked in. 'How many for lunch today, Joe?'

'Four, not including me. Five in all.'

'White Tower, as usual, Joe?'

'Yeah. One o'clock – sharp.'

'Okay, I'll have the car round the front at ten to.'

'Oh, no you won't! You'll have it round the back. You got me? Round the back.'

It was a glimpse of the consummate wheeler-dealer at work. The first Thatcher government, egged on by the more right-wing press, was already looking for scapegoats. After 'the year of discontent', no trade union was popular, least of all the NUM. For five officials to make themselves conspicuous in driving to lunch at an expensive restaurant, Nye Bevan's favourite haunt over twenty years earlier, would be asking for trouble.

After I had come to know him much better, Joe Gormley told me a story he swore was true; from my limited experience of the political scene, it has the ring of truth. On a far smaller scale, my work on behalf of authors had many similar moments. Anyone representing a group or an individual naturally wants to achieve the best results; it is doubly useful if he can demonstrate that he has done so. In that case, he needs room to manœuvre. As a practical example, let us say that he considers 7.5 to be a very acceptable result. If he is dealing with negotiators equally versed in the art, he will probably start off asking for 10, expecting them to counter with an offer of 5 and, after considerable haggling, end up at his preferred 7.5. He can then go back to his side and say, 'See what I've done for you? They offered 5 and I've managed to push them up to 7.5.' Applause all round.

By November 1973, only two years into the Gormley presidency of the NUM, deadlock had arisen over the wages claim. Already, there was a ban on overtime working in the mines and stocks of coal were beginning to run low. At the time, the electricity and gas generators relied very much more on coal than is now the case; the situation for the whole country had become difficult. Joe Gormley was torn two ways. He was a patriot without doubt but at the same time he had been elected to get the best conditions, including wages, for his men. In addition, he was surrounded on the Executive by members shoving hard from the left. If he was pushed out for being too soft, he knew that Arthur Scargill and his mates would ruin any chance of a peaceful settlement. So he had to 'box clever'.

On 21 November, the executive rejected the National Coal Board's revised pay offer, which was within the £44 million increase on the wages bill the board had already offered. The overtime ban was continued. The following day, the Prime Minister, Edward Heath, warned that there could be 'no surrender by the government'. Gormley challenged him to go to the country, adding, 'If we had been bloody-minded, I am sure we could have had the industry in a period of strike action by now.' Heath set up a crucial meeting for 28 November at 10 Downing Street. In spite of the venue, his role would be that of interested observer. The leading actors would be Joe Gormley as president of the NUM and Sir Derek Ezra, chairman of the

Coal Board. There was to be a preliminary and quite unofficial get-together, the Conservative equivalent of Harold Wilson's famed sandwiches-and-beer.

Joe Gormley described the first meeting to me – and what follows is as close to his actual words as memory will allow. 'Lovely fella, that Ezra. A real boy scout. Straight as they come – and decent with it. But . . .' – and here the George Robey-like eyebrows arched themselves and his eyes rolled skywards – 'I said to him, "Derek," I said, "you've got to make me look good. I wanna be able to go back to our men and tell 'em, 'Look what I done for you.' So, when we sit down across that table tomorrow, make me look good. Got it?"

'He smiled and nodded and I thought, "Right, he's got it." But what happens when we sit down next day? He says right off they'd done their sums backwards and forwards, and here was the final offer. No argument – it was the best they could come up with. The crazy thing was – it was a pretty good offer. We'd a bin happy to settle at that *if* he'd started lower and let himself be talked up.'

After three and a half hours, the meeting broke up in deadlock. Laurence Daly, the NUM's fiery General Secretary, had said the previous week, 'We are not going to Downing Street to be told by Mr Heath that we have to accept the Coal Board's offer.' Heath himelf described it, accurately enough, as 'a fair and generous offer'. The pity was that his honest broker did not indulge in the horse-trading that would have allowed both parties to leave Number 10 with a smile on their faces.

The coal strike began, to be followed on 2 January 1974 by the three-day week. Many of us will remember all too vividly huddling in overcoats at our office desks, trying to work in an unheated room by the light of a guttering candle. Back at home, young children complained of the cold – it was a bitter winter – while their mothers tried to cope with reduced and faltering electricity supplies. On 10 January, ASLEF, the train drivers' union, threatened to start a series of one-day strikes to put pressure on the British Rail Board to improve rates of pay for their men. On 21 January, TUC leaders announced that, if the miners' dispute was settled generously, other unions would not use it as an excuse for higher wage claims. Mr Heath refused the request.

For two more weeks, he remained stubbornly opposed to any improvement in the terms offered. Then, on 4 February, the NUM Executive decided to call an all-out strike from midnight Saturday 9 February. (In the ballot, over 80 per cent of the miners had voted in favour.) On the lines of 'Who runs this country?', Heath called a general election for 28 February, giving the various parties less advance warning than for any other general election this century. Harold Wilson, leader of the opposition, countered with, 'He is asking for a mandate to pay the miners *after* the election what he refuses to pay them *before* the election.'

It appears that the country wanted the Conservatives out more than it wanted the Labour Party in. The Conservatives lost twenty-six seats, emerging with 296, Labour gained fourteen to end up with 301 and the Liberals increased their holding from eleven to fourteen seats. Even so, Edward Heath hung on for a desperate three days, at first hoping to parlay a deal with Jeremy Thorpe as leader of the Liberals. On 5 March, two days after the new Parliament assembled, Michael Foot, as Secretary of State for Employment, offered the miners a settlement amounting to £103 million, backdated to the first of the month. It conceded their claim in full and was broadly in line with the Pay Board's recommendations, which Heath had indicated he would accept.

The Annual Register for 1974 made a telling comment:

> This decision to rush a mid-winter election proved expensive for his government and the Conservative Party; for he thus not only threw away his own majority prematurely but also created a situation which might keep his party in opposition until 1978 or 1979 – a heavy price to pay when a party leader calculates wrongly.

If only – a fit epitaph for all too many leaders. If only Sir Derek (now Lord) Ezra had not opened that fateful November meeting with the Coal Board's best offer but had deliberately proposed a lower set of figures and had allowed himself and his colleagues to be 'driven' upwards to the final sum; the NUM Executive would have departed with honour and profit, there might have been no three-day week and no threatened all-out strike, the Conservatives under Edward Heath could have continued in office throughout the decade and beyond – Heath was only in his early sixties in 1980 – there might have been no Margaret Thatcher swinging her prime-ministerial handbag, the history of Europe in that period would have been vastly different – and so on. But Heath 'calculated wrongly', and spent the next twenty years and more sulking in his political tent.

Jeremy Hornsby, the co-author of *Battered Cherub*, had worked with James Burke of the BBC on several important scientific programmes and was well versed in advanced technology. He prepared the text on his word processor and Christopher Sinclair-Stevenson, then managing director of Hamish Hamilton, who had acquired volume rights, edited it 'on screen'. The printing was done from the resulting disks, probably (in early 1982) the first time in Britain that the process was used for a casebound book. Sinclair-Stevenson calculated that about £1,500 in setting costs had been saved and with typical generosity agreed to pay Hornsby a substantial share on top of his royalty earnings.

Battered Cherub was published in the autumn of 1982 amid much publicity and a launching party at the Ritz Hotel, where, as the learned judge put it, justice is open to all – except perhaps beleaguered Prime Ministers. The advance sales were good, the champagne flowed and the book soon became a bestseller.

15

LATE CUTS

There are as many ways of acquiring clients as there are of skinning a cat. Disgruntled authors might point to the similar functions. Some agents derive them from a friend's recommendation, as with John Farquharson and James Hilton. Other agents will build a reputation in a certain area and find that one client – say, a mountaineer – will pass the word on to other mountaineers. Yet others discover that new clients come their way because the firm is known in writing circles. Many authors must have approached Curtis Brown because, apart perhaps from A.P. Watt, it is the only name known to the outside world. As mentioned earlier, George MacDonald Fraser sent the script of the first *Flashman* novel to John Farquharson Ltd because it was 'a good Scottish name'. The more aggressive agents may write a self-recommending letter out of the blue to established authors who happen to be total strangers.

One such was David Higham in the 1950s and 1960s. He had a standard letter which went off on Mondays to every new novelist who had received a good review in the previous day's *Observer* or *Sunday Times*. It said that, if the recipient already had an agent, would he please ignore the rest of the contents; but, if he were available, the Higham agency could offer this, that and the other service and, no doubt, bring him peace and prosperity.

Presumably the method obtained good results now and then but it did lay itself open to unflattering responses, as in the case of Stan Barstow. His first novel, *A Kind of Loving*, had just been published to an overture of high praise. He duly received the standard Higham letter and had great fun in replying. He thanked Mr Higham for his consideration and the flattering remarks. It was a pity, perhaps, that the same attitude had not been displayed nearly a year earlier when he had submitted the typescript of *A Kind of Loving* to Mr Higham's firm. He had heard nothing for over a month and then the script was returned with a printed rejection slip. At that point, he approached 'a good agent', Innes Rose of John Farquharson, who read the novel almost overnight, liked it greatly and promptly sold the British rights to Michael Joseph – with the results now known. In view of this short history, Mr Higham would no doubt realise that there was no prospect at all of his receiving the next Barstow novel, when ready.

One of the strangest ways in which I ever found a client – and a not inconsiderable one at that – was like this. In the distant past, Farquharson's often used the famous Mrs Hoster's secretarial training course for its permanent and temporary staff. One of the temps who came as a summer-holiday replacement was named Jane Eustace. Unlike most temps (and who can blame them?), she took a close interest in the agency's work, with the result that, when my regular secretary left shortly after her return from holiday, I offered Jane Eustace the job. She stayed for five years, she knew the workings of the firm intimately and, more importantly, knew and was liked by all my clients.

With her knowledge and ability, continuing as a secretary was clearly a dead end for her. She should be made an assistant director with a small client list of her own to start with; I discussed the point with Innes Rose. At that stage, we were equal in voting rights, each owning 50 of the company's 100 issued shares, but of course Innes was my senior by eight years in age and by many more in experience.

Patient and with a sense of humour, he was usually an

easy man to work with but beneath it all there were some old-fashioned attitudes, one of which emerged then.

'You don't promote the hired help,' he said.

I thought, you stupid clown. How else do people ever get on? You joined old Farky straight out of Cambridge as hired help – how come you're the boss man? Aloud, I argued in Jane's favour and even appealed to his Scottish instincts by adding that it would be cheaper to promote her from inside than acquire an experienced young agent, whom we would shortly need, from another firm. But all the time there came back that parrot cry – you don't promote the hired help.

Had I made it a resigning issue, no doubt I would have got my way. But the defeat would have rankled with Innes and the office atmosphere – there were only half a dozen of us in all – would have suffered, as would Jane's work in her new capacity. So I accepted his decision with ill grace. I knew that Hodder & Stoughton would shortly require a newcomer to run their subsidiary rights department and urged Paul Hodder-Williams to take on Jane Eustace, which he eventually did. That was in 1963. For the next five years or so, she handled the foreign rights of those Hodder authors who had no agent and paperback rights as well, since the firm had not then fully developed its own softcover outlet, Coronet Books. As I had expected, she carried out her duties with warmth and exemplary efficiency, and became well known in the publishing trade. She also became friendly with Mary Stewart, who dealt direct with Hodder's and was then one of the two bestselling women novelists in the country, the other being Agatha Christie. Jane would accompany Ms Stewart to functions like the *Yorkshire Post* Literary Luncheon.

As several of my clients were Hodder authors, I had occasion to keep in touch with her quite frequently. We would have occasional business lunches, and once or twice, when she was giving supper in her Primrose Hill flat for paperback publishers and magazine editors, she would invite me to make up the numbers. One Friday in the summer of 1970, it was, as far as I knew, a routine visit for supper when I rang the front door bell of her flat. The door was promptly opened – by John le Carré. I had met him once briefly at a party for his American publisher on a London visit and indeed I would have recognised him from press and trade photographs. Jane had kept her growing friendship with him a secret; they had first met, it seems, at a literary function.

We had a relaxed social evening at the Canaletto, a good Italian restaurant in Maida Vale, with David Cornwell (his real name) as host. He is a witty raconteur and one of the best mimics I have ever heard. In one anecdote relating to André Deutsch, he even managed to pronounce the *umlaut* in different vowel sounds. The hours danced by and not a word of business was spoken.

Early the following week, he telephoned me at my office, then in Red Lion Square, and invited me out to lunch with Jane.

I said, 'No.'

He said, 'What?'

I said, 'Sorry, let me start again. Of course, I'd love to have lunch. But you were the host last time. This time, it must be on me.'

Later that week, the three of us sat down to lunch at the Silver Grill in High Holborn, then probably the best steak house in London with an eclectic wine list. After various glasses of malt whisky, three bottles of Corton Clos du Roi and a *marc* or two to round things off, none of us was feeling the slightest pain as we stood on the corner alongside the brutal bulk of State House. Jane went off to look for their car. David turned to me and asked if I would like to be his agent. Swaying gently in the breeze, I had the temerity to wonder aloud whether it was the wine talking. I was quite wrong. Over many subsequent years and many encounters with different bottles in David's company, I have never seen him drunk nor lose the fine edge of his intellect through drink.

I had enough sense left to accept his offer. For the next sixteen years, we had a cordial relationship, which only ended with my retirement. Early on, I asked him why he had decided to leave his previous agent, A.P. Watt, and come to me. I knew, of course, that his main friendship had been with Peter Watt and that on Peter's untimely death he found himself among comparative strangers. Was that the reason?

No, he said, or at the most it was only a small part of the thinking that led to the decision. Jane had told him about me – and that had roused his curiosity. He had also quite enjoyed our first evening at the Canaletto, and found that he and I shared much the same background. But odd as it might seem, the big spur had been my refusal to accept a second free meal in succession. Ever since the success of *The Spy Who Came in from the Cold* it had been his practice to send a case of champagne as a gift to the directors and staff of A.P. Watt every Christmas. He had been abroad for much of the intervening time and only came briefly to London. He would telephone his agent for an appointment and the answer was likely to be 'Come along at three-thirty or four o'clock.' Too late for lunch and even too early for a pre-dinner drink; a cup of tea would have to suffice – and that in spite of the many thousands of pounds that had stayed with the agency as commission on his earnings.

I never had the good grace to go to Innes Rose, shake his hand warmly and offer my thanks. For it was really all his doing. If he had agreed with me to promote Jane inside John Farquharson Ltd, she would probably never have met le Carré – they became husband and wife after his first marriage was dissolved – and so never have the opportunity to introduce us.

The voice on the long-distance phone call might have been strained through gravel. It had that rasping pitch, the tone of the pedlar who over the centuries has had to make himself heard through the echoing din of the *soukh*.

'You George Greenfield?' I admitted it. 'Irving P. Lazar. You act for Jarn Lurker-Ray?' Americans, I had noted, even those who spoke adequate French, never could pronounce 'le Carré'. So again I admitted the fact. 'Wa'al, I reppresent Blake Edwards. Lemme tell you, sir, Blake Edwards is the best goddamn movie director in the world. Yessir. The best. In the world. Bar none. No kidding. He's in'erested in this last Lurker-Ray book – whatsitsname? He aims to buy the rights.'

He crackled on for some moments, extolling the merits of his client who, it seemed, combined the skills of Eisenstein, Kurosawa and Ophuls, although, to give him his due, my interlocutor gave no evidence of ever having heard of those *auteurs*. He ended with, 'You readin' me?'

'Loud and clear. But I must tell you two things. The first is – I don't handle le Carré's film rights, his New York lawyer does.' Then invention took over. 'The other is this. Talk of a coincidence. Last night, I had dinner with Mr le Carré. He'd just been to see the latest Blake Edwards movie. He told me it was dreadful – a load of shit. It's not up to me but I can't imagine he'd want your Mr Edwards within a mile of his film rights.'

The silence was fractional. That aged saurian, 'Swifty' Lazar, had developed too tough a hide over the years to be deterred by a direct rebuff.

'Ah, the hell with Blake Edwards,' he rasped. 'Wossay I reppersent Lurker-Ray in Hollywood for you?'

'Swifty' was one of the few surviving characters at a time when the megalithic structure of publishing and the linked activities that feed off it tend towards uniformity (or perhaps the myopic vision of old age fails to spot the nuances). One eccentric and yet successful New York agency that no longer exists was that of Littauer & Wilkinson. Ken Littauer, always known as the Colonel, had been a distinguished fighter pilot in the Escadrille Lafayette in the Great War. He carried a neatly furled umbrella and wore a furry bowler hat, bought from Lock's in St James's Street. In the firm's Fifth Avenue office, he sat at a rolltop desk with a threshing machine of an ancient typewriter in front of him. In another corner of the room sat his partner, the witty and sardonic Max Wilkinson, who, in a previous existence as a magazine editor, had the distinction of once being punched on the nose by a drunken F. Scott Fitzgerald. *Collier's* and the *Saturday Evening Post* were continually lending Fitzgerald money against the promise of short stories that either arrived many months late or never at all. On that occasion in the late 1930s, Max had gone out to

Hollywood in a genuine effort to sort out the troubled genius's writing affairs and help him prepare the long-overdue stories. Fitzgerald had gone on drinking and pestering him for more money on account of even more unwritten stories, which Max knew his finance department would never release. Suddenly Fitzgerald had hit him in the face and then burst into tears with the horror of his deed and the hopelessness of it all.

One of the firm's stranger clients was a journalist named Ken Purdy. At first glance, he was the original ninety-pound weakling, the one who lay skinnily on the beach while the big bully kicked sand in his face. He was very short-sighted and wore thick, horn-rimmed pebble glasses atop his snub nose. And yet he was a rally driver of some note and he doted on men of action, writing evocative articles about bullfighters and boxers and racing drivers. I got to know him in the early 1960s because Farquharson represented Littauer & Wilkinson in Britain and Purdy, then living in London, wanted to collaborate on a book with Stirling Moss, a friend of his.

When an English man or woman has had an outstanding career, the first-person story can be fraught with a sense of undue modesty. Muhammad Ali might proclaim 'I am the greatest!' and get away with it but a public-school background tends to bring on shrugs and a deprecating cough, and the stammered remark that the outright win was largely due to luck. When working with Moss on his autobiography, Ken Purdy had evolved a clever way of getting round that obstacle. They called the book *All But My Life* – Moss had once said when he recovered from his last near-fatal accident, 'I've given this so-and-so [motor racing] all but my life!' Purdy wrote half the book as a long biographical sketch of Stirling Moss in the third person and so was able to describe the man's driving skills and his courage without the brakes of modesty. For the other half, he tape-recorded and then edited Moss, speaking in the first person and often expanding with a personal insight on one or other of the episodes described in the biographical section. The method, which could be used again in similar cases, worked well and *All But My Life* was a substantial bestseller on both sides of the Atlantic.

Ken Purdy had written several articles about Ernest Hemingway as a big-game hunter and game fisherman, and after numerous interviews had become quite friendly with 'Papa'. One night, over dinner at the Steering Wheel Club on the edge of Shepherd Market, he told me a story which he swore was true. Gene Tunney became heavyweight champion of the world after the still-debated 'long count' against Jack Dempsey. Tunney soon retired from the ring; considering himself far more than a mere pugilist, he went in search of culture, travelling to England to meet Bernard Shaw and much later to Cuba to meet Ernest Hemingway.

It must have been a frustrating encounter because the ex-boxer only wanted to talk about the higher reaches of fiction whereas the novelist, who kept a boxing ring set up in his garden, only wanted to talk about his guest's various fights – and just how good was Dempsey as a fighter? At length, Hemingway asked Tunney if he would do him the great favour of sparring a couple of friendly rounds with him in the convenient nearby ring. What a thrill it would be, he declared, to tell his friends that he had exchanged punches – friendly punches, of course – with the world's undefeated heavyweight champ.

Tunney demurred. He had turned his back on the ring forever; indeed he had sworn an oath that nothing would ever get him back inside the ropes. In any case, after many months of travelling and sightseeing, he was completely out of training. But Hemingway kept on pressing him – almost to the point of hinting that he must have turned yellow to refuse a friendly bout with a rank amateur. At last, against his better judgement, Tunney was persuaded to strip down to a pair of bathing trunks, don the gloves and climb back through the ropes once more. There were to be two three-minute rounds and his host had summoned one of the servants to ring a bell at the start and finish.

When the first bell went, Hemingway came rushing out of his corner, throwing punches that only trained reflexes allowed Tunney to avoid. He suddenly realised from the savage gleam in his opponent's eyes that this was not to be boasted of as a friendly bout but rather as 'How I knocked

out the undefeated champion of the world.' He knew that
he was not fit enough to survive an all-out attack for more
than a minute or two. He did not want to hurt his host –
but self-preservation came first. So he swayed out of range
of the flailing fists, feinted a body-blow with his left and,
when Hemingway's guard instinctively lowered, hit him on
the point of the chin with a right hook. The famous novelist
went down – and out for the count, long or short. The story
was not recounted in *A Moveable Feast*.

My other abiding memory of Ken Purdy occurred a year
or two later, when he had returned to live in the States and
I was in New York on a business visit. Ken was something
of a connoisseur, and we had wined and dined sumptuously
at the Laurent. We were sauntering down Park Avenue on
its west side in a mellow silence induced by the food and the
drink when he paused opposite the Waldorf Hotel, hitched
his glasses up his ski-jump nose with a forefinger and gazed
up at the lighted profile soaring into the night sky.

He turned to me and said, 'George, do you know the tragedy
of life?'

Feeling in a philosophic mood and attracted by the thought
of a Socratic dialogue, I hiccuped gently and said, 'No.'

'Let me tell you. Look at the Waldorf over there – those
lit-up windows. There are 500 rooms there, wouldn't you
say?' I nodded. 'Right. Now statistics says that ten per cent are
unoccupied. That leaves 450. Half of those will be occupied by
businessmen on their own – more than half, probably – so let's
say that leaves 200. Over half are taken up by couples – men
with their wives or, more likely, their mistresses. I reckon that
would come to, say, 140. You agree the arithmetic so far?'

I was much impressed, being in no fit state to add or
subtract. I said, 'Yes, I'm with you.'

'Good. This is the point. Those sixty rooms are occupied by
women on their own. Two-thirds of them are too old or too
ugly or lesbian or something. But in that big building across
the street there are twenty gorgeous girls, tossing and turning
in their unfulfilled beds, writhing and twisting the sheets into
knots, desperate for a man like me to come and satisfy their
urges. And the tragedy of life, George, is twofold. They don't

know I'm down here on the sidewalk, rarin' to go, and I don't know their room numbers!'

In spite of his puny frame and pipestem limbs, there was a feeling of coiled and compressed violence about Ken Purdy. He was liable to flare up at the slightest provocation, and after a few drinks was quite likely to square up to someone much bigger and stronger than himself. In the end, after a cocktail party and a tiff on the drive home, he went straight into his study, locked the door, took out a handgun – he was a great gun fancier – and blew his brains out. There were many years of great descriptive writing left in him.

Another short-term client who 'was much possessed with death' was Donald Campbell. I had only been an agent for two years when we met at the beginning of 1955. Of medium height and erect bearing, he spoke in short, crisp sentences and, often wearing a neat double-breasted blue blazer, might have been taken for an RAF pilot off duty. Indeed, having been born in 1921, he wanted to enlist as a fighter pilot when war broke out but, due to rheumatic fever in childhood, had to be rejected as medically unfit.

He was the son of Sir Malcolm Campbell, a pre-war hero who had held both land and water speed records in cars and powerboats respectively, all of which were named *Bluebird*. Indeed, he was the first man ever to have travelled at more than 300 miles per hour on land. In the Great War, as a young infantry officer, he had transferred in 1916 to what was then the Royal Flying Corps and at a time when life for a pilot in one of those 'stringbag' aircraft could be measured in days, if not hours, he survived the next two years through his skill and courage. It was a daunting legacy to leave for a son.

An old story had it that the night editor of the *Daily Mail*, maddened beyond endurance by the drunken, loutish pranks of Randolph Churchill, whose father Winston had pulled strings to get him a job on the newspaper, blurted out, 'Randolph, your name begins with Ch- in *Who's Who* and Sh- in *What's What!*' Apparently, substituting 'Ca-' in the first part, exactly the same could have been said of Sir Malcolm. He was one of those men one meets from time to time in the fighting services whose personal bravery is based on a total lack of imagination. He must have possessed fast reflexes, considerable strength in forearms and wrists, excellent eyesight and a do-or-die mentality. But as a human being away from fast-moving vehicles, his imaginative lack permeated his conduct. Donald told me once that as a small boy he had accompanied his father to the deserts of Utah for an attempt on the land speed record. On one of the trial runs, Donald joined his father in the cockpit of the car. Most motorists will know the feeling of driving off a motorway after several hours of cruising at 70 miles per hour – or perhaps rather faster. Slowing down to 40 miles per hour gives one the fleeting impression of almost having halted. The sensation caused by hard braking from speeds in excess of 200 miles an hour must be that much greater. So near the end of that trial run, when the father told the son to 'hop out', the little boy, always keen to be in Daddy's good books, stepped out – and went bowling head over heels for two or three somersaults before coming to rest on the hot, hard desert sand.

Sir Malcolm did not pull the car to a complete halt and leap out to see if his son was hurt. He sat in the cockpit and roared with laughter, then told the shaken child he had learned a good lesson. Next time, he'd make damn sure the car had stopped before leaving it.

Donald's sister told me a nastier tale. The father was a serious womaniser when he was not breaking records, and his wife, their mother, fed up with his blatant behaviour, had left the family home. He occupied the master bedroom; Donald and his sister each occupied a single room on either side. They were then in their impressionable teens. Most nights, Sir Malcolm would bring a different woman home. The walls between were thin. The children in their narrow beds would lie rigid, listening to every sound on the other side as their father brought his temporary lady of the night to a wailing, groaning climax several times before morning.

In spite of his many hazardous record attempts on land and water, Sir Malcolm Campbell never so much as broke a finger. The Second World War put an end to his efforts to go ever faster and he eventually died peacefully in his bed. That left Donald with a double problem. The son of a famous father is usually faced with a huge boulder blocking his onward path; he can either try to force it to one side or clamber over it or turn back and find a different path to pursue. If he decides, as Donald did, to climb over it – to compete with it – and the father is no longer alive, the son will automatically face defeat. The famous dead are beyond competition. They will always be the best of their own generation.

Donald was physically compact but with great strength in the upper body and arms. He inherited his father's concentrated gaze and the hawk-like beak of a nose but, unlike the father, his mouth was soft and the chin rounded. His actions and his speech were always firm and decisive but somehow I felt that he was acting out a role. He often spoke of his father – 'the old man' or 'the boss', as he called him – and always with admiring affection. When I met him in the spring of 1955, he was thirty-four years old. With the expert help of Louis Villa, who had been Sir Malcolm's chief mechanic, he had developed a speedboat with a rudimentary jet engine to tackle the water speed record on the Ullswater lake that summer.

Such attempts are vastly expensive and, whereas his father had enjoyed the income from a stockbroking firm, Donald had no similar source to tap. Furthermore, as I soon discovered, selling exclusive visual rights was impossible. Any film unit or television crew could establish itself on either shore of the seven-mile-long lake and shoot away to its heart's content. Besides that, an actual record attempt over a measured mile lasted a matter of seconds. If successful, it would be a front-page story for the national newspapers next day but would not endure as a news item. I was able to sell book rights to Odhams Press and *Into the Water Barrier* was moderately successful on its appearance that autumn. (The title was a play on words, the 'sound barrier' having become established as a technical problem for jet speeds approaching the velocity of sound.)

I drove up to Ullswater in July a few days before Donald's first attempt at the water speed record and stayed in the same small hotel as he and his team were occupying. The hours were fraught with increasing problems. The jet engine was not developing full power. When that was put right, the additional surge affected the stabilisers, which in turn required adjusting. The surface of the lake had to be trawled at least once a day to ensure there was no floating driftwood. For *Bluebird* to hit a submerged log when flat out at over 150 miles an hour would send her cartwheeling end over end – and certain death for the pilot.

From early morning until late at night, Donald was as active as a whirling dervish. Repeated conferences with the engineers, test runs in the boat, friendly meetings with the press men who were beginning to gather, snatched meals, long-distance phone calls for spares and weather forecasts – he drove himself incessantly. He also drove a motorboat, which he used to ferry himself from the shore to where *Bluebird* was anchored a few hundred yards away, as if a sea monster were tracking him. He took me once for a ride on the lake and when the speed increased so that the bows lifted above the surface, it was like being shoved full tilt down a steep flight of stairs while sitting on a tin tray. The underside of the motorboat kept hitting the waves as though they were frozen into concrete dragon's teeth. What for God's sake must it be like, I thought, travelling at five times that speed in the monster that resembled a squat, wingless seaplane?

All the while, I could see the tension gnawing at Donald. Once, when I had to go to his room for a discussion, I found him doing chin-ups on the lintel above the door. Due to the jolting and jarring of high-speed driving in *Bluebird*, he had a chronically painful back – but it seemed to me that nervous tension might also affect the lumbar area. The need to keep his shoulders square and his back straight, not only in front of a growing crowd of well-wishers and journalists but also to quell any internal doubts he might have, was bound to put extra stress on the man at his very centre. I admired his courage. In the war, I had seen several unimaginative blockheads act without thought of danger to life and limb; they were called brave – as indeed they were. But to my mind then and since, the sensitive man who can vividly imagine the searing agony of a shell splinter or the fatal tattoo of a Spandau light machine-gun and who yet carries out orders is braver still.

A land or water speed record is made by taking the average miles per hour of two attempts over the measured mile, one in each direction, which have to take place within a limited time. Later that July, with a racket that echoed off the surrounding hills and a plume of steam and water that billowed out from the rear, *Bluebird* with Donald at the wheel bucked and flew over its double dissection of the previously placid Ullswater lake. The record fell. Before long, Donald Campbell was made a Companion of the British Empire, a valued award but one step beneath his father's knighthood. He spent the next eleven years scrabbling to find sponsors and other backers for the ever more expensive attempts to win and then lose and then win back both the land and the water records.

But he and I had long since parted, although remaining friends. I felt that once the Soviet Union had put sputniks and then Gagarin into space, ultrasonic air speeds were making private attempts at surface records redundant, even a quaint harking-back to speed for its own sake. And all the more I began to feel that Donald had seen 'the skull beneath the skin', that there would be only one end to his obsessed drive to compete with his father. So it proved. In January 1967, in yet another effort at the water record, the then *Bluebell* flipped up off the surface, somersaulted and broke into fragments. Donald's body was never recovered.

In July 1940, there was a cricket match at the army barracks in Lincoln. The opening batsmen for the home side were Staff-Sergeant Hutton, L., of the Army Physical Training Corps and Private Greenfield, G., of the Lincolnshire Regiment. Being the lowest form of military life, a private soldier never spoke to his seniors except in reply to a question or, more likely, an order, so I remained silent and with bowed head as we marched out to the wicket. It was almost two years since my partner had broken at The Oval Don Bradman's record for the highest individual score in a test match. As I had come to learn from regular PT drills he had taken, he was a dour, reticent creature with an accent as broad as the Yorkshire moors. With his lank hair, pale eyes and botched nose, he reminded me more of a professional boxer than a professional cricketer. A week or so later, he was to fall heavily off a set of parallel bars in the depot gymnasium and break his left elbow. When the arm healed, it would be permanently two inches shorter than the right one, which would require a complete change in his batting technique.

But on that bright summer's day, the precision, the certainty, of his strokes exuded greatness. There was a mellow ring to his bat as he drove the ball to the boundary or cut it square of cover point; and on the last ball of every over, whether it were a full toss or a long hop, he would steer it round the corner, call out, 'Come for one', and trot a single, thus monopolising the strike. We put on, as I recall, 116 for the opening stand, of which my share was eight runs – two boundaries slashed on the very rare occasions I actually faced the bowler. Indeed, greatly daring, I went up to him between overs and hinted that the batting task was supposed to be spread evenly between the two batsmen. He looked at me with those expressionless eyes and told me that he had come up through a hard school. When hardly out of his teens, he had first opened for Yorkshire with the famous Herbert Sutcliffe. If a really fast bowler was flinging them down, Mr Sutcliffe would quickly nudge a single and leave the boy to face the barrage. And again, if the bowling was friendly, Mr Sutcliffe would take that single off the last ball of the over and keep the batting to himself. That was the way the professionals did it. Yorkshire was the team every other county feared because they were a bunch of pros, not lah-di-dah amateurs with fancy-coloured caps and blazers.

Twenty years later, I occasionally played squash with my client Peter May, another superb batsman and England captain. Peter had a theory that squash sharpened the reflexes, being played at close quarters with a darting rubber ball. He was a natural games-player – as well as being an outstanding cricketer, he had been a soccer blue at Cambridge – but he never bothered to study the tactics of squash and just used it as strenuous exercise to speed up his reactions. Peter had a gracious modesty and droll sense of humour beneath a rather austere appearance. He did his National Service in the Royal Navy as a Writer, who is a kind of clerical worker. When playing cricket at Lord's for the United Services, he was put down on the scorecard as 'May, P.B.H.' with the abbreviation 'Wtr'. An elderly member of the MCC, with a face as scarlet as the garish club colour, who was sitting in the enclosure in front of the pavilion, misread the title and bellowed out, 'Hey, May, fetch me a gin and tonic!'

After the war, Hutton had suffered, along with his other English team-mates, at the hands of the Australians, who had won with ignominious ease. At last, in August 1953 at the Oval under Hutton's captaincy, there was a chance to reclaim the long-lost Ashes. Lindsay Hassett's Australian team should have made sure of at least drawing the series by winning at Lord's a few weeks earlier but on what seemed the verge of victory, they had apparently celebrated both prematurely and unwisely the night before and, thanks mainly to Watson and Bailey, the English rearguard had held out. Now, with England's second innings to come and only a handful of runs required, the tables were turned.

The Oval was, of course, Peter May's home ground and there was great applause when he went out to bat at second wicket down. He was in good form and hit a few boundaries, the latest one over the head of the bowler, who promptly stationed a fielder in the area where the ball had landed. Only about a dozen runs were needed for victory and eight wickets were yet to fall. A similar ball was bowled, Peter swung his bat as before, it sailed over the bowler's head and the fielder caught it. There was equal applause as the batsman returned to the pavilion. It had been a dashing little knock. But half-way up the stairs leading to the players' dressing room, Peter was confronted by a stormy captain, Len Hutton. 'What did tha want to do that for?' he demanded. 'It's not a game, tha know!'

During the 1960s, the Eyre & Spottiswoode Stragglers played – 'played at' is perhaps more accurate – an annual cricket match. We were a mixed bunch. Captained by John Bright-Holmes,

one of the three or four best post-war book editors, a man
of commanding stature and presence with a solid off-drive,
the team descended by abrupt stages from Stuart Turner,
then a lanky teenager and later a county all-rounder for
Essex, through Ronald Harwood, the playwright, whose
rudimentary batting technique was only matched by a sharp
eye and quick reflexes, and down to James Wright, another fine
editor, who more often than not when batting confused French
cricket with real cricket. It could be said with confidence that
we spanned the gamut of the summer game's talents from A
to A-minus.

Often our one match a year and certainly the most important
was played on the Lincoln College ground at Oxford against
Michael Sissons' XI. Michael, a formidable literary agent who
had learned his trade from the master, A.D. Peters, whose
firm he eventually took over, treated his games-playing with
equal gravity. The Stragglers may have been 'sons of grief'
but we certainly tried to be glad. We would foregather at
the well-known coaching inn, The George, at Dorchester-
on-Thames around noon on the day of the match. Pints
of country ale, several delectable bottles of wine, a hearty
lunch, even perhaps a few of Monsieur Hine's *digestifs*
and off we would set, ready for – often late for – the
fray. As we lurched out of our various cars, hiccuping
softly, we would see the Sissons team, already changed
and on the field, intent on catching practice and stretching
exercises. We would probably have lost the match in any
case but Sissons had a secret weapon, a demon fast bowler
named N'gendra. He was black; one end of the college
ground had no sight screen, only a murky line of hedgerow.
N'gendra always bowled from that end and, as the shadows
fell, all the batsman could see was the flash of his white
teeth as the dark ball came whipping out of his invisible
right hand.

After yet another shameful defeat in 1967, other members
of the Stragglers accused me of failing the cause. There was I,
agent for Norman O'Neill, Bobby Simpson, 'Slasher' McKay,
Peter May, Garfield Sobers, Frank Worrell. Why didn't I
get a few of them to join the team and put that so-and-so

Sissons in his place? I had to explain that in the English summer Australians and West Indians were either thousands of miles away in their own countries or fully occupied playing Test matches over here. But the idea stayed with me and germinated.

Over a decade earlier, Ron Roberts, a *Daily Telegraph* cricket correspondent and a client of mine, had introduced me to Richie Benaud. Ron was one of the best liked and most respected journalists among the players themselves; they would take seriously any recommendation he might make. Thanks to him, Richie came to me as a client. I handled his books, notably the outstanding *Tale of Two Tests* and later, on his retirement, his contract with the BBC. He was not only one of the finest spin bowlers of the past fifty years but probably the best captain over the same period. People tend to forget that the self-contained Don Bradman could never cope with rebels like Sid Barnes, who tried to run him out in a Test match, and Keith Miller. It was Richie who brought a scientific approach to fielding and bowling by initiating those plots of a batsman's favourite strokes. He applied the same intelligence to learning the commentator's craft. Unlike the garrulous clowns who cover athletics for the BBC, he understands the tact of allowing the action to tell its own story, intercut with a few shrewd and knowing comments.

He is also a man of great, if undisclosed, generosity. His good friend Ron Roberts died tragically young from a cerebral tumour in the mid-1960s, leaving a widow and two young children. Ever since, Richie, who will not thank me for revealing it, has arranged for part of his writing and BBC income to be passed to them at each accounting period.

He agreed to turn out for the Stragglers in their 1968 fixture against Michael Sissons and his fighting-fit team. It was the Sunday of the Headingley Test, where Richie, having retired a few years earlier from first-class cricket, was commentating for the BBC. He had to fly to Heathrow, to be collected by car and driven to Oxford via Dorchester-on-Thames, and return to Leeds on the last British Midland flight that same evening.

We had the usual convivial lunch at The George and, when we rolled into the Lincoln College ground somewhat late, we enjoyed the look of confused amazement on our opponents' faces when the great man, the new recruit, stepped out of my car.

Many years ago, a duchess, when informed that sexual intercourse was also enjoyed by the common people, was heard to say, 'Much too good for them.'

We fielded first and Richie's bowling was in the aristocratic class. It was 'much too good for them'. Where a Test match batsman would have been quick enough to get a touch and be snapped up in the slips, our opponents groped and hung out their bats, and the vicious legbreaks went fizzing past. None of them could spot his googly and if the 'flipper' thudded into a pad directly in front of the wicket, the opposition's umpire would shout 'Not out!' – often before we had appealed. It was caviar set before batsmen who only knew about baked beans.

When it was our turn to bat, Richie scored an elegant twenty or so. (Even connoisseurs of the game sometimes forget that he was an attacking batsman who once scored ninety-seven before lunch in a Lord's Test.) The light was beginning to fail and Sissons brought back his secret weapon, N'gendra, to bowl from the end without the sightscreen. In his opening over, he bowled a fast yorker that crashed into Richie's instep. He had to limp off – it seemed that a small bone in his left foot might have been broken. The match ended with our customary defeat, we changed, had a quick drink and then my task was to get the wounded hero back to Heathrow in good time to check in for the last flight to Leeds.

I had not reckoned with the narrow two-lane A423 road to Henley and the prevalence of Sunday-evening drivers, ambling along in close-huddled convoys at a steady thirty miles an hour; nor for the detours and cluttered streets of Henley itself, nor the delays in driving across the bridge on a late summer's evening. Finally, we hit the motorway and I probably broke several speed records as we tore along towards Heathrow. My son George, on vacation from university, had come along for the day. Time was running out; already, as we sped through the tunnel, the British Midland passengers must have been called forward for boarding. Richie just had to be in Leeds by early the following morning. The last train from King's Cross and St Pancras would have left long before we could cover the twenty-five miles from Heathrow.

The car slid to a stop outside Terminal 1 and young George, as arranged, sprinted ahead to the desk, shouting 'Please hold the plane for Mr Benaud!' while we extracted Richie's gear from the boot. The flight had already closed, indeed the aircraft with passengers on board had taxied to the end of the runway. But the British Midland attendants must have been cricket fans. They arranged for a car to take the wounded hero out to the aircraft, steps were placed in position, the door opened and he limped on board. My son and I smiled at one another as we watched the take-off. At much personal inconvenience and expense, the great cricketer had kept his promise to turn out for the Stragglers – and bore the scars to prove it.

Not many literary agents have been called as chief prosecution witness against one of their own clients. This is how it happened to me.

One day in 1975, our office switchboard operator buzzed me and said there was a Mr Norman Lee on the line. Normally, I was chary of taking calls from strangers who might want to sell me insurance or, worse still, insist on detailing the intricate plot of their latest boring novel, but I had known and liked an author of that name for whom I had acted many years before and with whom I had lost touch. So I asked her to put him on. I soon realised it was not the same Mr Lee but indeed a stranger. This one spelled his name Leigh. His voice sounded educated and there was a quiet assurance about the way he spoke. He had something to discuss which he felt might interest me quite considerably but it was a matter to be presented in person. Would I favour him with a brief appointment? My curiosity was aroused and we arranged for him to come in the following afternoon.

His appearance matched his voice. A high-domed forehead, small horns of hair brushed up over the ears, a neat bow tie with matching breast pocket handkerchief, a trim blazer with a froth of snowy handkerchief emerging from the left cuff, gleaming shoes with tassels – he was the epitome of an off-duty brigadier. And what was the matter of interest? Quite simple, really. He had an impeccable system for winning at roulette. Moreover, he had proved that it worked. He had trained a team of twelve ordinary people and, under his guidance, they had actually 'taken' the bank at the Nice Municipal Casino, winning so much that the casino authorities eventually banned them.

My attitude towards gambling is akin to that of the pre-war Chinese ambassador who refused an official invitation to the Royal Enclosure at Ascot on the grounds that 'in China it has long been recognised that one horse runs faster than another.' In Damon Runyan's words, life itself is a case of six-to-four against. I was sceptical – and said as much to my visitor. He could have my word that I would not divulge any secrets he told me but I had to know that his special system had a chance of working.

A chainsmoker, he lit another cigarette and pondered the point. Then, in those quiet military tones, he explained the method. It was a variation on the Reverse Labouchère gambit. The roulette wheel has six even-chance possibilities. They are red and black (*rouge et noir*), even and odd numbers (*pair et impair*) and high and low numbers (*passe et manque*). If the wheel were to be spun 100,000 times, red and black, for example, would each come up 50,000 times, give or take a few digits. But in the short term, one might find black turning up ten times running. The roulette player knows that 'runs' or sequences of this kind may crop up several times in an evening.

Norman Leigh's plan took advantage of the phenomenon. He split his players into two teams of six, one resting and the other playing all night. Each of the six members stuck to one of the even-chance possibilities, always putting on a modest bet, but if a run started, there was a special formula for increasing the amount with each spin of the wheel. And once the run ended, there was also a formula for cutting the next bet back to a low level. If, for example, a black five cropped up several times in succession, three of the six team members could be simultaneously on a run. To play the same narrow band of possibilities hour after hour throughout the night and yet always having to concentrate in case a run started must have been a mind-numbing performance. Norman Leigh's function was to act as team manager, moving about behind the players, encouraging them, watching out for potential runs and giving quiet advice, whenever needed, but never actually playing.

After a further meeting, I was convinced that there could be a good book in his exploits. He had held my attention throughout with his evident zeal for the subject and that quiet air of authority. He wanted to write the book himself and we left it that he would send me the first 20,000 words or so as soon as possible. That gave me the chance to make some independent enquiries. Deputy Assistant Commissioner Ernest Millen, the police officer who had been in charge of operations for the Great Train Robbery and who in retirement was chief security officer for the Casanova Club, was a client of mine. Through him, I had met Ben Barnett, the owner of the gambling club, who in his youth really had 'broken the bank at Monte Carlo'.

I asked Ben if the system Norman Leigh had described would work. He thought for quite a while before answering and then said that yes, in theory it was feasible. He himself had used a variation of the Reverse Labouchère system in his famous 'raid' on the Monte Carlo bank. But he reckoned that in practice, provided that the club or casino management stayed alert, it would not work for long. The authorities would spot quite quickly that a team was at work around the table – moreover, a team that by its modest appearance betrayed its lack of big funds. All the management had to do was close down the roulette table on some pretext and, when reopening it an hour or so later, announce that the minimum stakes had been substantially increased. That would not affect the wealthy heavy gamblers on whom the casino relied for its winnings but would wipe out the kind of small-time team a Norman Leigh might recruit.

In a strange way, his verdict encouraged me. He was speaking from the point of view of a successful West End gambling club, which had to be abreast of – indeed, ahead of – all the tricks of the trade. A municipal casino in a holiday resort in midsummer might well be a little drowsy on a hot afternoon. And the fact that the theory itself was sound, vouched for by an expert, gave me added assurance.

Norman Leigh's opening chapters proved a real disappointment. Stiffly and pompously written, they conveyed nothing of the excitement and suspense a book like that required. I had to tell him that unless a professional writer was brought in and, while keeping to the facts, given a free hand in the writing, I would have to give up the project. He reluctantly agreed – and I introduced him to Gordon Williams. A one-time journalist, an author of powerful novels such as *From Scenes Like These*, shortlisted for the Booker Prize, and *The Siege of Trencher's Farm*, filmed by Sam Peckinpah as the notorious *Straw Dogs*, and the co-author with Terry Venables of the private-eye book and TV series, *Hazell*, Gordon was well qualified as Norman Leigh's collaborator. He had the added merit of being able to interview closely three members of the team, whose names and addresses had been extracted from Leigh after much pressure and persuasion on Gordon's part. At least, those interviews endorsed the story, although the interviewees independently recalled much more modest winnings than the figures with which their leader had provided me. They reckoned that after deducting travel and hotel expenses, they were left with £100 at the most – a far cry from the many thousands put forward by Norman Leigh.

Thirteen Against the Bank was a graphic study of how the team was chosen, trained and taken to the south of France where it carried out its coup against the Nice Casino. In addition, Gordon Williams, with a touch of poetic licence, showed what effect the excitement and the access to sudden riches had on the developing relationships among the players.

Arthur Barker Ltd bought British book rights for an advance of £10,000 (worth over £40,000 in today's terms), William Morrow paid $35,000 for American book rights, there was a serial sale, several foreign rights sales and a film option or two. Steve McQueen, having had a success with *The Cincinnati Kid*, wanted to direct and act in a film of *Thirteen Against the Bank*. Or so it was rumoured. The total earnings were probably over £40,000.

All good things come to an end and for individual books the end can be an abrupt one. There was a flare of publicity on *Thirteen*'s appearance and, a year later, there were paperback editions on both sides of the Atlantic. But their selling time was brief; none of the options matured into a full film sale. By late 1976 the royalty income, which was of course shared with Gordon Williams, had dwindled to a dribble which itself soon dried up. At increasing intervals, there would be an occasional courteous letter from Norman Leigh, asking if further money was due to him and each time I had to respond with a regretful negative. Then for several years there was silence.

Early in 1983, I received a telephone call from a man in Lymington, Hampshire. He told me that his wife kept a small boarding house and that a rich client of mine, a Mr Leigh, had been staying there. When he left, he asked for his bill to be sent to me for settlement. His story was that, as a highly successful author travelling a great deal on research, he never stayed long enough in one place to open a bank account. He therefore only carried enough money on him for drinks and smokes, while I settled all his bigger bills for him. I had to tell my caller that I was holding no funds to Mr Leigh's credit and the situation was most unlikely to change in the near future. Unmollified, he rang off.

In the next week or so, two other lodging-house keepers in the Lymington area sent me unpaid bills on behalf of Norman Leigh and each time I had to return them with a covering letter, explaining that my firm was not his private banker. Then one afternoon the man who had telephoned turned up unannounced at Bell House and insisted on seeing me. He was in a belligerent mood – for which no one could blame him – and he obviously suspected that I was playing some game, using my wealthy client's funds for my own purposes. Normally, a client's accounts are kept strictly confidential but, as Norman Leigh had taken my name in vain, I had no compunction in calling forward his ledger cards and showing my visitor that there had been no income received for some three or four years. I felt sorry for the man and his hard-working wife – and indeed for the other couples who had been taken in by the clipped accent, the double-breasted blazer and the matching bow tie and breast-pocket handkerchief. In each case, he had run up a bill for around for £100 for bed and breakfast over a couple of weeks or so – big money for these modest people to lose. I told my caller his best redress was to report the matter to the police.

Not long afterwards, an officer from the Hampshire force called on me by appointment and took a statement. A few weeks later, I was summoned to give evidence at Lymington Magistrates' Court. I arrived early and sat in an area roped off for witnesses. Norman Leigh, who had surrendered his bail, entered, accompanied by a police officer, and gave me a cheery wave. He then came over and, until his escort abruptly moved him back, began a courteous chat, as though we were both members of the MCC sitting in front of the pavilion at Lord's. With the opening of the case, my evidence was simple and straightforward. It was to explain to the court that, as literary agent to the defendant, I was empowered to receive on his behalf moneys arising from the sale or licence of rights in his book, *Thirteen Against the Bank*; that no such payments had arisen in the past few years; and that there had never been an arrangement between us whereby I settled his bills and debited his account with John Farquharson Ltd. The solicitor acting for the defence subjected me to only a perfunctory cross-examination and was no more severe with the lodging-house witnesses who had been defrauded. It was an open and shut case. Norman Leigh was found guilty and sentenced to six months in prison.

That was the last I heard of him directly, although I often saw yellow handbills flyposted in the Covent Garden area, announcing that the author of that world bestseller, *Thirteen Against the Bank*, had an infallible system of winning at roulette, one which he was prepared to impart to anyone who cared to write to such and such an accommodation address. It seems he lived on in the Hampshire area in a residence for homeless people, supported by loyal friends, drinking whisky and being charming in the bar of The Golden Lion at Fareham – in the words of an acquaintance, 'always the perfect gentleman, splendidly dressed'. He died penniless of a heart attack on New Year's Eve 1992. There was a full-page article about him in the *Daily Mail*. He would have loved that.

Bernard Geis, a post-war American publisher who flourished for a while, was a character. His firm occupied two floors of a brownstone in the East Fifties. Others might use the elevator or the stairs but the agile Bernie had a hole in the connecting floor and a gleaming fireman's pole down which he slid when he wanted to descend to the lower level. He was also the only publisher I have ever met who had on the wall behind his desk what appeared to be three or four shelves of leatherbound, gilt-tooled volumes, which at the touch of a button swung back to reveal glasses and bottles set in a mirror-backed cocktail cabinet. Many 'mainline' New York publishers took their guests to the Century Club or the Harvard Club in the next street or the Yale Club on Vanderbilt Avenue. Bernie took his guests to the Playboy Club.

One evening, when he and his wife Darlene were visiting London – it must have been in the late 1960s – I was driving them through Camden Town and Chalk Farm up to Hampstead for supper. Harold Wilson's 'white heat of technology' had burnt down and no confident pipe-clenching appearances on television could ward off the severe slump that was gripping the country. Inflation was climbing step by step with unemployment, companies were reducing their staffs and public morale was slipping. We had reached Malden Road, that long straight road which must contain at least five public houses.

Darlene Geis said to me. 'I knew things were bad over here. But not to the point where the government has to exhort the people.'

'What do you mean, Darlene?' I said.

She pointed out of the car's window. There, high on the roof of the nearest pub and again on one some way up the road, blazed a sign in red neon: 'TAKE COURAGE'.

Thirty years later, the exhortation has stayed with me. For the young author, rising at dawn to write for an hour or two before going off to earn a living or returning tired out and forgoing the relaxation of the couch and TV set for a solitary spell of writing or for the one who is facing his fifteenth rejection slip or, if published, a complete absence of reviews, courage to keep going is the requirement.

Aldous Huxley said, 'Nature is monstrously unjust. There is no substitute for talent.' But talent is like cream. In the end, it floats to the top.

INDEX